Pioneers in Leisure and Recreation

HILMI IBRAHIM

and

JOSEPH BANNON
KATHLEEN CORDES
WILLIAM DEGROOT
ALAN EWERT
PHYLLIS FORD
GUS GERSON
CHARLES HARTSOE
RON HAVARD
JANE KAUFMAN
PAUL MCBRIDE
JANET MCLEAN
MOUNIR RAGHEB
S. ELAINE ROGERS
ALLEN SAPORA
RONALD SIMPSON
STEVEN SIMPSON
CARLTON YOSHIOKA

A Project for The American Association For Leisure & Recreation.

An Association of the American Alliance For Health, Physical Education,
Recreation, & Dance.

Copyright © 1989

American Alliance for Health, Physical Education, Recreation, and Dance
1900 Association Drive
Reston, VA 22091

ISBN 0-88314-423-9

Purposes of the American Alliance for Health, Physical Education, Recreation, and Dance

The American Alliance is an educational organization, structured for the purposes of supporting, encouraging, and providing assistance to member groups and their personnel throughout the nation as they seek to initiate, develop, and conduct programs in health, leisure, and movement-related activities for the enrichment of human life.

Alliance objectives include:

1. Professional growth and development—to support, encourage, and provide guidance in the development and conduct of programs in health, leisure, and movement-related activities which are based on the needs, interests, and inherent capacities of the individual in today's society.

2. Communication—to facilitate public and professional understanding and appreciation of the importance and value of health, leisure, and movement-related activites as they contribute toward human well-being.

3. Research—to encourage and facilitate research which will enrich the depth and scope of health, leisure, and movement-related activities; and to disseminate the findings to the profession and other interested and concerned publics.

4. Standards and guidelines—to further the continuous development and evaluation of standards within the profession for personnel and programs in health, leisure, and movement-related activities.

5. Public affairs—to coordinate and administer a planned program of professional, public, and governmental relations that will improve education in areas of health, leisure, and movement-related activities.

6. To conduct such other activities as shall be approved by the Board of Governors and the Alliance Assembly, provided that the Alliance shall not engage in any activity which would be inconsistent with the status of an educational and charitable organization as defined in Section 501 (c) (3) of the Internal Revenue Code of 1954 or any successor provision thereto, and none of the said purposes shall at any time be deemed or construed to be purposes other than the public benefit purposes and objectives consistent with such educational and charitable status.

Bylaws, Article III

Dedicated
To
The Many Pioneers
Whose Names Do Not Appear
In This Volume

Acknowledgement

The Editor and authors of this work would like to acknowledge the dedication of C. J. Dyer Hine who prepared the first draft of this volume. Mike Everman, AAHPERD Archivist, and Pam Hackbart, archivist of the National Recreation and Park Association, provided us with a number of the pictures used here. Special thanks goes to Mike Montgomery, and Scott A. Crabb for the final preparation of the manuscript, and to Cynthia Ibrahim for proofreading.

Preface

There are many people, both living and dead, who have contributed to the field of leisure and recreation. However, to write a volume on all the pioneers would require much more time and space than we have.

The 26 pioneers chronicled here are certainly considered among the most important. They span over two thousand years, and cross many cultures. Some are theorists, others are practitioners. But all of them have left their imprint on the leisure and recreation field.

When the Publication Committee of the American Association for Leisure and Recreation approved my proposal for a volume on the pioneers of leisure and recreation, I sent a memo to over 300 colleagues asking if they would like to contribute. Those who showed interest were students, followers, or chroniclers of some of these pioneers. In fact, three of the authors had written their Ph.D. dissertations on three of the pioneers.

What we hope to have achieved is to bring to the reader's attention the depth of commitment and the variety of approaches used by these extraordinary people to this extraordinary field.

Hilmi Ibrahim
Whittier, CA

Table of Contents

1

ARISTOTLE

384–322 B.C.E.

By Steven Simpson
Iowa State University

"Nature herself, as has been often said, requires that we should be able, not only to work well, but to use leisure well. . . Both are wanted, but leisure is more worth having. . ."

Politics, Bk. VIII, Ch. 3

Philosopher and educator Mortimer Adler claimed that philosophy is important for all people because it helps them to understand even better than they do now the things that they already know. "For that purpose," he wrote, "there is no better teacher than Aristotle. . . Plato taught Aristotle how to think philosophically, but Aristotle learned the lesson so well that he is the better teacher for all of us." (Adler, 1978: ix–x)

In a volume presenting the accomplishments of the pioneers of recreation and leisure, Aristotle obviously cannot be credited with heading a recreation agency or founding a professional organization. Instead, Aristotle conveyed ideas and, more importantly, ideals concerning the role of leisure in humankind's quest for a good life. Had Adler been limiting his discussion to leisure and recreation, he might have also said that in order to understand the classical presentation of leisure, there is no better teacher than Aristotle.

Aristotle was born in 384 Before the Common Era, at the Macedonian city of Stagira, about 200 miles north of Athens. His father, Nicomachus, was physician to Amyntas, King of Macedon and grandfather to Alexander.

Although Aristotle may have lived his early years recklessly and not made his way to Plato and the Academy until the age of 30, most accounts claim he went to Athens in his late teens and studied under his master teacher for a full 20 years. Plato recognized the talents of this man nearly 50 years his junior, for he called Aristotle "the reader" and "the mind of the School." (Durant, 1926: 41, Kaplan, 1958: xi)

In spite of Aristotle's recognized genius, the chance that he would succeed Plato as head of the Academy was nonexistent. Such an honor could not go to a nonAthenian. Aristotle, therefore, left Athens, and after a few years of teaching in Assos in Asia Minor and on Lesbos, King Phillip of Macedon called for him to tutor his son, Alexander.

The association with Alexander proved to be both a benefit and a detriment to the thinker. When Alexander ascended to the throne, Aristotle returned to Athens and founded the Lyceum. With Aristotle's reputation as a student of Plato and a teacher of Alexander, his new school immediately surpassed the Academy in prestige. It was noted for its teaching of biology and the natural sciences, and large donations from Alexander supported the school and its scientific study. This was a productive time for Aristotle, and much of his written work was done during his years at the Lyceum.

Athenian citizenry, however, now under the rule of Alexander the Great, was at odds with Aristotle for his association with the Macedonian ruler and for his support of Alexander's efforts to unify Greece. When Alexander unexpectedly died in 323 B.C.E., the Macedonian party in Athens quickly fell. A chief priest of Athens brought an indictment against

Aristotle for impiety. Choosing not to endure the same fate as Socrates, Aristotle left Athens, saying he would not give the city-state a second chance to sin against philosophy. Arriving at Chalcis, he took ill and only a few months after fleeing Athens, Aristotle died. (Kaplan, 1958: xii)

In *Ethics*, Aristotle asked himself to identify the highest of all practical goods. In response, he wrote, "Well, so far as the name goes, there is pretty general agreement. 'It is happiness' say both ordinary and cultured people." (*Ethics*, Book I, Ch. 4) The reason for this was that of all worthwhile goals, happiness was the only one desired for its own sake and for no other. Undertakings such as medicine and architecture were honorable, but in themselves, were only means to an end and had purposes other than for their own sakes.

If there existed one end for which all other ends were means, then this would be the ultimate goal. For Aristotle, this was happiness. He wrote:

> So if there is only one final end, this will be the good of which we are in search; and if there are more than one, it will be the most final of these. Now we call an object pursued for its own sake more final than one pursued for something else;. . . and that which is always choosable for its own sake and never for something else we call final without any reservation. Well, happiness more than anything is thought to be just such an end, because we always choose it for itself, and never for any other reason. It is different with honor, pleasure, intelligence, and good qualities generally. We do choose them partly for themselves, but we choose them also for the sake of our happiness, in the belief that they will be instrumental in promoting it. On the other hand nobody chooses happiness for their sake, or in general for any other reason. (*Ethics*, Bk.I Ch. 7)

Even if Aristotle's premise concerning happiness is accepted, what then does this have to do with leisure? The answer is best addressed by looking at the classical definition of leisure.

In the ancient Greek, the work for leisure was *schole*. Dare, Welton, and Coe defined *schole* not as a period of time (as time remaining after work), but as a state or condition of being free from the necessity of work. (1987: xvii)

Barker carried this a bit further and identified *schole* as an activity, and as an activity:

> it is therefore contrasted not with activity, but with 'occupation' (*ascholia*)—in other words with the sort of activity which is pursued not for its own sake (as the activity of leisure is), but for the sake of something else. . . it also contrasted with, or distinguished from 'recreation' (*anapausis*) and 'amusement' (*paidia*—'the sort of thing children do'). Amusement and recreation mean rest after occupation, and preparation for new occupation: they are thus both essentially connected with the idea of occupation. Leisure stands by itself, in its own independent right. Aristotle thus operates with three different notions; the notion of leisure; the notion of occupation; and the

notion (in one sense intermediate between the two, but in another sense closer to the latter) of amusement and recreation. (1946: 323–324)

For Aristotle, then, occupation was an activity executed with a purpose in mind; in contrast to leisure which included activities performed for their own sake. Leisure, therefore, or the freedom from having to be occupied, was the necessary condition or activity for happiness.

Aristotle believed the goodness of anything was found in the actualization of its uniqueness. This applied to humans as much as anything else. And for human beings, the most unique of functions was the power of reason. Not surprisingly then, Aristotle believed a life of contemplation was the route to happiness and the proper use of leisure. In *Ethics*, he wrote:

. . . that what is best and most pleasant for any given creature is that which is proper to it. Therefore for man, too, the best and most pleasant life is the life of intellect, since this life will also be the happiest. (*Ethics*, Bk X, Ch.7)

One other activity was singled out as being as noble as contemplation, and that activity was music. Considered by Greek society to be the highest form of culture, Aristotle lauded music because it, like contemplation, best fit the definition of the activities leading to happiness; i.e., it is done for its own sake and is without ulterior motive or purpose. (*Politics* Bk. VIII, Chs. 5–6)

Limiting the proper use of leisure to only contemplation and music, however, would certainly condemn all but a small educated leisure class to an unhappy existence. To a large degree, this accurately describes Aristotle's view on the subject. The highest levels of happiness were available to only a few. He did, however, soften his philosophy a bit by recognizing happiness as a matter of degrees. In *Politics*, he wrote:

Happiness is an end, since not all men deem it to be accompanied with pleasure and not pain. This pleasure, however, is regarded differently by different persons, and varies according to the habit of the individual. The pleasure of the best man is the best, and springs from the noblest sources. (*Politics*, Bk. VIII, Ch. 3)

Among the activities Aristotle held in high regard, even if below contemplation and music, were leading a moral life and working in politics; a moral life because acting justly and bravely joined contemplation as uniquely human experiences; politics because it included the fine goal of bringing happiness to the state. (*Ethics*, Bk. I, Ch.2 and Bk. IX, Ch. 9)

As mentioned earlier in defining *schole*, among the activities Aristotle specifically excluded from those connected with happiness and the proper use of leisure were play and amusement. For the most part, this was because amusement was not an activity for its own sake, but rather a period of relaxation designed to restore the person for more toil. Furthermore, simple amusements excluded themselves from activities for happiness because of their superficiality. In other words, the ultimate goal of life ought to be more than diversion. As Aristotle wrote, "the happy life seems to be lived in accordance with goodness, and such a life implies seriousness and does not consist of amusing oneself." (*Ethics*, Bk. X, Ch. 6)

Aristotle understood that external things, including material goods, were prerequisites to leisure. Freedom from the worries of poverty, for example, was necessary if contemplation was to take place. The list of external needs even included friends, judged the most nobel of the external aids because sharing with friends directly enhanced happiness. (*Ethics*, Bk. X, Ch. 8).

Yet as would be expected concerning the use of these external goods, moderation was necessary. Just because a person could not be happy without external goods, "it must not be supposed. . . it will be necessary to have many of them on a grand scale to be happy at all." In fact, Aristotle suggested that the happy man would be perceived by the masses as odd, lacking the materialistic outward appearances upon which people are generally judged. (*Ethics*, Bk. X, Ch. 8)

Perhaps the least expected and most elusive of the necessary external goods was peace. Throughout Aristotle's discourses on leisure, peace is frequently discussed. For one thing, leisure and peace were compared with each other, as one was the goal of toil and work, the other the purpose for war. For another, peace was in itself a means to an end in that it was a necessary condition for leisure. Leisure was impossible for those constantly on guard for their lives and the sovereignty of their nation. (*Ethics*, Bk. X, Ch. 7, *Politics*, Bk. VII, Ch. 14)

The responsibility of the government in regards to leisure, however, ran much deeper than merely striving to end war. Being at peace and having the basics of food and shelter, although important, were not enough to ensure the proper use of leisure. After these preliminary necessities have been met, the final key tool to leisure is a populace educated in the proper use of leisure. According to Aristotle, this responsibility, like peace, belonged to the state.

Aristotle, in fact, went so far as to claim that the fall of nations was a result of a failure to train for leisure. A nation skilled at training for war may well have a populace illiterate in leisure. Once peace is achieved, education must change dramatically, or the nation will crumble from within. Aristotle cited Sparta as an example, but could have been forecasting the demise of future empires as well. Certainly Rome fits the description. (*Politics*, Bk. VII, Chs. 14–15)

As de Grazia stated it:

> Courage in battle is a virtue of limited use in peacetime. The legislator is to blame if he does not educate citizens to those other virtues needed for the

proper use of leisure. . . A citizenry unprepared for leisure will degenerate in prosperous times. (1962: 12)

Governments have not been good at educating for leisure, and one reason may be that educating for leisure, unlike educating for war or business or good citizenry, lacks apparent practical value. Aristotle's response to this was a reminder that learning pursued for its own sake is better than that pursued as a means to something else. The highest functions of education go beyond the practical life, and "to be always seeking after the useful does not become free and exalted souls." (*Politics*, Bk. VIII, Ch. 3)

To fail to educate for leisure leaves a citizenry unskilled at contemplation, insensitive to moderation, and unaware of productive uses of leisure. An excellent illustration of this is the recently retired person who is at a loss as to what to do with his or her time. As Burnett points out in his book on Aristotle and education, it is also what turns people to meaningless diversion rather than proper uses of leisure. (1936:10)

Aristotle did not include women, the working class, or those of limited vision among the people deserving leisure. He held leisure in the highest regard, but reserved it for a small, free, male leisure class. These are major faults in his philosophy and cannot be ignored. Aristotle not only recognized slavery and the strict subordination of women, but relied upon them for support of the leisure class. For a recreation profession attempting to be many things for all people, and for a society based upon equal opportunity, it is valid to wonder whether a philosophy linked to elitism and sexism has any value at all.

Dare, Welton, and Coe's answer to this dilemma is that the student of Aristotle can view his writings in one of two ways.

From one perspective (absolute) the good life is reserved for the few; from another (relative), the process of history holds out the possibility of expanding contemplation (and leisure) throughout society, given changes in economic, moral, and social circumstances. (1987:39)

In other words, should the baby go out with the bath water? In ancient Greece, leisure for the few probably was the only possible scenario. The contemporary reader of Aristotle's views on leisure should bring his ideas into the 20th century to take on an egalitarian flavor.

In summary, Aristotle felt the ultimate goal of each individual was happiness. Happiness was accomplished through leisure. Leisure involved serious endeavors, the greatest of them being contemplation. The government must support the individual in regards to leisure, not only by striving for peace and self-sufficiency, but by encouraging moderation and teaching the proper use of leisure. The result would be elevating leisure activity from simple amusement to the basis of culture.

PARTIAL LIST OF ARISTOTLE'S PUBLICATIONS

Aristotle wrote volumes, addressing just about every subject of science and philosophy known to Greek civilization. For his ideas on leisure, this short manuscript relied entirely upon *Politics* and *Ethics*.

The History Of Animals (Historia Animalium)

Metaphysics (Metaphysica)

Nichomachean Ethics or Ethics (Ethica Nichomachea)

On Generation and Corruption (De Generatione et Corruptione)

On the Generation of Animals (De Generatione Animalium)

On The Heavens (De Caelo)

On the Parts of Animals (De Partibus Animalium)

On the Soul (De Anima)

Organon

Physics (Physica)

Poetics (De Poetica)

Politics (Politica)

Rhetoric (Rhetorica)

REFERENCES

Adler, M. J. (1978). *Aristotle For Everybody*. New York: Bantam Books.

Aristotle, *Ethics*.

Aristotle, *Politics*.

Barker, E., trans. (1946). *The Politics of Aristotle*. London: Oxford University Press.

Burnett, J., ed. (1936). *Aristotle on Education*. London:Cambridge University Press.

de Grazia, S. (1962). *Of Time, Work, and Leisure*. New York:Twentieth Century Fund.

Dare, B., G. Welton and Wm. Coe. (1987). *Concepts of Leisure in Western Thought*. Dubuque, IA.: Kendall/Hunt Publishing.

Durant, W. (1954). *The Story of Philosophy*, 2nd Edition. New York: Simon and Schuster.

Kaplan, J., ed. (1958). *The Pocket Aristotle*. New York:Washington Square Press.

2

CICERO
106–43 B.C.E.

By Hilmi Ibrahim
Whittier College

"This ought to be my happiest time, *my* otium cum dignitate.**"**

From a letter to Quintas

Marcus Tullius Cicero was born on January 3, 106 Before the Common Era, to a wealthy landowner in the municipium of Arpinum, 60 miles southwest of Rome. He was educated in Rome and in Greece, and after military service, he first appeared in court as a defender at age 25. His reputation at the bar led him to a public career as a Quaester in 75 B.C.E.

As a praeter in 66 B.C.E., he made his first important political speech and was elected as consul in 63 B.C.E. He persuaded the Senate to prosecute Cataline who planned an uprising. His announcement to the crowds outside the Senate that the conspirators were executed was the climax of his career.

As the star of Caesar was rising, Cicero's descended. He was exiled, sometimes without a position, other times as governor of a far away province. He devoted a good part of his life to writing. His philosophy came in 900 letters he wrote to his friends from 67 to 43 B.C.E.

A philosopher, statesman, orator, and poet, Cicero was very much affected by the Greek schools of thought, but identified himself primarily with the Academy. He admired the Stoa and the Lyceum, but rejected Epicureanism. Cicero's philosophic writings, however, were not mere copies of Greek originals, for they represent a coherent, unique system of thought. Perhaps his greatest contribution was in the union between philosophy and rhetoric.

A great man, according to Cicero, is a man who is master of both philosophy and rhetoric. To him, philosophy supplies knowledge and rhetoric provides persuasion. Both are the instruments for the effective use of knowledge, for one alone is not sufficient. Such use is the only way for guiding human affairs.

These are the ideals needed for a free society. A free society is a constitutional republic in which persuasion and not violence is the tool of political power. Rome had the seeds for such a society. (Delacy, 1984:113–114)

Cicero's most unique contribution was in transmitting to Rome, and therefore Europe, its philosophic vocabulary—terms such as quality, morality, induction, and infinity. Most of his philosophic works were presented as dialogues preceeded by introductions. His speakers were distinguished Romans and their conflicting views were presented.

As an orator, Cicero made his reputation in politics and in the law courts. He was eclectic, refusing to adhere to either school of oration: the Asian with its rich grandiose style, or the Atticist with its simple form. He tended to end his speeches with rhythms. Cicero believed that the tools of an orator should be thorough knowledge of literature, a ground in philosophy, a storage of history, and legal expertise.

As a poet, he applied rhetoric to his treatment of poetry and refined the use of hexameter, using words of two or three syllables at the end to ensure coincidence of natural word accent. Although his best known poems survived only in fragments, they influenced many individual contemporaries. Cicero is one of those poets who made possible the achievements of Virgil, the greatest Roman poet ever.

According to de Grazia (1964:19), the ideal of leisure went into Rome through the works of Plato, Epicurus, and Aristotle. The Roman word for leisure was *otium*, the opposite of *otium* being *negotium*. In Rome when one was occupied with the affairs of state, army, or business, one was in *negotium* and for that he needed *otium*. *Otium* then was not for its own sake but for *negotium's* sake. Conceived as such, Rome's *otium* is not similar to Greece's *schole*. (Ibrahim, 1979:72)

According to Barnes (1984:38), influenced as he was by the Greeks, Cicero pushed forward the ideal of scholarly leisure, unintelligible to both the commoner and the aristocrat alike. His training under the Greeks led him to adopt this position. Among the Greeks, he quoted Pythagoras, who opined that life is like a great public festival. In festivals, some come to participate in athletic contests, others come to debate and discuss, others just simply come to observe and contemplate. The same happens in life. Some struggle for glory, others seek superiority, but those who have wisdom scorn lesser pursuits and give themselves to thought and study. This is *otium cum dignitate*, a devotion to intellectual pursuits and the cultivation of congenial friendships and of fame, contemporary and posthumous. (Petersson, 1920: 291–292) It was during a two-year stay in Greece and Asia that Cicero enjoyed the leisure for the intellectual and spiritual pursuits which he later called *otium cum dignitate*: rhetoric, philosophy, and debate. Referring to the Catilinarian conspiracy of 65 B.C.E., Cicero believed that he had saved the state and thus had earned his honorable leisure. (Petersson, 1920: 288)

According to Petersson (1920:218), Cicero was too ambitious and active to give any of his time to other pleasures. When others were noisily celebrating public holidays, giving dinners of many courses, gambling, or playing ball, "he sought to serve his own home town, Arpinum."

The *otiosi*, men of leisure, should remember that the life of a student is easier and safer than that of a public servant. It is also less subject to envy. They should know also that intellectual life, if divorced from action, is a maimed and incomplete thing. One finds his highest activity in his relationship with his fellow men.

According to de Grazia (1964:19), Seneca, who knew Cicero's world well, indicated he took to leisure during political difficulties or when he was in a petulant mood, feeling that he was not appreciated by his associates. Pliny corroborated Seneca's analysis when he suggested that Cicero wished for leisure, enjoyed it, and worried too often about *inertiae crimen*, the guilt of inertia. Seneca arrived at the conclusion that Cicero sought *otium* not for itself but because he was fed up with *negotium*.

de Grazia believed that Cicero, like Loyola and Thoreau, conceived of leisure as retreat, repose earned by work, to be taken to prepare a person to better cope with life in the city. (1964:395)

REFERENCES

de Grazia, S. (1964). *Of Time, Work, and Leisure*. Garden City: Anchor Books.
De Lacy, P. H. (1984). Cicero, Marcus Tullius. *Encyclopedia of Philosophy*.
Ibrahim, H. (1979). Leisure in the Ancient World. Ibrahim H. and Shivers, J. *Leisure: Emergence and Expansion*. Los Alamitos, CA: Hwong Publishing.
Petersson, T. (1920). *Cicero: A Biography*. Berkeley: University of California Press.

3

SENECA

4 B.C.E.–65 C.E.

By Hilmi Ibrahim
Whittier College

"**B**ut if that state which we dream of can nowhere be found, leisure begins to be a necessity for all of us, because the only thing that might have been preferred to leisure nowhere exists."

Liber VIII Ad Serenum *De Otio*

Lucius Annaeus Seneca was born in Corduba, Spain and was taken to Rome as a boy to be educated in law and for an official career. He studied under Pythagorean, Stoic, and Cynic philosophers and gained fame for his eloquence. He served in the Senate until he was accused of intrigue and was banished to Corsica. He became a tutor to a boy who later became Emperor Nero, and was able initially to keep Nero within the bounds of humanity. Seneca left public life and retired into the country to live a simple life, yet he was implicated in a conspiracy and was ordered by Nero to commit suicide, which he did in 65 C.E. (McCrea, 1984:550)

Seneca wrote many essays embracing "dialogues" on Tranquility of Mind, on Anger, on the Happy Life, and on Leisure. He also wrote seven books of *Naturales Quaestiones* on physics and left nine tragedies.

McCrea (1984: 550) believes that Seneca was undoubtedly "an earnest seeker of truth, yet he acquiesced to Nero." His real contribution is in being the man of letters of his time. His style varied from Cicero's in that he loved short and epigramatic sentences. He was more of a Stoic than anything else, sympathetic to ethical principle and may have been a Christian.

John W. Basore (1932) translated the *Seneca Moral* Essays, among which is Liber VIII *De Otio*, on Leisure. Seneca started by deriding the way humans lead their lives. ". . . we find pleasure first in one and then in another, and the trouble is that our choices are not only wrong, but also fickle." (Basore, 1932:181) The Stoics suggested that one should, for the common good, stick to the affairs of state until the end of his life, that there should be no leisure before death. Seneca rejected this notion and claimed that he was not betraying his own philosophic orientation, becoming more of an Epicurean in that he was not revolting against the teachings of the Stoics by praising leisure. The Epicureans accepted the doctrine that a man, from his early life, can surrender himself totally to the contemplation of truth and to the search for the art of living. Also, upon retirement, a man is entitled to turn his mind to quite different activities. (Basore, 1932:185)

In fact, claimed Seneca, both the Stoics and the Epicureans direct us to leisure, but by two different roads. Epicurus says "the wise man will not engage in public affairs except in emergency." Zeno the Stoic says "he will engage in public affairs unless something prevents him." The cause preventing one from engaging in public affairs may be ill-health or the corruption of the state. But man can serve his fellow man through leisure by concentrating on liberal studies. If he does not benefit his fellow men, he will benefit a few; if not a few, those who are near to him; if not those, himself. (Basore, 1932:187)

There are two commonwealths: the vast one which embraces alike gods and men and is measured by the path of the sun, the other is the one to which one is assigned by birth (Athens or Carthage). Some serve both the greater and the lesser at the same time, some only the lesser, some only the greater. One is able to serve the greater commonwealth even better in leisure. "We are fond of saying that the highest good is to live according to nature. Nature has begotten us for two purposes—for contemplation and for action." (Basore, 1932:189) How great is our desire to gain knowledge of the unknown, queried Seneca. Nature has bestowed upon us an inquisitive disposition and begotten us to be spectators of her mighty array. She wished us not only to behold her, but to gaze upon her as well. "She has not only created man erect, but in order to fit him for contemplation of herself, she has given him a head to top the body. . . " (Basore, 1932:191)

Nature intended us to be both active and contemplative, asserted Seneca. "And I really do both, since even contemplative life is not devoid of action." (Basore, 1932:195) Seneca suggested that he did not resort to leisure because it is pleasant and has its own charms. Action *sans* leisure is like wealth without virtue; all of these must be combined and go hand-in-hand. Why defy action? There are great men who accomplished great things without leading an army, holding a public office, or framing a law. Their work did not benefit one state, but the whole human race. Their leisure is benefitting for the good men.

According to Seneca, there are three kinds of life. One is devoted to pleasure, a second devoted to contemplation, and a third devoted to action. Which is best? All of them come under the same name. "For he who sanctions pleasure is not without contemplation, nor he who surrenders to contemplation without pleasure, nor is he whose life is devoted to action without contemplation." (Basore. 1932:199) It is clear that contemplation is favored by those who seek pleasure and by those who pursue action. Some men may make contemplation their aim. For Seneca it is a roadstead, but not the harbor.

PARTIAL LIST OF SENECA'S PUBLICATIONS

Ad Lucilium Epistulae Morales. (1917). Translated by Richard M. Gummere. 3 volumes, New York: Putnams.

The Complete Roman Drama. (1942). Translated by George E. Duckworth. New York: Random House.

Naturales Quaestiones. (1971). Translated by Thomas H. Corcaran. Cambridge: Harvard University Press.

Petronius. (1916). Translated by Michael Heseltine. New York: Putnams.

REFERENCES

Basore, J. (1932). *Seneca: Moral Essays Volume II*. Cambridge: Harvard University Press.

McCrea, N. (1984). Seneca, Lucius Annaeus. *The Encyclopedia Americana International, 24*. Danbury, CT.: Grolier Incorporated.

Sorrensen, V. (1984). *Seneca: The Humanist At The Court Of Nero*. Chicago: University of Chicago Press.

4

IBN KHALDUN

1337–1408

By Hilmi Ibrahim
Whittier College

" **F**inally are the desires connected with leisure, the desire for amusement, relaxation, and laughter, the desire to hear rhythmic tones, and the desire for learning. "

Mahdi, 1964:179

21

The Khaldun family originated from the southern Arabian tribe of Kinda. A branch of the family established itself in Seville and later moved to Tunis in the middle of the 13th century. Khaldun was educated under Moroccan teachers. He became a royal secretary at the age of 20 and continued that profession for 20 years. He acted most of the time as an advisor, ". . . sometimes he was in high favor, sometimes under suspicion, sometimes was thrown into prision. . . " (Sarton, 1956:176)

In 1374 he entered a monastary, where he remained for four years, and it was there that he wrote the first draft of his masterpiece, *The Muqaddama*. He returned to Tunis apparently to obtain some information in the libraries of the city. Most probably with the same purpose in mind, he headed east in 1382. He was persuaded by the Sultan of Cairo to remain in that city and was appointed *grand quadi* (Supreme Court Judge) in 1384. After he lost his family and fortune in a shipwreck, he devoted his life to his studies. He died in Cairo in March of 1408.

Ibn Khaldun was a prolific writer. Most of his early writings were summaries of previous works, but he will always be remembered for his *Kitab al Ibar*, a collection of origins and information concerning the historical development of many societies. It is divided into three parts: a philosophical introduction; a history of the Arabs and other Semites such as the Jews, Copts, and Persians, along with the history of the Greeks, Romans, Turks, and Franks; and the history of the Berbers and the Muslim dynasty of North Africa.

Ibn Khaldun suggested a new science, the purpose of which is to examine the nature and causes of the human society and to reveal the internal aspects of the external events of history. (Mahdi, 1964:171) The relationship between the new science and history is revealed in three ways: in a sequence through which the mind achieves knowledge where the new science comes after history; in the art of the historian where history and the new science should be combined; and in the order of being where the object of the science of culture comes before the objects of history.

The study of the new science requires the study of five major problems: primitive culture and its transformation into a civilized one; the State; the City; the economic life; and the Sciences. But it should be understood that culture is not an independent substance, but a property of another substance—man.

To Ibn Khaldun, the human faculties are innate capacities to desire. The desires of the human soul are capable of infinite variations from the simplest instinctive urge for the satisfaction of hunger and thirst to the most intricate, complex, and specialized desires developed in a highly civilized order.

He classified them as follows (Ibrahim, 1988):

Bodily appetites to satisfy hunger and thirst, the need for warmth and coolness, sex and reproduction. These desires are necessary for existence and vary little in time and place, only in form and degree.

The desires for safety, prosperity, and calm come next. In general, humans seek the absence of serious causes of alarm which allows for confidence and hope. Otherwise, they may be struck with fear or anger and desire vengence.

The desire for affiliation with others who are either related or resemble one comes third. Accordingly, humans tend to want to live together in companionship and fellowship.

After the formation of human associations and organizations as modes of relations within society, the fourth type of desires are fulfilled. Among these is the desire to be victorious and superior, and the desire to obtain wealth. Such desires may be the source of conflicts and wars. But something positive may come out of them—the feeling of pity and the lending of assistance.

Finally, humans seek to fulfill three sets of desires connected with leisure. The first set of desires includes the desire for amusement, relaxation, and laughter. The second set includes the desire for rhythmic tunes, and the desire to experience objects of hearing, tasting, touching, smelling, or seeing which leads to delight and delectation.

The last set includes the desire to wonder, to learn, and to gain knowledge.[1]

When the community of necessity which provides food and safety is established, it generates the forces that could lead to its destruction. Men cooperate to feed themselves. Such cooperation and the division of labor among them lead to opulence which transforms the community of necessity to a community of luxury. Men start to transgress the property of others. The injured, driven by anger, react, and the result is conflict and confusion, and existence is threatened once again. But the most able among them restrains them and reconciles them, and forces them to follow his directive. He becomes their ruler and institutes kingship (sultan), and the state.[2] The state is thus natural and necessary because society which is also natural and necessary cannot exist without the state.

Once the state comes into being, it follows the natural laws of growth, maturity, and decline. It passes through five distinct stages (Mahdi, 1964; Rosenthal, 1958):

1. A period of establishment when *assabiyya* (solidarity), based on kinship and religion, preserves the state.
2. The ruler succeeds in monopolizing power and becomes an absolute master. As any well-disposed body, the state should consist of a heirarchy of powers. Solidarity is replaced by a paid army and a bureaucracy.
3. A stage of leisure and tranquility follows. Crafts, fine arts, and science are encouraged and they flourish.

4. Having reached its zenith, a period of contentment will follow. Ruler and ruled believe that their luxurious lifestyles and the advantage of civilization have always existed and will continue to exist forever.

5. The habit of comfort and luxury generates physical weakness and vice. People no longer make long range plans and the birth rate drops. The entire population lives in large crowded cities, becoming subject to diseases and plagues. Prodigality and waste set in. The state has reached old age and is doomed to slow or violent death like a wick dying out of a lamp whose oil has gone.

The city exists for the satisfaction of man's desire for luxury, refinement, and leisure. (Mahdi, 1964) When a powerful state comes into being, it establishes or takes over cities. The long struggle for building the state having ended, the group looks for rest and seeks the enjoyment of their efforts. Cities reflect the state that founds them. The longer it took to build the state, the more time the city will have to grow and establish its institutions. First feverish expansion takes place. The state benefits from this progressive trend for it increases income.

A new social structure emerges which is radically different from that of a primitive culture. It is characterized by the decline of the original *assabiyya* of small, closely knit, and relatively isolated communities. The various classes of rulers, bureaucrats, artisans, traders, and learned men tend to group themselves according to political and economic interests.

The inhabitants of the city become accustomed to life in luxury and waste and become slaves to their habits. They depend on the walls of the city and on mercenaries for their protection. They eat a variety of food stuff, weakened by cooking and spices that do not fit the humors of the body. They do not have the opportunity for physical activity and open air. They strain their intelligence to invent ways to occupy their now idle life. Prostitution and sodomy spread, leading to the decline of natural relations and compassion among members of the family. By this time both the state and the city are decaying. If not attacked from the outside, the city will slowly disintegrate.

Ibn Khaldun used two terms to operationalize leisure: *Faraqh* and *dia*. The first could also mean free time which he used to describe the fifth layer of desires that humans seek to fulfill. The second term which could also mean to feel lost, was used to describe a state lacking the necessary elements to build a civilized culture.

Ibn Khaldun seems to agree with Huizinga (1950) and Peiper (1952) in that leisure is the basis of culture, since he placed leisure as the third stage of his five-stage theory on the establishment of the state. While influenced by Aristotle, Ibn Khaldun did not adopt completely his views on leisure (*schole*) in which contemplation and music are the highest forms. Ibn

Khaldun's leisure is closer to Aristotle's *paidia* (amusement) and *anapausis* (recreation). (de Grazia, 1964) In addition, Ibn Khaldun lists the desire to wonder, to learn, and to gain knowledge as leisure. He is, in this case, in agreement with Cicero's *otium* (scholarly leisure). (Petersson, 1920).

Roger Callois suggested that *"ludus* is not the only conceivable metamorphosis of *paidia."* (1979:33) He was suggesting that certain cultures may direct play activities differently enough that the western mind may not conceive of it as ludic. In fact, he used the Chinese culture to show that a different variety developed there. Similarly, a different form of metamorphosis might have taken place in Medieval Islam, the one(s) suggested by Ibn Khaldun in his fifth layer of human desires connected with leisure.

PARTIAL LIST OF IBN KHALDUN'S PUBLICATIONS

Al Muquaddama (in Arabic)
Kitab Al Ibar (in Arabic)

REFERENCES

Callois, R. (1979). *Man, Play and Games.* New York: Schocker Books.
de Grazia S. (1964). *Of Time, Work, and Leisure.* New York: Anchor Books.
Huizinga, J. (1952). *Homo Ludens: A Study of the Element of Play in Culture.* Boston: Beacon Press.
Ibrahim, H. (1988). Leisure, Idleness, and Ibn Khaldun. *Leisure Studies, 7,* 51–58.
Mahdi, M. (1964). *Ibn Khaldun's Philosophy of History.* Chicago: University Of Chicago Press.
Maslow, A. (1970). *Motivation and Personality.* New York: Harper and Row.
Petersson, T. (1920). *Cicero: A Biography.* Berkeley: University of California Press.
Pieper, J. (1952). *Leisure: The Basis of Culture.* New York: Pantheon Press.
Rosenthal, F. (translator) (1958). *Ibn Khaldun The Muqaddimah: An Introduction to History.* New York: Bollinger Foundation.
Sarton, G. (1956). *Introduction to History of Science.* Baltimore: William and Wilkins.

[1]It is rather intriguing how similar Ibn Khaldun's list of human desires is to Maslow's heirarchy of needs. (1970: 35–58)

[2]It is interesting to note that many contemporary anthropologists are advocating the same using the term "primitive state." (Service, 1975)

5

FREDERICK LAW OLMSTED
1822–1903

By Ron Havard
Ithaca College

Courtesy National Park Service, Frederick Law Olmsted National Historic Site

"*The primary purpose of the Park is to provide the best practicable means to healthful recreation for the inhabitants of all classes.*"

Olmsted & Kimball, 1970:44

Frederick Law Olmsted was born the 26th of April, 1822 in Hartford, Connecticut to Charlotte Law (Hull) and John Olmsted, in a secure place, by his right, in the city founded by his ancestors and in the community formed and sustained by seven generations of his family.

During the 81 years of his life, Frederick Law Olmsted tried many professions: clerk, cabin boy, farmer, writer, journalist, traveler, editor, politician, government official, and landscape architect, the profession he created. This variety of experience contributed to his understanding of his time, which he translated into projects to meet future urban needs. (Wurman, et al, 1972:6)

Raised in an affluent New England environment, Olmsted had a vision of a gentle reasonable society whose citizens and their democratically-elected representatives, working together, would design the best possible setting for themselves and their descendants.

Olmsted regarded his childhood as instrumental in awakening his later interest in making the natural environment a component of the expanding urban one. By the time he was 14, Olmsted had lived and studied with rural preachers and explored the New England countryside around their homes. While his friends were entering college (which he was advised against because of temporarily weak vision), Olmsted took up what he called "a decently restrained vagabond life" in the course of which he attended lectures at Yale for a year. (Wurman, et al, 1972:6) During the period 1838–1840, Olmsted studied topographical engineering with Frederick A. Barton, spending two years learning surveying, collecting rocks and plants, and drawing plans of imaginary towns.

Through Olmsted's life "the insistant presence of sickness and death [was] commonplace in domestic life of the past century. Olmsted lost his mother, brothers, and sisters in his childhood; his closest friend, his brother John, in his youth; and was himself intermittently seriously ill throughout his long life." (Wurman, et al 1974:30) Olmsted had been by all accounts, a rather lonely lad, much given to long rambles in the country. His mother died while he was so young that he had "but a tradition of memory rather than the faint recollection of her." (Olmsted & Kimball, 1970:46) Not that Olmsted was deeply scarred by his mother's premature passing. He quite liked his father, brother, and stepmother, people, as he put it, "of silent habits" that suited his own solitary temperament admirably.

When he was 24, Olmsted joined the crew of a ship sailing to China; upon his return, he apprenticed himself to two farmers. In 1848, his father bought him a farm on Staten Island, where he was able to try out his ideas about farming on a small scale. After two years, his desire for travel resurfaced, and he embarked on a walking tour of England with his brother John and a friend, Charles Loring Brace. Impressed by English rural life and fascinated by the planning and construction of deceptively natural park landscapes, he wrote *Walks and Talks of an American Farmer in England,* which was published in 1852. (Wurman, *et al,* 1972:6)

> Olmsted had an intense interest in the out-of-doors and had developed skills in boating, camping, and so on. As a young man, he spent many hours thinking, dreaming, and studying the outdoors and how it affected man. He also devoted much time to reading about people and nature, philosophy and agriculture, the science and art of landscape gardening. He then became a farmer, raising the traditional agricultural and horticultural crops, and practiced landscaping gardening as well. (Jubenvile, 1976:31)

In fact, environmental planning was only his second career. By the time he finally committed himself to it, Olmsted was already an established writer, journalist, and social critic. He had helped launch *The Nation,* a respected liberal journal still in publication. He also wrote two influential books. One of these, *The Cotton Kingdom* (1861), was based on his dispatches as a *New York Times* correspondent. These dispatches were entitled: "A Journey in the Seaboard Slave States," "A Journey Through Texas," and "A Journey in the Back Country." They are one of the most accurate and vivid accounts of life in the pre-Civil War South.

His career as a planner and designer spanned more than a generation, from his appointment in 1857, at the age of 35, as the superintendent of an as yet undesigned Central Park, to his retirement in 1895. Throughout, Olmsted was known as a landscape architect. In the park and public sphere, Olmsted has, of course, become a hallowed figure. Name any city and its most prominent landscape feature probably bears the name of the father of the profession. (*Time,* 1972:98)

Olmsted created Central Park, his first and most famous work, from a wasteland on New York's outskirts. Much of it was swamp, "steeped," Olmstead reported, "in the overflow and mush of pigsties, slaughter-houses, and bone-boiling works, and the stench was sickening." But when a competition was held in 1857 for the park's design, Olmsted, a farmer-turned-journalist who had been hired to supervise the clearing of the land, teamed up with British born architect Calvert Vaux to produce the winning plan. (Kern, 1972:80)

"Greensward" as the Olmsted-Vaux plan was called, surmounted every difficulty with such imaginative brilliance that later generations have often been lulled into presuming that the architects did little more than preserve what was already there. In fact, Greensward created a naturalness that the original land never possessed. The commissioners awarded it the grand prise and promoted Olmsted to architect-in-chief of Central Park on May 17, 1858.

The following year, he married his brother's widow, Mary, and adopted her three children. A year later, the first of Olmsted's own three children was born. However, a carriage accident which shattered Olmsted's knee and killed his infant son blighted Olmsted's happiness.

Olmsted in 1861 became the general secretary of the newly created United States Sanitary Commission (later to become the American Red Cross), and for two years struggled with the monumental task of providing troops with medical and sanitary supplies. The results of this experience made him an ernest advocate of pure water, adequate sewage treatment, and disease prevention during the post war era.

At the age of 41, when he was the head of a growing family and deeply in debt, he was unexpectedly offered a lucrative position as general manager of the Mariposa Company, a gold mining company in California. His reputation as the designer for Central Park brought a flurry of requests for his services. He surveyed Yosemite Valley and in September, 1864 was appointed Commissioner of Yosemite and Mariposa Big Tree Grove. He also designed some estates and a cemetery, and provided a plan for the Berkeley campus of the University of California.

In 1865, at the urging of Vaux and lured by the opportunity of working on Prospect Park in Brooklyn and on the weekly review, *The Nation*, Olmsted returned to New York to officially take up a career as a landscape architect. Repeatedly frustrated by political interference and bureaucratic stupidity—often accompanied by several resignations and reappointments, Olmsted transferred the major part of his energy from New York to Boston, and moved permanently to Brookline in 1883. The Boston period of his career, which began in the late 1870s, included Montreal, the Biltmore estate, and the World's Columbian Exposition in Chicago. (Wurman, *et al,* 1972:7)

Yet when Olmsted retired 40 years later, nearly every state and territory in the Union carried examples of his handiwork or marks of his influence. He had instructed the nation in the necessity of striking a healthy balance in its daily environment between the natural world and the man-made world. And he had trained a generation of experts in areas like suburban design and regional planning, which had not even existed until Olmsted invented them.

In the late 1890s, Olmsted became incapacitated by failing memory, followed by gradual mental disintegration. He spent his final years until his death on August 28, 1903, as a patient at the Mclean Asylum in Waverly, Massachusetts. Ironically, he had designed the grounds himself, almost 30 years before.

To have accomplished as much in a single lifetime as Olmsted did is astonishing. There is no label quite broad enough to cover Olmsted's activities. He built the first parkways, for instance, and even coined the word. He was the first to use overpasses and underpasses to keep the movements of pedestrians and vehicular traffic separated, a notion that has only lately become accepted as a principle of urban design. At the other end of the scale, Olmsted fought to conserve America's virgin wilderness. He and Vaux helped save Niagara Falls from commercial exploitation, and as the first commissioner of Yosemite Valley Park in California (1893), Olmsted spelled out his ideas in a brief that became the official creed for the entire national and state park systems.

The prototypes were, naturally, English. Olmsted had absorbed the lessons of the "picturesque" on his first visit to England and Europe in 1850—that mode of articulating a landscape or a park so that it seemed not designed, but modulated into a suggestive wilderness. He was the first American planner to think holistically, in terms of complete systems. Architect, sociologist, ecologist, engineer, and conservationist, he felt an abiding concern for the refreshment of human life by an interaction with nature, but with a nature that was planned or preserved.

What most concerned Olmsted, however, was to make nature accessible to the millions imprisoned in the big cities. Even the major cities, luckily, still had space available for parks, and the success of Central Park set off a mania for park building. Over the years the sophisticated landscapes that were Olmsted's trademark sprouted up across the country— Belle Isle Park in Detroit, Cherokee Park in Louisville, and Lake Park in Milwaukee. In Boston and Buffalo, Olmsted did even better, creating whole systems of parks connected by landscape corridors weaving through the urban grid. " 'The Emerald Necklace' concept of a string of green space around the city, bringing recreation areas close to every citizen, was introduced in Boston in 1888 by Charles Eliot and Frederick Law Olmsted." (Knudson, 1980:170) At the same time, Olmsted foresaw the migration to the suburbs. Long before community planning came into fashion, he designed complete commuter villages—notably Riverside, near Chicago—which are still regarded as models of suburban design.

Olmsted also did his share of more conventional landscape planning, including private estates and college campuses such as Amherst, Trinity, West Point, George Washington, and Stanford. He was the obvious choice to improve the grounds of the Capitol in Washington, D.C. in 1874. But even his private projects had a way of turning a profit for the public. His efforts for George W. Vanderbilt on his vast wooded estate, Biltmore, near Ashville, N.C. led to the founding of the U.S. Forest Service. And his setting for the Columbian Exposition of 1893 was deliberately planned so that the site would revert afterward into another pleasant Olmsted park, for the people of Chicago to use and enjoy. (Kern, 1972:8)

"In 1870 an early advocate of city planning, Frederick Law Olmsted urged the importance of a comprehensive city plan that would make provisions for physical and mental health, safety and transportation needs in commercial and residential districts, proper housing and recreation, and even the aesthetic proclivities of the people." (Fisher, 1986:2) Olmsted applied his "organic principle" to the whole city, saying that since the city is always in a process of growth, it needs a rational, comprehensive plan to direct that growth for the well being of all. Olmsted was aware of the detrimental effects of urbanization but was convinced also that cities produce a better quality of life than rural areas. He viewed parks as a countervailing influence that should be integrated into the city to produce a new, higher, organic urban whole. (Stach, 1988:125)

This nation's most comprehensive environmental planner and designer contributed to the development of cities and regions, of a national park system, and of the United States Forest Service. It was always worth a commitment to social democracy that he completed his prototypical designs for such planned environments as urban parks, parkways, suburban communities, and campuses. His work, or examples of his influence, are still evident in every region of the United States and Canada. (Fein, 1972:3)

With the establishment of the National Association for Olmsted Parks in 1980, and the eight affiliates in Atlanta, Baltimore, Buffalo, Louisville, Massachusetts, New York, Rhode Island, and Seattle, there has been a movement throughout the country to identify, inventory, and revitalize Olmsted's works.

SELECTED LIST OF OLMSTED'S PUBLICATIONS

Walks and Talks of an American Farmer in England (Vols. 1–2). (1852). New York: George P. Putnam.

Walks and Talks of an American Farmer in England. (1859). Columbia, OH: J.H. Riley & Co.

A Journey Through Texas, or A Saddle-Trip on the Southwestern Frontier with a Statistical Appendix, (1857). New York: Dix, Edwards, & Co.

Journey in the Back Country. (1860). New York: Mason Brothers.

The Cotton Kingdom (Vols. 1–2) (1861). New York: Mason Brothers.

Mount Royal, Montreal. (1881). New York: G.P. Putnam's Sons.

REFERENCES

Fein, A. (1972). *Frederick Law Olmsted and the American Environmental Tradi-tion.* New York: Braziller.

Fisher, I.D. (1986). *Frederick Law Olmsted and the City Planning Movement in the United States.* Ann Arbor, MI: UMI Research Press.

Jubenville, A. (1976). *Outdoor Recreation Planning.* Philadelphia, PA: W.B. Saunders Co.

Kern, E. (1972, December 8). He Saw Democracy in Dirt. *Life, 73,* pp. 80-5.

Knudson, D. (1980). *Outdoor Recreation.* New York: MacMillan.

Olmsted, F.R. Jr., and Kimball, T. (1970). *Frederick Law Olmsted, Landscape Architect, 1822–1903*. New York: Benjamin Blom.

Stach, P.B. (1988 Winter) A Revolution in Land Use Regulation? [Review of *Frederick Law Olmsted and the City Planning Movement in the United States*]. *Journal of the American Planning Association, v. 54*, pp. 125–126.

Wurman, R., Levy, A. & Katz, J. (1972). *The Nature of Recreation*. Cambridge, MA: The MIT Press.

The Prescient Planner. (1972, December 11). *Time, v. 100*, pp. 98–99.

6

JOHN MUIR
1838–1914

By Phyllis M. Ford
Michigan State University

© 1971, Flying Spur Press

"The sun was up, but it was yet too cold for birds and the few burrowing animals that dwell here. Only the stream, cascading from pool to pool, seemed to be wholly awake. Yet the spirit of the opening day called to action."

The Mountains of
California, 1911:31

Yosemite National Park in California
Courtesy National Park Service

In the mid-1800s, America was a country of great diversity. On the east coast were cities with opera houses, hospitals, auditoriums, universities, and many people. In the western part of the nation there were few people, many miles of open space, acres of forests, unexplored areas, and vast expanses of untold beauty. In the center of the country were acres of prairies, forests, and small towns made up of laboring farmers eking out their livings through the toil of claiming the land for agriculture.

On the east coast and as far west as the Mississippi River, people's concerns were focused on the social issues accompanying the influx of thousands of immigrants, the new ideas brought about by standardized education programs, and the need for social control to alleviate the problems of those crowded into the cities. The last half of the century witnessed the Civil War, the Industrial Revolution, the invention of the automobile, progressive education, and the events that eventually culminated in the first two World Wars. Basketball and baseball were invented, as were the telegraph and the telephone. Names such as Ralph Waldo Emerson, Henry David Thoreau, John Burroughs, and Walt Whitman filled the literary appetites of the nation. The great botanist, Asa Gray, and the geologist, Louis Agassiz, were counted among the faculty at Harvard University. John James Audubon filled his canvasses with life-size paintings of birds, while railroad magnate Avery Harriman filled his banks with dividends earned from the great expansion of railroads that were built across the country. Teddy Roosevelt was well on his way to earning the political respect of the nation. Born in the late years of the 19th century were Jane Addams, Joseph Lee, Luther Gulick, and Henry Curtis who were later to shape America's values toward municipal provision of areas and programs for children's play. Also late in the century, events occurred that brought to America such organizations as the YMCA, YWCA, Boy Scouts, and Girl Scouts. In 1911, Luther Gulick and his colleagues succeeded in founding the Campfire Girls.

In the forests and prairies west of the Mississippi there were few cities. Seattle, Portland, San Francisco, and Los Angeles were the major ones and they were 3,000 miles west of the industrialized, historic cities of Boston, New York, Philadelphia, and Baltimore, and 2,000 miles west of Chicago and St. Louis. The concerns of people living in those thousands of miles of uninhabited land were focused on survival and conquering land. While those on the eastern seaboard exhibited concern for conservation, there is no evidence that those on the west coast had any intentions of preserving the land. Their values were clearly related to the belief in the "myth of super-abundance," as Stewart Udall was to call it 100 years later. These people believed there was more than enough of every type of natural resource that Americans could ever want. Trees, forests, prairies, animals, soil, water, and fresh air were there for the taking, the using, and the exploiting.

Into this period of American history entered an 11-year old boy who was destined to change much of the thinking of America about the land and the preservation of its resources. It is often said that people are the product of their environments, but it appears that, in the case of John Muir, he was the analyst of his surroundings and the prophet of their future.

John Muir came to America in 1849 from Scotland with his father, 9-year-old brother, David, and 13-year-old sister, Sarah to start a farm in Wisconsin. As soon as the farm was manageable and the home was inhabitable, the father sent for his wife and the other four children: the eldest sister, Margaret, and the three youngest, Daniel, Mary, and Anna. There on the Wisconsin farm, John toiled beside his siblings for 11 years. While he had had good and consistent schooling in Scotland and was well-prepared to read the classics, cipher, and write, John spent only two months in school between 1849 and 1859. The childhood days of John Muir were controlled by his stern, religious father who flogged the boy daily for the sake of righteousness.

By the time John was 17, his family had moved 6 miles to the southeast because the thin soil of the original farm had given out. It was at this new farm that a well digging accident almost cost John his life. At that time, rural families usually procured their drinking water from springs, streams or rivers. Eventually, water came from wells dug by hand to the depth of the water table or a water-bearing crack in the rock. The Muir's second farm had no water and it was deemed necessary to dig a 90-foot well to reach the underground source of water.

Mr. Muir and David would have John climb into a large bucket and then they would lower him into the opening and let him down until he reached the bottom of the spot where he had been on the previous day. John filled the bucket with the sandstone chips he had loosened the day before and the bucket was raised and emptied, while John laboriously loosened another pile of chips. At lunch time, the bucket was lowered for John and he was raised to the surface. After lunch, he was lowered into the shaft again and the morning chips were lifted to the surface where the bucket again rested until John was ready to come up at the end of the day.

One morning, when John had reached 80 feet below the surface, he became faint and failed to fill the bucket with the chips from the previous day. His father yelled to him, asking him what was wrong, and got no response. In one of the passages from *The Story of My Boyhood and Youth*, Muir tells the reader that seeing a sapling burr oak against the sky revived him enough to call to his father to get him out of there. After several attempts and much yelling from the father, John managed to get into the bucket and was hauled up, having nearly suffocated from the carbonic gas that sank to the bottom of dry wells. One of the neighbors came by and explained that the gas, called "choke-damp," could be dispelled by throwing water down the shaft or by agitating it by lowering a bunch of light brush tied to a rope and stirring it around several times every morning. As soon as he was able, John re-entered the well (after agitating the air thoroughly) and dug to the 90-foot mark where at "last I struck a fine, hearty gush of water. Constant dripping wears away stone. So does constant chipping, while at the same time wearing away the chipper. Father never spent an hour in that well. He trusted me to sink it straight and plumb, and I did, and built a fine covered top over it, and swung two iron-bound buckets in it from which we all drank for many a day." (Teale, 1954: 50)

Muir's early days were spent toiling on the farm, receiving his daily whipping, saving money, buying books by Shakespeare, Milton, Cowper, and others of similar quality, and by inventing. It was the desire to read that led him to invent. Muir's father refused to allow John to read at night and insisted that he go to bed at the same time as the rest of the family, for he hated irregularity. Evidently, the night he issued this decree, John was reading about the history of the Church and his father gave in to the point of adding, "If you will read, get up in the morning and read. You may get up in the morning as early as you like." (Teale, 1954:52)

The first morning, the excited boy rose to read and, looking at the clock, found it was one o'clock in the morning. He had gained five hours to go on with his reading, but the idea of reading in the zero temperature of an unheated house caused him to postpone the books while he invented a self-setting sawmill so he would waste no time in chopping. The making of the saw required designing his own tools and the working of an old piece of steel for a blade. Since he worked in the basement right under his father's bed, he had to be quiet so as not to wake him. Actually, the father knew what was going on, but he had given John permission to rise early, and his Christian ethics forbade him to go back on his word.

It is from the writings of his boyhood, remembered in later years and laboriously transformed into essays, that we get a glimpse of four characteristics that seem to have served Muir well throughout his life. His deeply founded religion; the love for literature; exposure to hard work, pain and discomfort; combined with an unusual ability to observe and deduce the greater marvels of nature. These qualities appear and reappear throughout Muir's writings, and have given us great insight into the man whose works are still read by thousands. While a religious man, Muir had no creed, but was constantly expressing his appreciation for the Creator.

He became interested in transcendentalism after reading Thoreau and Emerson.

In 1860, John Muir left home with the blessings of his parents to take his inventions to the state fair. He may never have returned home again until the end of the century for we know that soon thereafter, he entered the University of Wisconsin where he studied for two years. During this time he studied the writings of Louis Agassiz, the scientist, and learned of Thoreau and Emerson from Dr. and Mrs. Carr for whom he worked. Poor and hungry though he was, Muir spent four years at Madison, taking courses in chemistry, mathematics, physics, Greek, Latin, botany, and geology instead of working toward a degree. He left in 1863 to go on what he called "a glorious botanical and geological excursion, which . . . lasted nearly fifty years . . ." (Teale, 1954:72) and traded the University of Wisconsin for the University of the Wilderness. While he earned no degree from his studies there, 34 years later, the University of Wisconsin awarded him the honarary LL.D. degree

He left the University of Wisconsin with the intention of entering the medical school at Ann Arbor Michigan, but evidently, because his draft number for the Civil War was not called, he chose to wander north to Canada studying plants and doing odd jobs. In order to test more inventions and to become employed, Muir accepted a job in a Canadian factory making broom handles where his inventiveness increased the output of the factory. When that factory burned down in 1866 (and with it, Muir's draft of a first book), he left for Indianapolis, a city chosen for its numerous factories as well as its proximity to some of the finest hardwoods in America. He found work at the wagon wheel factory of Osgood, Smith & Company and was so successful in both inventions and administrative skills that he was offered a partnership after his first year. That spring, however, the cornea of his right eye was pierced when a file slipped from his hands. For a short time, Muir lost his vision in that eye and later became blind in both eyes as a sympathetic nervous reaction set in. The accident caused such pain, fear, and annoyance that, upon recovery, he was convinced never to work again inside or with machines. At that point, John Muir began his famous 1,000-mile walk, and traveled from Indiana to Kentucky, Tennessee, Georgia, and Florida where he contracted malaria. The 4- × 6.5-inch notebook that he tied to his belt on the trip has since been edited (1916) and appears under the title of *The Thousand Mile Walk.* He had planned to keep going to South America, however, he was only able to find a boat going to Cuba and then to New York, a place he later admitted he would like to explore if only it was clear of its inhabitants. From New York he journeyed by boat to California via the Panama Canal.

In 1866, Muir arrived in San Francisco and took the quickest way out of town. He headed east over the Pacheco Pass toward the land that he always remembered as the most beautiful he had ever beheld. He was able to find a job as an escort to a sheepherder, and soon became a supervisor of shepherds. It was during this time that he realized sheep were "hooved locusts" devouring the fragile mountain lands as he watched "flowers being turned into mutton." The journal he kept during this time became Muir's fourth book, *My First Summer in the Sierra,* published in 1911 when he was 71. The walking and writing trips he started in Indiana were to continue throughout his life.

In 1869, his friends from Madison, the Carrs, moved to California where they renewed their acquaintance with Muir. Professor Carr had taught geology and chemistry at Madison and had became a faculty member at the University of California. Jeanne Carr influenced Muir to write, and helped him get his articles placed in such well-known journals as the *Overland Monthly, New York Tribune, Sacramento Union, San Francisco Bulletin, Century Magazine,* and *Atlantic Monthly.* From conversations with the Carrs, Muir came back to his interest in the work of Ralph Waldo Emerson and read and reread his 1870 book of prose as he traveled the High Sierras, often writing in the margins when his opinions differed from those of the author.

Because of their eminence, the Carrs were able to convince Emerson to visit them when he was in California in 1871. They introduced Emerson to Muir who they thought was the best person to interpret the natural history of the Yosemite region. The traveling companions of the 71-year old Emerson insisted on staying in a hotel and holding the discussions indoors. The 33-year old Muir was quite disappointed by this behavior for only through camping out, he believed, could one really understand nature. He developed new respect for Emerson during the visit, however, and continued to read his works, especially the nature essays and articles on Transcendentalism. After Emerson returned to the east coast, Muir spent the summer studying the glaciation of Yosemite.

The following summer, Muir took a job as caretaker in a Yosemite hotel and spent much of the fall continuing those studies. His theories that glaciers had carved out the Yosemite Valley and that a subsequent dropping of the land had created the formations found in the area were quite controversial, particularly among those who insisted the area around the valley was created by a vast uplifting. Years later, Muir's theories were proven to be correct. He left Yosemite in 1873 to return to Oakland and spent the next ten months writing, but he took time that summer to climb Mt. Whitney's east side, becoming the first white man to make the ascent.

In 1864, President Lincoln had signed a bill ceding Yosemite to the state of California for public use, resort, and recreation. Muir had noticed how over-grazed and over-logged the beautiful area was and began his campaign to save the park for posterity. He introduced bills in the 1860s to save Sequoia and to enlarge Yosemite, but still took time away from his political activities to travel. In 1879, curiosity again consumed him and he went to Alaska where he and S. Hall Yound became the first white men to explore the glaciers. Muir Glacier in Glacier Bay is named after him and for his explorations. With his never-ending drive to learn more, his weight dropped to below 100 pounds as he chose to travel, explore, and write rather than to cook and eat. In all, he made five trips to Alaska: 1879, 1881, 1890, and 1899.

Upon his return from Alaska, Muir evidently felt he should lead a more normal life. He decided to settle down and in 1880, at the age of 41, he married Louise Wanda Strenzel of Martinez, California. He borrowed money from his father-in-law and leased a farm where he raised grapes. A prudent farmer, Muir was an early riser who always took his crop to the railroad station before the other farmers and found that he had his choice of shipping boxes. By selecting carefully, Muir insured that his grapes were always in the newest, cleanest boxes and his produce always seemed to sell first. He is credited with being the first person to export grapes from California to Hawaii. In the ten years of operating the farm, Muir cleared $10,000 per year, carrying his weekly profit to the bank in a laundry bag. With $100,000 in the bank, he gave up farming to spend his time writing. His wife understood his need to return to the outdoors and urged him to do so whenever she noticed him becoming despondent or restless from too many months sitting at his desk. Consequently, he frequently left his wife and daughters, Helen and Wanda, for several weeks at a time. People who wonder how Muir could have spent so much time in the woods probably do not realize that his trips were of relatively short duration and that he returned to the comforts of home and solid meals while he wrote his articles and essays.

In 1889, he campaigned in *Century Magazine* for the preservation of Yosemite National Park. He spent 17 years in his attempt to have the area returned to the federal government and remain a national park inviolate to destruction by man. He had to convince both the federal and state governments of the merit of the idea. In 1890, he sponsored a forest reserve of over a million acres around Yosemite Valley and Sequoia and General Grant National Parks. Eventually, he convinced President Theodore Roosevelt to re-cede Yosemite to the federal government. By 1890, there were three national parks: Yosemite, Sequoia, and General Grant (now King's Canyon). Muir gave credit to an editor, Robert Underwood Johnson, as the "originator of Yosemite." Muir is credited with saving the Grand Canyon and the Petrified Forest. He is further credited with playing a significant role in the establishment of Sequoia, Yosemite, Mount Rainier, Crater Lake, Glacier, and Mesa Verde National Parks, as well as 12 national monuments including Grand Canyon and Olympic which became national parks at later dates. In 1892, he founded the Sierra Club to explore, preserve, and enjoy the mountains of the coast, and served as its president until his death 22 years later.

Edward H. Harriman, the railroad magnate, organized an expedition to Alaska in 1899 and invited 124 well-known scientists, among whom were Louis Agassiz, John Burroughs, and John Muir. For an entire summer, this august group explored, compared notes, discussed, argued, and wrote. Muir knew Alaska well, thus he was often the leader of the scientific discussions. Muir liked to philosophize that Harriman never had enough money and worked, therefore, all his life. Muir, on the other hand, was time-rich and he had no need to work and that made him free to travel and write as he wished. He probably could have become a millionaire had he not left the Indianapolis wagon wheel factory, and certainly could have become wealthy had he continued farming. After his $100,000 savings, he invested his money carefully for his family and was able to spend the rest of his life on his campaign for preservation.

In 1892, at the age of 56, Muir wrote his first book, Mountains of California, and followed it in 1901 with Our National Parks. His 1913 book, Boyhood and Youth, was dedicated to one of the stenographers at Harriman's ranch in Klamath Lake, Oregon. The dictation took 1,000 typed pages, giving testimony to Muir's prodigious memory and his enthusiasm for the activities of his early life. Between 1901 and 1913 were Stikeen (1909), My First Summer in the Sierra (1911), and Yosemite (1912). Travels to Alaska was published posthumously as were four other books, papers, and memoires.

With all his outdoors activities, Muir possessed few camping skills and we may wonder today why he did not die from hypothermia or an accident. He wore just a coat and sometimes carried a blanket to ward off cold and snow while he slept. He built fires only to heat his coffee or tea and carried little food other than bread, which rapidly became hard. Muir told of dropping his canvas sack of bread and kicking it before him as he walked until he broke off a small piece to dunk into his tea to soften it enough to be edible. He was unafraid of danger, hardship, wilderness, being alone, facing death, public opinion, work, poverty, or hunger. He knew them all. He never carried a gun, for the outdoors was not something to fear, it was a laboratory for research and a temple for worship.

Muir never shaved his reddish brown beard and, in spite of the earlier eye injury, impressed his listeners with his bright blue eyes. Listeners all agreed that they had to be just that—listeners—not conversationalists, for Muir could talk for hours at a time. It took four hours to finish breakfast with one colleague and John Burroughs told of Muir telling a story of his dog, Stikeen, with "the whole theory of glaciation thrown in." (Teale, 1954: xvii)

It is said that Muir is the only outdoor writer who has been able to produce good literature and scientific facts simultaneously. This man with only five years of formal schooling became a botanist, an entomologist, a geologist, and an ornithologist. He might be called an early ecologist. He wrote his first book at the age of 56 and only two more by the age of 70. With his constant travels and magazine articles, it is a wonder that he wrote any books at all. He took notes throughout his life and published them laboriously. To his sister, Sarah, he wrote, "My life these days is like the life of a glacier—one eternal grind. . . ." (Teale, 1954:xiv) What he wrote was done by hand in a barely legible penmanship and the books that were published after his death consisted of what the transcribers could ferret out of his scrawl.

During the late 1800s and early 1900s, Muir traveled extensively, visiting Egypt, Russia, Scotland, Australia, New Zealand, Japan, and Brazil. He also returned to Wisconsin, and visited the areas around Boston where Thoreau and Emerson lived. His wife died of lung cancer in 1905 and Muir spent the rest of his life alone, either traveling, writing, or working on the cause of preservation. In 1914, he contracted pneumonia and was taken to the hospital by his daughter, Helen, where he passed away on Christmas Eve at the age of 76.

There is no doubt that John Muir will be remembered for the founding of the Sierra Club and for his literature. The club continues to be one of America's champions for preservation. Other reasons that the park and recreation profession should remember Muir are the two events that made Muir unpopular with many and a hero with others. Each event was eventually a failure and a great disappointment to Muir, yet each has lasting value to those involved in management of recreational resources.

Twenty miles north of Yosemite Valley, but within the national park, lay the Hetch Hetchy Valley that was reputedly as beautiful as Yosemite Valley. The valley was considered by the citizens of San Francisco to be the best sited location and the cheapest for a source of water power for their city. Muir fought a long and often lonely battle to save the valley from destruction and lost when, in 1913, the bill was passed permitting the building of a dam across the Tuolumne River, thus flooding the valley and losing the splendor forever.

The lesson to be learned from this failure is that the government does have the power to violate the land established for national parks by revoking the statutes. Only through the efforts of people working together to save our preserves will they be spared. Muir had thought that he could influence thousands of people with his writing and hundreds more by showing them the beauty of the areas. America needed many more advocates to speak out with him. Further, the American public needed to be educated about the wilderness and the necessity to preserve pristine regions. No land is safe unless the believers of the land organize to protect it. The responsibility lies with those who believe in the land to educate others. The lesson of Hetch Hetchy was a painful one, but if it is ever forgotten, America's precious preserves will be doomed.

The second event relates to his association with Gifford Pinchot who is known as the Father of American Forestry. While Muir was battling to save the forests of the west from destruction, Pinchot was struggling to introduce new forestry methods that would include select cutting, replanting, and the monitoring of cuts. Pinchot had been concerned about the overlogging and complete loss of forests in Indiana, Michigan, Wisconsin, Minnesota, and other midwestern states and realized the same thing was occurring in the forests of the west. Pinchot and Muir worked together to establish forest preserves until Muir realized that Pinchot was interested in conservation, or the wise use of resources, including grazing and cutting, while Muir was interested only in preservation of the land which meant no economical use at all. This may well have been the first clear differentiation of the single purpose national parks system and the multiple-use policies of the U.S. Forest Service. It is quite possible that Aldo Leopold, who read John Muir's writings, was influenced by this point of view when he suggested the Gila Wilderness Area, the first in the nation to exist within a national forest. This clear difference between conservation and preservation reserved Muir's respects for Pinchot, and the two became opponents. It is the understanding of the philosophical differences that should be retained today as related to decisions regarding land use.

The Sierra Club and the books written by Muir may endure time longer than the examples of advocacy for preservation, for objects are easier to preserve than are ideas. Nevertheless, the zeal of the preservationist as exhibited by John Muir is his greatest contribution to parks and recreation as a profession. As long as the ideas and values exist, Muir will be one of the field's greatest contributors.

PARTIAL LIST OF MUIR'S PUBLICATIONS

The Mountains of California (1911). *Century Magazine*. New York.
The Story of My Boyhood & Youth (1913). New York: Houghton.
The Yosemite (1914). New York: Houghton.
A Thousand Mile Walk To The Gulf (1916). New York: Houghton.
Rambles Of A Botanist (1974). Los Angeles: Dawson's Book Shop.

REFERENCES

Brockman, C.F. and L.C. Merriman, Jr. (1979). *Recreational Use of Wild Lands*. New York: McGraw Hill Book Co.

Jensen, C.W. (1985). *Outdoor Recreation in America, (4th ed.).* Minneapolis: Burgess Publishing Co.

Knudson, D.M. (1984). *Outdoor Recreation.* New York: MacMillan Publishing Co.

McCall, J.R. and V.N. McCall (1977). *Outdoor Recreation: Forest, Park, and Wilderness.* Beverly Hills: Bruce, Benziger, Bruce, and Glencoe, Inc.

Nash, R. (1973). *Wilderness and the American Mind.* New Haven, CT: Yale University Press.

Sax, J.L. (1980). *Mountains Without Handrails.* Ann Arbor: The University of Michigan Press.

Sharpe, G.W., C.H. Odegarde, and W.F. Sharpe (1983). *Park Management.* New York: John Wiley and Sons.

Teale, E.W. (Ed.) (1954). *The Wilderness Way of John Muir.* Boston: Houghton, Mifflin Co.

Udall, S. (1963). *The Quiet Crisis.* New York: Holt, Rinehart, and Winston.

7

THORSTEIN BUNDE VEBLEN

1857–1929

By Mounir G. Ragheb
Florida State University

"*From the foregoing survey of the growth of conspicuous leisure and consumption, it appears that the utility of both alike for the purposes of reputability lies in the element of waste time and effort, in the other it is a waste of goods. Both are methods of demonstrating the possession of wealth, and the two are conventionally accepted as equivalents.*"

1899:85

47

Thorstein B. Veblen was born and raised in Cato, Wisconsin. His parents, who migrated from rural Norway to the United States ten years before he was born, resided on a farm. There were 12 children in the family, and the family was alienated from the rest of the society due to language and cultural differences. Veblen's parents were more attached to their old cultural and peasant ways of life. For example, Veblen's father did not learn English as a means to be integrated in the new society. This in turn worked as a barrier for the parents and other family members to get adjusted and accommodated to the new culture and the new American way of life. As a result, Thorstein's school progress was limited due to difficulties with language and probably led him to be critical, later, of the American society, capitalism, industry, and high class. In his childhood, Veblen was a teaser and was fond of coming up with nicknames. As a scholar this tendency continued as he developed expressions such as "conspicuous leisure" and "conspicuous consumption."

Veblen's higher education performance was marginal. He graduated in 1880 from Carleton College in Minnesota. He received two Ph.D.s, the first in philosophy from Yale in 1884. For the next seven years he was unemployed and worked on the farm, read and refined his language skills. In 1891 he started his second Ph.D in economics at Cornell. He then moved to the University of Chicago where he taught for 14 years. He went from Chicago to Stanford, where he served from 1906–1909. Once again he was unemployed, though only for one year, and moved on to teach at the University of Missouri for seven years. In 1918, he left academe to work in other environments. In 1926 he retired in California and died three years later at the age of 72.

Veblen was critical of the modern capitalist institution and its surrounding culture, but took no direct part in social movements. Claiming the role of the detached observer, he felt himself above the conflict. This might be attributed to his family's isolation, detachment, and inability to adjust to the American culture. Veblen's scholarly work was developed in the course of 40 years. Some products of his era that had great impact on his writings included: agriculture, industry, Karl Marx, Darwinism, and play theory. "Culture Lag" was a major and critical notion which Veblen revived. It was actually originated by Marx and Darwin and later refined by Ogburn. Veblen realized that technology and industry can change faster than social institutions and that their laws and norms can control their applications. In other words, social developments are usually far behind technological advancements, which in turn creates cultural lag.

Veblen's attention throughout his writings was on the development of the American economic institutions. He had a great influence on many of his students, though most of them disagreed with his views. Veblen and Freud resemble each other in some respects. Veblen revealed some of the dark sides, mechanisms, and secrets of society and Freud revealed the inner dark tendencies and secrets of the individual. Both of them relied on instincts to explain their theories. In their times, both were considered radical and as a result their ideas were rejected. Although their notions did not lend themselves to scientific verifications and investigations, they stimulated research in their respective fields. Freud challenged psychology and social psychology, while Veblen challenged economics and sociology. The following are some comments which reflect a diversity of assessments of Veblen's work:

This (The Theory of the Leisure Class) classic of economic thought and sociology—Thorstein Veblen's first and best-known work—defines the social attitudes and values which condone the misuse of wealth and observes the variety of ways in which the resources of modern society are wasted. Chief among these is the practice of conspicuous consumption, a pattern of behavior that more than survives to the present day. With exquisite irony, Veblen discusses the hollowness of our canons of taste and culture and considers the emptiness of those habits of life and thought which many of us like to regard as our strength.

In his first and most fascinating book, The Theory of the Leisure Class, Veblen was mocking a process as old as civilization. . . . He expressed his skepticism in a roughhewn prose style which made him the most impressive American satirist of his day.

Time

Thorstein Veblen is the best critic of Americans that America has produced.

C. Wright Mills

Veblen has worn well. Very little in him dates. . . . The years since his death in 1929—years of economic and cultural disintegration and dynastic war— have borne out the main lines of his thought. They have strengthened the conviction that Veblen is the most creative mind American social thought has produced.

Max Lerner

Veblen founded no school. He influenced many scholars and public officials (often former students), but nearly always they differed from him more than they resembled him . . . Veblen's influence has been less pervasive among sociologists than among economists.

Arthur K. Davis

Nevertheless, The Theory of the Leisure Class contains a great deal more than social satire. In a way the outraged economists and sociologists who condemned Veblen for sloppy scholarship, maligned intentions, and unsupported utterances were somewhat closer to Veblen's major intentions.

A. Lekachman

The first book to be published for Veblen was *The Theory of the Leisure Class* (1899). Veblen's speculation was centered around the observation that the higher class members, the wealthy, the bourgeoisie and the rulers demonstrated their power and elitism through the possession of leisure— being free from work and its commitments. It is important to note that when Veblen referred to leisure, he meant in essence free time, to be free from labor or drugery and its duties and obligations.

Veblen was influenced by the industrial revolution and by the European feudal and Renaissance eras. In Veblen's words, in order to gain and hold the esteem of men, it is not sufficient merely to possess wealth and power. The wealth or power must be put in evidence . . . leisure as a means of gaining the respect of others . . . the characteristic feature of leisure-class life is a conspicuous exception from all useful employment. The possession of leisure was considered a status symbol and a higher class identity. The leisure class derived its high status and prestige from work inactivity.

The Theory of the Leisure Class equates leisure with nonproductive consumption of time. Time is consumed nonproductively (1) from a sense of worthiness or productive work, and (2) as an evidence of pecuniary ability to afford a life of idleness. The gentlemen of leisure spend their time in privacy, not before the eyes of spectators; but in the meantime providing evidence of their leisure in the form of immaterial or cultural products. Immaterial evidences of leisure are quasi-scholarly or quasiartistic accomplishments. That is in the form of advancements in linguistics, knowledge, music, arts, and sports. Leisure or (free time) is used by the higher class to produce and preserve high culture.

Veblen's theory on the leisure class was not an attempt to explain leisure as a social and behavioral phenomenon, but to interpret the economics of the upper class, its spending patterns, consumption, standard of living, and status. In essence he did not mean to interpret and explain the leisure phenomenon as a societal force or domain. Granted, higher classes could use, spend, and waste more time, money, resources, and products, in every era. But this could change from one era to another.

Recently the middle class started to have access to all those resources and aspects due to high automation and mass production. Kelly (1982) comments on leisure consumption saying,

Thorstein Veblen proposed that at the end of the nineteenth century it was the conspicuous consumption of leisure that distinguished the upper class. Today it may be that boat, second home, recreation vehicle in the driveway, vacation trip to Europe, or lavish entertainment that yields community status in the suburb which most people leave when they work and where homes look very much alike. Leisure consumption may symbolize having more than enough to get by in a world where cars, houses, and jobs tend to be almost indistinguishable. (1982:125)

Materialistic products change in their meaning, value, and importance, as time and society change. The American society is like its citizens, moving in Maslow's hierarchy of needs from the lower levels toward the direction of self-actualization and fulfillment.

The theory does not apply to the contemporary era, especially the end of the 20th Century, because the material consumption of the higher class, observed by Veblen, has become the norm and the style of life of the middle class. The contemporary era has been witnessing more free time for all classes than in the past. Automation, technology, and the flow of information have changed the course of history, which makes Veblen's theory outdated and inaccurate. It does not apply to all societies and all eras. The Theory of the Leisure Class attempted to explain the free time of the elite—which is less than 5 percent of the American society.

According to Kraus, "His [Veblen's] analysis is not as applicable to contemporary life as it was to the time when it was written, since the working classes today tend to have far more free time than industrial managers, business executives, and professionals. . . . Thus, with the exception of a small group of jet setters, the class he criticized no longer exists." (1978:40)

PARTIAL LIST OF VEBLEN'S PUBLICATIONS

The Theory of the Leisure Class: An Economic Study of Institutions. Rev. ed. (1899, 1959). New York: New American Library.

The Theory of Business Enterprise. (1904) New York: Scribner.

The Instinct of Workmanship and the State of the Industrial Arts. (1914) New York: MacMillan.

Imperial Germany and the Industrial Revolution (1915, 1964). New York: Kelley.

An Inquiry Into the Nature of Peace and the Terms of Its Perpetuation (1917, 1964). New York: Kelley.

The Higher Learning in America: A Memorandum on the Conduct of Universities by Business Men (1918, 1957). New York: Sagamore.

The Vested Interests and the Common Man: The Modern Point of View and the New Order. (1919, 1964). New York: Kelley. First published as The Vested Interests and the State of Industrial Art.

The Engineers and The Price System (1919, 1963). New York: Huebsch.

Absentee Ownership and Business Enterprise in Recent Time: The Case of America (1923, 1945). New York: Sagamore.

REFERENCES

Kelley, John R. (1982). Leisure. Englewood Cliffs, N.J.: Prentice-Hall, Inc.

Kraus, Richard (1978). Recreation and Leisure in Modern Society. Santa Monica, CA: Goodyear Publishing Co., Inc.

8

JANE ADDAMS

1860–1935

By Paul W. McBride
Ithaca College

Courtesy University of Illinois Library at Chicago Circle Campus, Jane Addams Memorial Collection

"It is as if our cities had not yet developed a sense of responsibility in regard to the life of the streets, and continually forget that recreation is stronger than vice, and that recreation alone can stifle the lust for vice."

1909:19

The late historian Richard Hofstadter once observed that the United States had been born in the country and moved to the city. Perhaps no American figure, male or female, so personifies the magnitude of this national transformation than Jane Addams. When Jane Addams was born in Cedarville, Illinois, on September 6, 1860, Abraham Lincoln was running for president. There were only 30,000 miles of railroad track in the country. Slaves outnumbered free industrial laborers who worked mostly in small foundries of fewer than 20 workmen. Americans over-whelmingly lived in small towns or rural areas. By contrast, in 1900 there were no slaves, the industrial work force had increased nearly 400 percent to over 8 million, there were over 1,000 industrial plants which employed between 500 and 1,000 workers each, and 14 which had work forces exceeding 6,000. In 1913 alone, 25,000 workers died of job-related injuries and 100,000 more were injured. (Filipelli, 1984:52) By 1920, for the first time in American history, a majority of the nation's citizens lived in cities, many of them recently arrived from southern and eastern Europe. When Jane Addams died from cancer on May 21, 1935, President Franklin D. Roosevelt was preparing to sign the Social Security Act into law amidst the Great Depression. Benito Mussolini and Adolph Hitler were in power in Europe. Automobiles congested the cities and airplanes had crossed the ocean.

When Jane Addams was two years old, her mother, Sarah, died giving birth to her ninth child. Only 4 of the 9 lived beyond their 16th year. Not until six years later did Jane's father, John Huy Addams, marry Anna Haldeman, widow of a prominent businessman. Thus, during her early childhood, Jane Addams fixed her attention upon her father. John Addams was prominent in his own right, being president of a nearby bank, owner of two mills, and a member of the Illinois Assembly where he was a friend and colleague of Abraham Lincoln. One of Jane's most cherished stories was of the letter which Lincoln had written to her father addressed to "My dear double-D'd Addams." (Addams, 1910:31)

Her childhood was marred by a nagging spinal problem which troubled her all her life. She thought herself misshapen and uncomely and she feared that her father was ashamed of her. John was a Quaker who held to a rigid code of personal morality and conservative political maxims. When Jane pleaded to attend recently opened Smith College at age 17, her father insisted that she enroll instead at nearby Rockford Female Seminary, which she did. From 1877 to 1881, Jane excelled at Rockford where she began to grapple with philosophical, economic, and social issues which confronted the first generation of college-educated women in America. She resisted the missionary bent of Rockford, steeped herself in classical and contemporary literature, and studied the social commentary of Carlyle, Ruskin, Darwin, Comte, Tolstoy, and other leading intellectuals and critics. She was especially concerned that she had not properly come to terms with religion and at one point complained that "I only feel that I need religion in a practical sense." Her personal dilemmas unresolved, she graduated from Rockford in 1881, a few months before her beloved father died of a ruptured appendix. Her father's death sent Jane into an eight-year crisis of depression, illness, and indecision which did not end until she and Ellen Gates Starr founded the Hull House settlement in Chicago on September 18, 1889, a few days after Jane's 29th birthday.

Hull House soon became the capitol of the settlement community in the United States and Jane Addams its undisputed first lady. No problem escaped her attention and comment. She wrote and lectured about child labor reform, unhealthy and dangerous working conditions, slums, tenement house codes, garbage removal, the corruption of boss politics, the need to regulate industry, urban education, immigration and assimilation, the need to foster the arts among city dwellers, the problem of prostitution, the disintegration of the family, the responsibility of the new woman and the necessity that she vote, the importance of organizing leisure and recreation for city dwellers, pacifism, and many other issues. Her articles appeared in nearly every important journal and magazine of her age and her books received the praise of political and social leaders of all persuasions.

Always at the center of her activities and writings was Hull House. Inspired by a visit to Toynbee Hall where a group of dedicated reformers had established a home amidst the slums of east London, Jane decided to find a home in the heart of an American urban slum, reside there with like-minded volunteers and befriend and help the poor and displaced with whom they shared the neighborhood. In the 30 years since Charles Hull had built his country home on the then outskirts of Chicago in the 1850s, it had become surrounded by sprawling, densely packed, unsightly, deteriorating immigrant slums, Chicago's 19th ward. His heir granted Jane and Ellen Gates Starr a rent-free, four-year lease and the Hull country home became Hull House.

From the beginning, Hull House was the center of every imaginable social and intellectual activity. It served generally as a halfway house for the largely immigrant slum dwellers who could seek advice, avail themselves of child care, find temporary shelter, attend lectures and classes on nearly every topic, become a part of a chorus, dance, or drama group, discuss great and near great literature, learn English, or take part in a veritable Chinese menu of physical activities and recreational programs and games. The activities of Hull House were so encompassing in part because its residents, as the settlement workers were called, confronted all the complex problems wrought by industrialism, urbanization, ethnic diversity, and conflict. Moreover, Jane Addams' universal tolerance and humane outlook propelled her to explore the needs of humanity in all of its facets. She insisted that "whatever good the settlement had to offer should be put into positive terms, that we might live with opposition to no man, with recognition of the good in every man, even the most wretched." (Addams, 1910:273)

No need was beyond Miss Addams' notice. If working mothers could not care properly for their children, Hull House offered a day care center. There were kindergarten classes in the morning, classes and clubs for teens in the afternoon, and adult education programs in the evening. In addition, Hull House provided college extension classes and a summer college program at Rockford College for working women. To supplement the more or less formal education which these programs provided, Addams arranged literally hundreds of lectures on topics ranging from politics, economics, and philosophy to education and travelogues. The first building besides Hull House to become part of the complex was an art museum, gallery, and studio donated by a local supporter in 1891. The same year, responding to the needs of single women to live in a wholesome environment near their workplace, Addams founded the Jane Club, a cooperative apartment building. The year before, she had established the Working People's Social Science Club which brought together neighbors, in this case usually male, and social thinkers of all stripes. The illustrated lectures on Sunday evenings filled to capacity the 750-seat auditorium in Bowen Hall, which Louise de Koven Bowen had built for Hull House to serve the Women's Club. There, John Dewey gave a series of lectures on social psychology, and specialists conducted classes on Shakespeare, Dante, Plato, Browning, and others. Her most insurmountable problem, Addams confessed, was to find enough lecturers who could avoid "the dull terminology of the classroom." (Addams, 1910:431)

Of course, Jane Addams did not think that all education had to be formal or academic. Hull House held classes in English for foreigners, cooking, dressmaking, millinery, woodworking, iron and brass work, commercial photography, printing, and telegraphy. Moreover, in an attempt to preserve the pre-industrial skills and crafts of her immigrant friends and to teach them the continuities between their skills and modern industry, Addams inaugurated the Hull House Labor Museum. There she recruited many of the neighborhood residents to demonstrate and produce the fruits of their crafts for display and preservation. It was one of the most popular activities of Hull House. Further, Addams was a national leader in promoting industrial education in the public school system and a persistent lobbyist on behalf of federal aid for industrial education. Hull House, in fact, ran its own apprentice school in bricklaying during the off season.

Hull House met with spectacular growth and success. It grew from its original two residents in 1889 housed in one building, to 15 residents five years later, and finally to as many as 40 in a 13-building complex by 1915. However, not all Hull House ventures were successful. More idealism than practicality characterized the coal cooperative, the carpenter shop, the labor exchange, and the attempt to create a colonization movement to get immigrants out of the city. But even in her failures, Jane Addams demonstrated her perspicacity in recognizing social problems even though some of her solutions were short of the mark.

It soon became apparent to Jane Addams, as well as to the entire settlement movement, that the slums did not exist in a vacuum and that if reform were to come about it would necessitate involvement in politics at all levels. Moreover, it also became clear that the way to reform was through legislation, lobbying, and factfinding. Thus, Jane Addams became a garbage inspector for the 19th ward, conducted studies on the causes of the spread of tuberculosis in the tenements, plumbing, overcrowding, child labor, cocaine sales and juvenile addiction, truancy, the plight of newsboys and shoeblacks in the streets, and many others. Every problem was studied with a view toward finding legislative solutions.

But legislation inevitably led to dealing with corrupt political bosses. In her efforts to undermine the boss, Addams met with decisive defeat. After three unsuccessful attempts in the 1890s to unseat John Powers, powerful boss of her district, she was forced to surrender. She learned a lesson, however, which remained with her throughout her life—that political leaders must respect the democratic process and spring from popular roots. Reformers and elites, however well intentioned, must not impose their ideas from above. "Would it be dangerous to conclude," she queried in 1902,

> that the corrupt politician himself, because he is democratic in method, is on a more ethical line of social development than the reformer, who believes that the reformer must be made over by 'good citizens' and governed by 'experts'? The former at least are engaged in that great moral effort of getting the mass to express itself and of adding its mass energy and wisdom to the community as a whole. (Addams, 1902:270)

Few reformers, particularly settlement leaders, could have brought themselves to ask such a self-indicting question as this.

It was precisely because of her abiding love of democracy, and her deep respect for the sense of community that is necessary to make it work, that Jane Addams devoted so much effort to the promotion of urban recreation. Democracy could not work, she saw, when children were forced to labor from dawn to dark to support families cut off from their traditions. It could not find nurture in street gangs. It would not long prosper among citizenry which could not see beyond its own personal needs. It could not thrive in the Sodom and Gomorrah atmosphere created in the modern city with its open prostitution, crimes of violence and dens of sexual overkill. Democracy could not be bequeathed to a generation of children formed in such a devilish kiln as the American city.

Carefully managed recreation and supervised athletic events were central to her efforts to save the children from the effects of the city and to prepare them to take a productive and positive place in the democratic process. She saw all about her the exploitation of children. She noted their dismal drop-out rate from the school system. Each month at least one child from the neighborhood perished in a tenement fire, a job accident, a street gang battle, or simply from disease or neglect. From the youngest age, children of the city slums were exposed to the influences of houses of prostitution, alcohol, and drug abuse, and were victimized by family disintegration and chaos. Moreover, when they turned their youthful enthusiasm, imagination, and energy to play, they had nowhere to turn except to the street with all its pitfalls. It was apparent to Jane Addams and to the child welfare movement that there was much to be done. Compulsory school attendance, minimum working age requirements, maximum hour legislation for youthful workers, and industrial education programs were a few of the causes which occupied the attention of the child welfare activists. Jane Addams was in the forefront of them all. But she also led the movement to organize recreation.

Jane Addams entered the field of recreation quite early. In 1893, four years after she founded Hull House, Addams acquired a nearby building, formerly a saloon, which she converted into a coffee house and gymnasium. That same year, a shamed slumlord gave his tenement to Hull House on condition that it be run as a model tenement. Jane Addams prevailed upon him to allow the building to be torn down and a playground installed. It was an immediate success with the community and by 1903, Addams and her associates had successfully lobbied for the building of public playgrounds in Chicago, the first being the Hull House playground which the city took over.

Addams was in the forefront of a national movement. The same thing was happening all over the country, especially in large eastern and midwestern cities. In New York, for example, settlement workers were prominent in founding the Society for Parks and Playgrounds in 1890. Similar societies appeared in many cities in the decade that followed. By 1898, the society changed its name to the Outdoor Recreation League which opened New York City's first playground in 1899 and turned it over to the city four years later. By 1906, the playground movement had become nationally organized with the establishment of the Playground Association of America (PAA). One of the founders of the PAA, a member of its first executive council and its first vice president was Jane Addams. (Cavallo, 1981: Chapter 1)

The philosophy behind the need for playgrounds was simple and the evidence for their necessity stark. There was a direct connection, settlement leaders believed, between adolescent juvenile delinquency and the stunting of the play instinct in children. "If we want decent adolescent boys, we must give playgrounds to ten year olds" wrote one settlement leader. Another stated bluntly that a "young offender's presence in court may be traced to a play impulse for which there is no safe outlet." (Davis, 1967:60) Jane Addams saw recreation as critical to the stemming of crime and violence but, more than that, as the vehicle through which youth might foster and strengthen the creative instinct. Therefore, she argued that recreation was more than sport, more than physical education. Indeed, it was the wellspring of creativity itself. Thus, for Addams, recreation consisted of dance, art, music, pottery, crafts, and sculpting as well as the more obvious areas of physical activity and games. At times, her thoughts on recreation bordered on mysticism. The purpose of teaching recreation, Addams wrote, was "to give every child in our schools the ability to use his hands with ease and pleasure . . . in order to retain that power of unfolding human life which is implicit in the play instinct." (Addams, 1930:358) Put another way, Addams believed that the proper nurturing of recreation skills both retarded criminal instincts and fostered creative ones.

Even more critical, organized play and managed recreation, according to Addams, served as a training ground for democratic citizenship. Skills taught on the ball field or the playground, under proper supervision, enabled boys and girls to understand the necessity of following rules, acting decisively, and sacrificing their own interests to those of the group. All of these attitudes and aptitudes were essential to the working of democracy, and they were struggling for support within the hostile environment of traditional rugged individualism which stifled social consciousness and ethnic enclaves which retarded commitment to the general welfare. Thus, in properly taught team sports, players and spectators were caught up in the community of the crowd and the compulsion of team loyalty which demonstrated "the undoubted powers of public recreation to bring together all classes of a community in the modern city unhappily so full of devices for keeping them apart." (Addams, 1909:96)

Among the most insidious devices for dividing the populous were gangs and their offspring, corrupt political machines (despite their democratic leanings). The only possibility of overcoming the enormous influence of peer group pressure toward gangs was to rechannel it toward more wholesome, communitarian ends. In this effort, Jane Addams saw no more important ally than organized sport and recreation because it created countervailing forces within the peer group itself. Sport was "the only agency powerful enough to break this intensified and unwholesome life," she wrote. In fact, she had seen on the playground and the ball field that the dominating influence of the gang leader was neutralized by the rules of the sport and the expectations of "the athletic director." In such a setting, Addams argued, "a rude sort of justice developed" which "may become the basis for new citizenship which will in the end overthrow both the gang leader and the corrupt politician." (Addams, 1930:366–7)

As was her bent, Jane Addams was not satisfied with theorizing. She set her ideas to action at Hull House where she exhibited the full gamut of her interest in recreation. Within its confines were taught classes in art, pottery, rhythm and dance, music, and chorus. In addition, despite the priggishness of the times, Addams allowed Hull House guests to play cards, bowl, and shoot pool (even on the Sabbath) and to engage in all sorts of sports. The Greek immigrants in the neighborhood even convinced the unflagging pacifist to allow wrestling and military drill! Her tolerance for leisure was so complete that she grievously wounded the sensibilities of some of her more religious neighbors. When a Methodist college inquired of Chicago's religious leaders whether it would be proper to grant the founder of Hull House an honorary degree, it was advised that Hull House "permits on the Sabbath day the playing of cards, billiards, and other amusements . . . I do not think the cause of Christ would gain advantage by giving such a degree." (Davis, 1973:118) Miss Addams did not get the degree.

Nor did she curtail her dedication to recreation. Each Saturday evening, the gymnasium was set aside for athletic contests and the neighborhood attended in large numbers. Addams preferred events which involved "a matter of character" and which fostered "abstinence and the curbing of impulse" as well as those contests which required that the participants must keep their minds and bodies "close to the rules of the game." To see "in rhythmic motion the slim bodies of a class of lads," she gushed, "one is reminded of the old prayer, 'Grant them with feet so light to pass through life.' " The prayer neatly encompassed her approach to recreation. (Addams, 1910, 442–3)

For her own life, however, lighter feet than fate allowed were necessary. As the world broke into warfare in 1915, Jane Addams and the whole reform generation stood in utter dismay and disbelief. Was it not a dogma of the progressive creed that war was unthinkable? As the nation slowly edged toward war, then finally took the plunge in 1917, Jane Addams found herself at loggerheads with her nation, its people, and the inevitable war hysteria. She was ridiculed for her unswerving pacifism, reviled for her criticism of the policies of the Wilson administration, and declared one of the nation's most dangerous women by a New York State legislative investigation. Nationalism and intolerance painfully transformed Jane Addams from an American saint to an unAmerican villian.

In the aftermath of the war, the Red Scare, the decline of immigration in the face of quota restrictions, the disintegration of the progressive reform spirit, and the Freudian mood of the 1920s left Jane Addams out of step with her times and her people. By the time of her death in 1935, the increasing role of the federal government in the field of social welfare, coupled with the bureaucratic professionalization which slowly transformed settlement workers into social workers, made even the shrine of Hull House somewhat an anachronism. However, the visionary goal of Jane Addams remains one of the nation's most inspiring. She fought to make a society comprised of many diverse peoples into a cohesive, democratic, and egalitarian community. Moreover, her reading of early 20th century social problems was, and remains to this day, sophisticated, well-rounded, and convincing. Finally, her extraordinary insight into the importance of recreation in an urban, industrial, and multiethnic setting set the stage for the next two generations of sport and recreation theorists.

PARTIAL LIST OF ADDAMS' PUBLICATIONS

Democracy and Social Ethics (1902). New York: The MacMillan Company.

Public Recreation and Social Morality (1907, August). *Charities and the Commons, v. 18.*

The Spirit of Youth and the City Streets (1909). New York: The Macmillan Company.

Twenty Years at Hull House (1910). New York: The Macmillan Company.

A New Conscience and a Social Evil (1912). New York: The Macmillan Company.

The Long Road of a Woman's Memory (1917). New York: Macmillan Company.

Peace and Bread in Time of War (1922). New York: The Macmillan Company.

The Second Twenty Years at Hull House (1930). New York: The Macmillan Company.

REFERENCES

Ashby, L. (1984). *Saving The Waifs: Reformers and Dependent Children, 1890–1917.* Philadelphia: Temple University Press.

Cavallo, D. (1981). *Muscles and Morals: Organized Playgrounds and Urban Reform, 1880–1920.* Philadelphia: University of Pennsylvania Press.

Cremin, L. (1961). *The Transformation of the School: Progressivism in American Education.* New York: Knopf.

Davis, A. F. (1973). *American Heroine: The Life And Legend Of Jane Addams.* London: Oxford University Press.

Davis, A. F. (1967). *Spearheads for Reform: The Social Settlements and the Progressive Movement 1890–1914.* London: Oxford University Press.

Dulles, F. R. (1940). *America Learns To Play*. New York Appleton-Century.

Filipelli, R. L. (1984). *Labor in the USA: A History*. New York: Knopf.

Goodman, C. (1979). *Choosing Sides: Playground and Street Life on the Lower East Side*. New York: Schocken Books.

Lagemann, E. C. (1985). *Jane Addams on Education*. New York: Teachers College Press.

Lasch, C. (1965). *The New Radicalism in America*. New York: Knopf.

Lasch, C. (1965). *The Social Thought of Jane Addams*. Indianapolis: Bobbs-Merrill.

Levine, D. (1971). *Jane Addams and the Liberal Tradition*. Madison: State Historical Society of Wisconsin.

Linn, J. W. (1935). *Jane Addams*. New York: Appleton-Century.

Lubove, R. (1965) *The Professional Altruist*. Cambridge, MA: Harvard University Press

Mrozek, D. J. (1983). *Sport and American Mentality, 1880–1910*. Knoxville: The University of Tennessee Press.

Schmitt, P. J. (1969). *Back to Nature: The Arcadian Myth in Urban America*. New York: Oxford University Press.

9

JOSEPH LEE

1862–1937

By Allen V. Saporo
University of Illinois

Courtesy National Recreation and Park Association Archives

"*In truth the play of children is in the main not play at all in the sense in which grown people use the word. It is play in the sense of being spontaneous, agreeable, undertaken for its own sake and not for ulterior motive.*"

1915:2

Charles Riverbank Playground, Boston, MA, c. 1900.
Courtesy National Recreation and Park Association Archives

Joseph Lee was born March 8, 1862, in Brookline, Massachusetts. His parents were descendants of the old Puritan gentry that came to Boston during colonial days. Lee's ancestors were successful merchants and businessmen and his father had accumulated a great personal fortune. His ancestors remained staunchly religious, though Lee and his father, Colonel Lee, abandoned the traditional Calvinistic Congregationalism in favor of Unitarianism. The family members were leaders in the business, spiritual, and social life of Boston.

The Lee homestead was large and pleasant, although not famous as an outstanding mansion. Their summer home at Beverly Farms, on the North Shore, also provided an excellent play environment, affording Lee and his six brothers and sisters a very happy childhood. Later, reflecting on his early years, Lee stressed the great importance of family life. (Sapora 1952: 48)

After attending Noble's private preparatory school near his home, Lee entered Harvard in 1878 at the age of 16. During this period he experienced many new recreational activities, including boxing, sailing, riding, participating in club sports, music, drama, and dance, and he developed his skill in painting. Mrs. J. F. Moore, a member of the crowd to which Lee belonged had this to say about him:

> He was one of the most amusing persons I ever knew. We all used to like to hear Joe talk . . . he did not tell stories, but in his inimitable manner he could recite poetry and prominent speeches in such a way one would just split with laughter . . . Joe was one of the most popular boys in the crowd . . . (Sapora 1952: 64–65)

At Harvard as an undergraduate, Lee studied political science and philosophy under Josiah Royce and William James. He received the AB degree in 1883 and left immediately for a year of study and travel in Europe. Lee's Scottish tutor, who had a liberal, or perhaps socialistic philosophy, had much to do with the development of Lee's liberal thinking, especially his ideas regarding the ultimate values in life. Lee's letters from Europe to his father showed clearly that he was not only undecided but also quite disturbed emotionally about the selection of a career. His father hoped that he would decide on business, since he was the only son left to follow in his footsteps as the senior partner in Lee, Higginson and Company. After his return from Europe in 1884, Lee spent the summer in his father's office. In the Fall he entered Harvard Law School. He received his law degree in 1888, but the problem of his career remained undetermined.

In 1889 Lee resigned a position he held in a law firm in Boston. His father became impatient with him, for he was a nonconformist, lived modestly, paid little attention to his attire, and rarely participated in any formal social life, preferring informal activities and public service projects.

To gain time to think, he spent a year during 1889–1890 in Europe traveling and visiting friends. He had personal conferences with Leo Tolstoy in Russia and with other eminent people who reinforced his interest in social reform.

In 1889, Lee began his famous ten-year study of child delinquency in Boston with Zelpha Smith, which was edited and released by Lee in 1899. (Lee 1903: 409–13) He prepared the State of Massachusetts Bureau of Charities and Corrections' Report to be presented at the World's Columbian Exposition in 1893. His detailed analysis of all state social services in Massachusetts was recognized as one of the most complete and informative reports on sociological activities of any state.

By 1900, Lee had become a nationally-known social worker, devoting his life and his considerable personal fortune to the solution of social problems. He learned that he could not remain only a philanthropist giving money to charity. He must become a professional student of social problems, meticulously prepared for the questions with which he dealt, constantly aware of the interrelatedness of the social ills of his time. He felt guilty about having so much, and knew from observing the conditions around him that so many had so little of the basic needs for a decent life.

Lee's work and the extent of his writings, public appearances, and association with social reform groups between 1890 and 1910 clearly show that his contribution to the social reform movement was noteworthy. (Sapora, 1952:144–147) In the year 1906, for example, the scope of his work and influence was particularly evident. He was the heart of the Massachusetts Civic League and personally led the fight for medical inspection and health laws of public schools passed by the Massachusetts Legislature in 1906; he was operating the model playground at Columbus Avenue and was doing pioneer work establishing new methods of administration and conduct of a year-round program in public recreation; he was conducting a state campaign to get enabling legislation to permit Massachusetts communities to conduct recreation programs; he was instrumental in the establishment of the Boston Juvenile Court and in preparations for the establishment of the Probation Commission; he was active in solving the tramp problem (care of the homeless) in Massachusetts; he was active in the work of the immigration restrictionists and was chairman of the session on this work at the Conference of Charities and Correction. He gave of his time and energy to several other social problems in which he played a minor part, such as his work with housing, drunkenness, billboard legislation, and newsboy licenses. Lee was truly a tower of strength among social workers. His intense desire was to serve others and his unselfish attitude inspired all who came in contact with him.

In his early work with the Massachusetts Civic League, he learned the techniques of organizing volunteer groups to work for needed reform, methods of securing the necessary funds for a broad attack upon social problems, acquired techniques of dealing with the electorate, as well as with state and local governing bodies. He sharpened his organizational shrewdness which became obvious in later contributions to the development of the Playground Association of America. It was his involvement in social work that broadened his outlook, enriched his background, and contributed a great deal to his general understanding of the basic social problems of his day.

That Boston played an important role in the development of the public playground movement in the United States is now a matter of record.

> The evidence studied is unmistakably in support of the view that the initial action in provision for play in Philadelphia, Chicago, New York, and other cities was the result of the impulse derived from the experience of Boston. (Rainwater, 1922:43–44)

The famous Boston Common of 1634, the opening of ten public swimming and vacation schools in 1886, the Boston sandgardens initiated in 1885 and operated until 1907 by Ellen Tower, and the creation of the famous Charlesbank outdoor gymnasium at Harvard by Dr. Dudley Sargent are significant landmarks of the play movement.

In 1892, the first major Metropolitan Park System in the United States was formed which included Boston and 36 other neighboring cities and towns. The immediate provocation of Lee's attack in 1898 upon the problem of providing adequate play areas in these parks were: the State Law of that year authorizing $500,000 for 22 "big boy" playground areas by the Boston Park Department for general outdoor play and baseball; and the formation of the Massachusetts Civic League (MCL). Beginning with his ten-year study of children's needs with Zelpha Smith, already mentioned, Lee did considerable research on play in Boston playgrounds, sandgardens, and in the streets, making descriptive maps and compiling statistics, including the relations by district between play and density of population, play and law breaking, and the reaction of people in various neighborhoods to the social and economic conditions. Furthermore, Lee became more interested in playground operations during his trips to Europe, in his consultations with play leaders in various cities in the United States, and very importantly, because of the activities of his wife, Margaret Cabot Lee, who was a student of the principles and teachings of Froebel, the father of the kindergarten. But Lee's interest was far deeper than the problem of delinquency. He had experienced a rich play and cultural life as a child and youth; he thought that every child needed play experience; and he felt an obligation to help children experience the type of free play he had in his childhood. He readily saw the value of play as a means of human expression as well as a positive approach to education following Froebelian principles.

But to the astonishment of Lee and everyone, the activities in the new park areas differed only slightly from the ones on the streets. Much of the activity was confined to fighting, card games, and crap shooting; older boys and men monopolized the baseball and games areas; and gang bullies prevented the smaller children from using the grounds. Lee pondered the problem and came to the conclusion that supervision and leadership were needed. He realized that money and volunteer help would be absolutely necessary. The Playground Committee of MCL was organized with Lee as Secretary. In February, 1900 he proposed that the Committee sponsor a model playground in the North End Park, one of the new park play areas. The use of the park was approved and an organized playground program began under the supervision of Lee and the MCL Playground Committee. (MCL,1900: 1–7)

The North End Playground was a flat, barren two-acre site having a bath house and beach on the Charles River. Lee supervised the development and installation of play equipment; had areas marked off for different age groups; and designated areas for informal play. Two paid leaders (Harvard students) and several volunteers met weekly with Lee before the playground opened in May and programs were outlined. Despite the limited area available and the lack of understanding by the local neighborhood, the program attracted over 300 children per week and proved to be an excellent model for further planning.

In 1901 the program was moved to the Columbus Avenue playground, a well landscaped park area of five acres. For the next six years this unique and never before operated type of playground program was mostly financed and personally planned and supervised by Lee, his staff, and the MCL Playground Committee. Since there was no equipment on the grounds, Lee designed the entire area with the help of the Narraganset Machine Company. (Sapora 1952: 243) A fenced-off children's corner and an area for older boys and girls were designated to provide a logical place for children of different ages, which reflected Lee's philosophy, later included in his book, *Play in Education.* There were sand boxes and individual model gardens, swings, slides, teeters, slanting poles and ladders, a coast (slide), gymnastic apparatus, basketball court, three marked off baseball diamonds with backstops, a roped off running track, two football areas with goal posts, minor apparatus for track events, and an indoor gymnasium with six built-in showers. Winter facilities included flooded areas for skating and hockey; and the street arc lights were often slanted to provide light for late-evening football games. (MCL 1902: 1–18) The facilities were rearranged and apparatus redesigned as program experiences indicated. This research provided models for new playground designs that were copied by other cities throughout the United States.

Leadership, according to Lee, was the most important factor in playground operation. Although he was involved in many other social projects, he worked on the playground project tirelessly, visiting the grounds daily, observing operations, taking detailed notes, and visiting with and evaluating leadership personnel. He met regularly with the six paid and specially trained recreation leaders, discussing the administration of programs. Fifteen boys and girls were chosen by the participants to represent the children's interests, which was one of Lee's ideas for teaching democracy in action. One woman half-time staff member spent most of her time visiting people in the neighborhood, promoting the program, and recruiting adult participants and volunteers. (Sapora 1952: 226–233)

Rainwater (1922: 55–70) discusses the work done in several pioneer playgrounds and relates the many contributions of Joseph Lee in his model program. He refers to Lee's book *Constructive and Preventative Philanthropy* which clearly indicates that he was a very competent authority and wrote as conclusively on model playgrounds as did any other leader engaged in this type of program. However, it should be pointed out that the early public-supported model playgrounds of New York, Pittsburgh, and Philadelphia were rigidly controlled by the schools. Lee's philosophy and personal motivation provided a unique and more informal program. The formal control in other cities precluded the considerable amount of research that was possible on the playgrounds administered and financed by philanthropic groups. For example, the South Parks of Chicago, which started three years after Lee's first playground in Boston, spent the first year of their operation centering on the problem of meeting mass needs by emphasizing the more formal indoor and outdoor programs in gymnastics and apparatus play. On the contrary, the conditions surrounding Lee's pioneer work in Boston were, from the very first, experimental. Other than having to get permission to use the Park Department land, Lee had complete freedom to develop the experimental program without interference from the city, park, or school officials. The general control of the research was vested in the Massachusetts Civic League Playground Committee, which Lee found completely cooperative and of inestimable help.

Lee's experimental playground work was particularly representative of actual possibilities under conditions existing in many cities badly in need of playgrounds. Although New York's Seward playground cost over two million dollars and the Chicago South Park playgrounds needed huge budgets, Lee's program was truly a neighborhood playground, with an average budget of approximately $5,000 per year, and its area and facilities more closely fitted to the needs of the average town or city throughout the country. Hence Lee's plan of administration, his standards for neighborhood facilities, and his budget for operations were more plausible, more applicable, and more encouraging to people in communities attempting to start playground programs. Lee was truly a great pioneer in the development of early playgrounds.

After completing seven years of experimental work at the Columbia Avenue playground, Lee gave his major attention to promoting the modern recreation movement. In 1907 he repeated his earlier objective that

popular support is essential. . . not only to get the playground used, to make it a true popular and neighborhood institution, affecting social life and ideals as well as individual health, but also for the practical reason that our object is to get the city to introduce similar work in all the public playgrounds, our function being merely to carry the work through the experimental stage. (MCL, 1900: 8)

It is difficult to capture Lee's total contribution in this abbreviated review of his work. However, his major work may be explained through his activities in three general phases: (1) His leadership in recreation in New England after 1907 and his early work with the Playground Association of America (PAA); (2) His outstanding leadership as president of the National Recreation Association (NRA) and his promotion and broad development of its program for 27 years; (3) The effect of his financial contributions to promote the movement; and his accomplishments as the leading philosopher of the early movement.

While the PAA was being organized by Curtis and Gulick [presented later] in 1906, Lee was very busy with recreation matters in Boston and New England. He felt there still remained much follow-up work to be done in Massachusetts. He traveled extensively to meet with community groups. Unable to keep pace with the great number of requests in the entire state, he engaged Thomas Curley full time in 1910 to act as supervisor of the MCL State field work consultant office, a service he supported financially for 20 years. He wrote and published a comprehensive set of instructions for initiating a local playground and recreation system, which was used not only by Curley, but nationwide. (Lee: 1908) Lee's experimental model playground in Boston in 1900 led to what he had hoped and planned for—to get others to introduce similar operations in public playgrounds. The movement had spread throughout Boston, New England, and then across the entire country.

In 1904, Lee had accepted the post as head of the Recreation Department of the newly formed American Civic Association based in St. Louis. In that position he offered consultation nationally in parks and recreation. In June of 1907 the very effective National Play Congress was held in Chicago. Lee attended reluctantly, but once there, played an important part in the meetings. The PAA became the national leader under Luther Gulick as president from 1906 to 1910. Lee became more active in the PAA each year and succeeded Gulick as president in 1910. He did not seek the office but it was soon evident that he was going to do everything in his power to promote the Association, which changed its name to the Playground and Recreation Association of America in 1910 (PRAA) and later to the National Recreation Association (NRA) in 1926.

Between 1910 and 1912, there was an immediate administrative organizational task to be accomplished. The Association had a constant problem of readjusting its operations to give adequate service to the rapidly expanding field of recreation. Lee, with his legal and management background, called for a complete reorganization of the PRAA structure. He received unusual powers from the Board of Directors but delegated operational duties to Howard Braucher who had been hired as Executive Director in 1909 [presented later]. Many top-level decisions and negotiations needed to be made in the name of the Association and Lee was delegated to investigate these operations personally.

In 1917, a critical need developed to provide recreation services in communities near military installations. Lee, as PRAA president, showed his organizational genius as he was instrumental in creating a joint coordinated plan through which War Camp Community Services (WCCS) and the Association secured and helped train recreation leaders and organize programs to meet the growing needs of many local communities during and after World War I.

During the 1920s to almost the time of his death in 1937, Lee was an inspiration to the PRAA (NRA) staff and Board members, and his influence was also felt in local recreation systems. Local leaders thought of the entire movement on a higher plane because they knew that quietly and without seeking anything for himself, Lee was devoting his abilities to the problems of the movement.

Joseph Lee had inherited a considerable fortune from his father, and his financial support of the movement should not be minimized. He virtually financed the entire ten-year study of needs of children with Zelpha Smith from 1889 to 1899, already mentioned. Although the MCL was supportive of his model playground work, Lee personally financed most of the costs so he could do exactly the type of experimental work he wished to do. Between 1910 and 1914 the PRAA was almost abandoned after its original $20,000 gift from the Russell Sage Foundation was depleted. Lee gave of his time and personal fortune to increase the Association's budget from $11,000 in 1910 to over $90,000 in 1914. He later revised The Normal Course in Play for Professionals, and helped provide funds for Clark Hetherington's one-year visitations during 1910–1911 to various universities to encourage them to develop professional leadership degree training programs. Lee promoted leadership training in the Boston Normal School and personally financed the MCL New England Park and Recreation State Consultant Service for over 20 years. He was influential in the establishment of the Harvard Graduate School of Education. His greatest interest, however, was in the School's courses in play and recreation that helped school superintendents and recreation administrators understand the philosophy as well as the practical aspects of the expanding field of public recreation. In 1915, Lee recruited George E. Johnson, prominent recreation leader and superintendent of Recreation at Pittsburgh, Pennsylvania, to join the Harvard faculty, and paid his salary while there. Professor Johnson taught what were probably the first graduate courses in play and recreation, with Lee serving as a lecturer. By 1930, Professor Johnson was offering four general recreation courses and it appeared Lee's ultimate objective of building a recognized professional recreation graduate training curriculum would be attained. But the development of this curriculum at Harvard, based on the PRAA Normal Course, was abruptly halted by the untimely death of Johnson in 1931 and the courses were not offered thereafter.[1] (Sapora 1952: 197)

During Lee's 31 years with the PRAA (NRA) he gave over $360,000 to the Association, as well as paying all of his personal and travel expenses incurred in Association work. He also showed aggressive leadership in getting others to help raise money for the cause. The fact that the Association had a benefactor who was so familiar with its real needs was undoubtedly one of the main factors in its success throughout the years. And he did all these things quietly and never wished to bring any special credit to himself. (Braucher 1937: 540)

Although Lee contributed much to the growth and development of the recreation movement through his functional administration work, his role as the philosopher of the early play movement is thought by many to be his greatest contribution. It is pointed out that a modern philosophy of play had not as yet been expressed by the turn of the century. (Hetherington 1931: 89) In 1897, Lee was married to Margaret Cabot, who studied the work of Froebel. As early as 1903, during his model playground work, Lee accepted the philosophy of Froebel, and his writings on play are based upon Froebel's fundamental laws of child development, self-activity, symbolism, and the educational and the possible values of play. Lee's philosophy was also a mixture of the idealism of Royce, the ideas of Ralph Waldo Emerson, as well as the works of William James, Karl Groos, and William McDougal on the biological impulse to play. Lee did not appreciate the views of the behaviorists Watson and Thorndike, and also assailed at times the views of John Dewey. (Letter, Lee: 1919) He made an extensive study of the interaction between play and Hall's concept of recapitulation and emphasized the fact that play was a fundamental way of helping children in their process of self-education. Joseph Lee was truly

---

[1] A course on the Sociology of Play was started at the University of Southern California about this time (See Neumeyer).

the philosopher of the modern recreation movement, a man who explained more convincingly than anyone else, the importance and the potential value of recreation in modern life.

Lee's ability to communicate his ideas was perhaps his greatest personal asset. In this regard, and in many other ways, he was different from the other play movement pioneers. He travelled worldwide and appeared almost weekly at some national, state, or local meeting of lay or professional leaders. He wrote extensively about social work and philanthropy, and felt the economic system must be understood before social problems could be ameliorated. In many of his writings he explained his efforts to study the conditions that caused the need for developing public play programs and recreation services. He wrote of democracy and his philosophy that in order to live in a free society, the individual should be educated to participate in and contribute to that society. His informal poems mirrored a variety of social problems as well as his ideas on play and recreation.

In addition to his two books, *Play in Education* and *Constructive and Preventive Philosophy,* he wrote much about his personal experiences and ideas. He published more on play and recreation than anyone else before 1940. Among his total publications on all subjects were approximately 45 pamphlets, 192 magazine articles, 800 newspaper articles, numerous memoranda, and personal letters. Many of these are listed in Sapora (1952 :396–447), in many other original sources (Marian Snow Lee Scrapbook), the Massachusetts Civic League files, and in several recent publications.

Lee was successful in his professional relationships to a great extent because of his personal charm and humor and his inimitable style of expression. He wrote and spoke with authority and said some of the most significant things that have ever been said about the recreation movement in the United States.

> During the World War I, Joseph Lee gave himself so completely to the work of the Association that he sometimes thought the war (WCCS) might cost his life, but he found himself in better health at the end of the war than at the beginning. (Braucher, 1937:540)

> Lee was awarded the Distinguished Service Medal by the War Department for his work with War Camp Community Services. (Butler, 1965: 4)

> Joseph Lee, the choice of the Association (PRAA) for President, was the first man in America to write a book on the subject and was one of the first promoters of the movement in Boston. He has always been, also, the one philosopher of the movement. . . If there is any one man who may claim to be the Father of the American Playground Movement, it is undoubtedly Joseph Lee. (Curtis, 1917:18)

This was corroborated during an interview with Dr. Curtis at Ann Arbor, Michigan in 1951. (Sapora 1952: 333)

His (Lee's) method of helping the Harvard School of Education was characteristic. He quietly gave the school men (faculty) and then left them strictly alone. For five years he paid my own salary . . . he paid the salary for five years of Professor Johnson, following the theories of Froebel . . . as a teacher of play and recreation. (Holmes, 1937:528)

On National Joseph Lee Day, July 28, 1938, *The Lens,* Massachusetts Civic League, XVI No. 4 published this statement by Franklin D. Roosevelt, President of the United States:

Today in the far flung communities of a great nation children are happier, youth is better served, and men and women have a chance to live more richly because of the life work of Joseph Lee. No greater tribute could be paid to him than to have a share in helping to strengthen and build further this vital part of our community and of our national life.

On the other hand, a number of studies viewed his work negatively. The studies claim that during the reform conscious Progressive Era between 1888 and 1920, the work of recreation pioneers and other reformers most often resulted in negative and more disruptive social conditions rather than ameliorating the conditions they set out to correct.

The basis of playground specialization was a body of social propaganda promoting character development and physical development as a means to maintain the existing social order. The qualities of play itself generally were not considered important . . . Play was never valued in its own right. (Dickason 1979a: 254)

The movement failed to make any effort to analyze societal problems that caused the need for developing public play programs. Progressives treated the symptoms, not the causes. (Finfer 1974: 287–288) It increased dissension and caused disruption among children and their immigrant parents, as well as in neighborhoods near play areas. Play organizers attempted to replace the family authority. (Cavallo, 1981:122–125) It aimed to develop adaptive behavior rather than encouraging individual initiative and the American laissez-faire competitive capitalistic philosophy. (Cavallo, 1981: 54) It failed to recognize and promote the philosophy and concept of play for play's sake; used play only as a means of "influencing the lives of a menacing population." (Dickason, 1979b: 2)

Due to the limitation of space, the above positive and negative comments about Lee's work in the play movement cannot be discussed at length. However, through the years there has been unparalleled recognition of Lee as the outstanding leader in the early years of the movement. Most of the negative conclusions about Lee's work are unjustifiable. In some instances, his methods in attempting to meet the social needs of the day may be subject to criticism, but not his motives. The personal interviews conducted by the author with his contemporaries and the long study of his life shows that he was primarily a selfless humanitarian. His experimental playground and later his leadership in the movement were basically concerned with selected educational objectives through guided play as well as the basic principle of play for play's sake, as more recently described by Hunnicutt. (1972: 87) He was the most prominent and influential progenitor of the present-day leisure services systems in the United States.

PARTIAL LIST OF LEE'S PUBLICATIONS

Juvenile Law Breakers in Boston. (1903, September). *American Statistical Association Publication, VIII*, pp. 409–13.

How to Start a Playground (1908). New York Playground and Recreation Association of America.

A letter by Joseph Lee to his daughter, Susan Lee, Susan Lee File, NRPA Library, June 23, 1919.

Play in Education (1915). New York: The Macmillan Company.

The Massachusetts Civic League (MCL). (1900). *The North End Playground*. Boston: The League Playground Committee, pp. 1–7.

The Columbus Avenue Playground Program. (1902). The MCL Committee Report, 1902 pp. 1–18.

Constructive and Preventive Philanthropy (1902). New York: MacMillan Co.

REFERENCES

Braucher, H.S. (1937). Joseph Lee and the National Recreation Association. *Recreation. v. 31*, p. 540.

Butler, G.D. (1965). *Pioneers in Public Recreation*. Minneapolis, Minnesota: Burgess Publishing Company.

Cavallo, D. (1981). Muscles and Morals. *Organized Playgrounds and Urban Reform, 1880–1920*. Philadelphia: University of Pennsylvania Press.

Curtis, H. (1917). *The Play Movement and Its Significance*. New York: MacMillan.

Dickason, J.G. (1979a). *The Development of the Play Movement in the United States: A Historical Study*. Unpublished Dissertation for the Ph.D., New York University.

Dickason, J.G. (1979b, October 28). *Summary of the Development of the Playground Movement in the Untied States: A Historical Study*. Paper presented at the NRPA Research Symposium.

Finfer, L.A. (1974). *Leisure as Social Work in the Urban Community: The Progressive Movement, 1890–1920.* Unpublished Dissertation for the Ph.D., Michigan State University.

Goodman, C. (1979). *Choosing Sides: Playground and Street Life on the Lower East Side.* New York: Schocken Books.

Hardy, S. (1982). *How Boston Played.* Boston: Northeastern University Press.

Hunnicutt, B.K. (1972). *Playground Reform: The Recreation Movement in America from 1880–1920.* Unpublished Thesis for the Master of Arts Degree, University of North Carolina.

Hetherington, C.W. (1931). Development of Recreation Philosophy. *Recreation, v. 25,* p. 89.

Holmes, W. (1937). Prophet in Education. *Recreation v. 31,* p. 528.

Knapp, R.F. (August 1972 to November 1973). Play for America. *Parks and Recreation;* one of seven articles, Part II, *Founding Years—Joseph Lee, Philanthropist and Social Worker.* 7, 10, pp. 20–24.

Knapp, R.F. and Hartsoe, C.E. (1979). *Play for America. The National Recreation Association—1906–1965.* Arlington, Virginia: The National Recreation Association.

Rainwater, C.E. (1922). *The Play Movement in the United States.* Chicago: The University of Chicago Press.

Rainwater, C.E. (1922). A summary of the origin and development of model playgrounds, pp. 55–70.

Sapora, A.V. (1952). *The Contributions of Joseph Lee to the Modern Recreation Movement and Related Social Movements in the United States.* Unpublished Dissertation for the Ph.D., University of Michigan.

[1]A course on the Sociology of Play was started at the University of Southern California about this time (See Neumeyer).

10

LUTHER H. GULICK

1865–1918

By Phyllis M. Ford
Michigan State University

Courtesy National Recreation and Park Association Archives

"**P**lay is more than a name applied
to a given list of activities: it is an attitude which may pervade every activity."

1920:11

Each spring, a professional in the fields of health, physical education, recreation, or dance is the recipient of the highest award given to members of the American Alliance for Health, Physical Education, Recreation, and Dance—the Luther H. Gulick Award. Each year, faculty in college and university recreation departments across the United States extol the contributions of Luther Gulick to their field, and point out passages in the texts referring to the man. A health educator looking into the history of health texts finds the name Luther Gulick on every volume of the Gulick Hygiene Series of the early 1900s. A camp director marvels at the longevity and national reputation of 80 years of the Gulick Camps in Sebago, Maine. Students in classes in the administration of recreation and leisure services from 1945 to 1980 memorized the Gulick principles of administration, learning them by their initials, PODSCORB, which stand for planning, organizing, delegating, staffing, coordinating, reporting, and budgeting. Since 1900, the human services professions have turned to the Russell Sage Foundation for support of and information regarding social welfare. A man at Springfield College in Massachusetts was credited with the invention of a game called basketball.

What is this all about? Was there one person behind all these scenes or is this a list of several unrelated events by different individuals? What makes the name Gulick stand out so much in the fields of health, recreation, physical education, dance, and even basketball and human services? Who or what is the common connection that links all these topics?

These questions and their answers comprise the content of this article. The author is indebted to Eleanor Eells, an acquaintance of Gulick's wife, Charlotte, and of their son, J. Halsey. for the two weeks spent in 1978 discussing Gulick's life and writing the tale of Gulick's contribution to the early history of organized camping. The records on Luther Gulick are not clear; dates vary from book to book. Many organizations claimed him; some, concurrently. Even if he had lived in a jet age, he would have had trouble accomplishing so much. He was like a rubber ball, bouncing from idea to idea and from project to project.

In order to understand the circumstances that led Luther Gulick to influence and to be influenced by so many people, one must know something about the geographic locations in which he lived and worked and the manner in which he was able to make the acquaintance of so many prominent people. Throughout his lifetime, Luther Gulick was able to travel by train between Boston, New York, Chicago, and points in between. In the early part of the 20th Century, commuter trains ran frequently between Boston and New York with intervening stops in Springfield, Massachusetts. Gulick could, thus, work part of the week in one city and the rest of the week in another city with no interruption by traveling on the overnight Pullman sleeper cars.

In the early days of physical education, recreation, and youth camping in this country, there were relatively few professionals and the majority of those lived between Boston and New York. Analysis of the history of any of those fields gives one the names of Lee, Curtis, Wood, Sargent, Meylan, and others, all of whom resided and worked in New England or New York. Further west in Chicago, the names of Jane Addams and Jacob Riis appear in the literature and it is known that those people journeyed to the same meetings in New York that attracted Gulick. Further, the eastern contingent of leaders often traveled to Chicago and frequently met to discuss common concerns. The fact that Gulick rubbed shoulders with so many others about whose accomplishments we can still read is really not so amazing given their geographical proximity, the ease of travel on trains, the paucity of strong leaders, and the common zeal with which all seemed to attack their own interests in the field of human services. What is interesting about Gulick is the fact that his influence spanned so many fields of endeavor.

Gulick's formal education was frequently interrupted, for throughout his youth he accompanied his family to missionary posts in Spain, Italy, and Japan, never spending much continuous time in school. At 16 he entered Oberlin (Ohio) Academy to prepare for college and spent two years there. Health problems, including migraine headaches and eye trouble, as well as the necessity of spending time with his ailing mother, had prevented his earning a high school diploma. The health problems persisted and later interfered with his college work. He left college periodically to follow new ideas and never earned the Bachelor's degree.

Nash wrote of Gulick,

> He was described in these words: clear blue eyes under a shock of red hair, a tall wiry form, quick in movement, a tongue that can snap like a wit and sometimes with sarcasm, the glorious impatience of unlimited energy, the incarnation of the unexpected, a personality that, coming into a room, sends a crackle through the atmosphere like an electric current, a laugh that is its own infection, and, with it all, an exhilaration like the wind from the bills and a boyishness that makes people love him, even when he startles them. To be with him is to learn a new meaning for the old phrase about coming to life, and when one leaves him one whispers to oneself, 'I have been in the presence of a man.' (1960:46)

Others have noted that he was mischievous, active in games, and skilled in sports and gymnastics. He evidently loved music and was accomplished at improvising at the piano. Long walks, alone or with a friend, were important to him (but never on a Sunday). He was full of ideas and always experimenting or trying something new. It was this last characteristic that enabled him to contribute so much to his field.

At Oberlin College, Gulick studied under Dr. Delphine Hanna in the first co-educational teacher training program in the Midwest. Dr. Hanna, a graduate of the Sargent School (of Physical Education), exerted a deep and lasting influence on his life and career. She believed that gymnastics teaching should be scientific and result in health and body building. Gulick and his roommate, Thomas Wood (who later convinced physical educators to include health in their classes and became known as the "Father of Health Education"), seem to have held lengthy discussions on their courses and how the knowledge should be applied. It was evidently on one of his long walks with Wood that Gulick worked out what should be his course of action in physical education. Since Dr. Hanna had been so greatly influenced by Dr. Dudley Allen Sargent, Gulick dropped out of Oberlin and spent the winter of 1886 studying with Sargent at Springfield College in Massachusetts. Sargent's brief influence convinced Gulick to leave school again and in April, 1886, he became a physical director for the Jackson, Michigan, YMCA. He retained a life long friendship with Dr. Sargent as can be validated by Sargent's later writings concerning Gulick's personality and successful endeavors in all he attempted.

The brief six month period at the Jackson YMCA convinced Gulick that it was "not only undignified and unethical but unChristian for the YMCA to proclaim that they cared nothing for the body as such and 'only used the gymnasium as a bait or allurement to draw souls to Christ.' " (Sargent, 1918:421) He was particularly concerned, for the instructors the Y hired to lure young men to their doors were "circus performers, ex-athletes, ex-pugilists, and old soldiers." (Sargent, 1918:421) Gulick felt that the physical director must be a Christian gentleman of high moral standards and with the basics of education and physical training. This seems to show the results of his missionary background and the influences of Dr. Hanna and Dr. Sargent. Recruiting and training such men was to become an important part of his life work with the YMCA, on both the national and international scenes. His commitment to this work contributed ultimately to his early death. To prepare himself for his work further, he left Michigan and enrolled in the first class in medicine in New York University in 1887, receiving the M.D. degree two years later in March of 1889.

The year of 1887 was an eventful one for a man just beginning to pursue a medical degree. He married Charlotte Vetter, also of missionary parents, and, with her as partner, opened a family camp for colleagues and their families at Gales Ferry, Connecticut. This camp was a cooperative effort with the work shared by the parents and the expenses divided at the end of the summer. The site on the Thames River afforded good swimming and sailing, while the countryside invited long walks and explorations. Forty tents were scattered among the trees with ample space for recreation. It was a closely knit community with many interests in common but with sufficient diversity to spark lively discussions. Here the Gulicks spent the next 20 summers where many lasting friendships were formed. After Dr. Gulick's death, friends' recollections of him were of wonderful stimulating summers, of stories told and poetry read around the campfire, and of Sunday services led by Dr. Gulick in that Connecticut setting.

The year 1887 also marked the start of Dr. Gulick's 13 years of teaching at the School of Christian Workers in Springfield, Massachusetts (later the International YMCA College, now Springfield College.) Imagining how he managed to start a family camp in Connecticut, and to commute by train between a new part-time job in Massachusetts and medical school in New York leaves one a bit breathless. At Springfield he saw the opportunity to influence the YMCA and to lay the foundations for the new profession of physical directors; and he is credited with heading the first YMCA training school.

It was at Springfield in 1891 that Gulick conceived the idea and initial rules for the game of basketball and gave them to a young instructor, James Naismith, to develop. Most books state that Naismith invented the game; but in Spalding's 1894 Sports Book there is a quotation from Naismith who avows that Dr. Gulick "gave me the rules and had me develop the game." (Spalding, 1894) That passage is in a section titled, "Basketball by James Naismith and Luther H. Gulick." In a sports encyclopedia of 1904, one can read that Gulick helped Naismith, but in the next edition the name Gulick was dropped and the credit has since been given to Naismith.

Butler gives the history of the game as:

> Dr. Gulick was interested in the qualities essential for a successful game and attempted to work out the elements required for various types. His only notable success was in the case of basketball. According to his own account, he listed seventeen conditions essential to produce a game 'that would be interesting to spectators, so there would be money to support it, that beginners would have some fun in playing, yet in connection with which a great deal of skill could be used, and that would hold interest year after year.' He urged Dr. James Naismith, a member of the staff at Springfield College, to develop such a game. Basketball, invented for 'certain, exact, precise conditions' was the result. (Butler, 1965: 63)

It was earlier, in 1890, that Gulick had designed the YMCA triangle embodying mind, body, and spirit which he felt should be the three interrelated and inevitable components of all YMCA physical directors. The motto, "Spirit upheld by body and mind" persists today. (Nash, 1960:60) A dynamic teacher, Gulick not only imparted information, but raised the sights of his students to service to people and to professional growth. He based his teachings on the "concept of the coordinate unity of the physical, intellectual and spiritual in man." (Nash,1960:60)

At the turn of the century, Dr. Gulick's interests widened into the field of childhood education and concern for the problems of adolescence. Three years (1900–1903) as principal of a progressive school, Pratt Institute in Brooklyn (now Pratt University), were followed by five years as director of Physical Education of the New York City public schools. He reorganized the city physical education classes from a compulsory 20 minutes of gymnastics and 10 minutes of recess to 15 minutes of gymnastics and an equal time for games and free play (endearing his name to the recreation field).

During his five years in the New York schools, he introduced many innovative programs which included classes in hygiene, the New York schools' athletic league (intramurals on the elementary level), a girls' branch of the league, and the mandating of folk dance as part of the curriculum. Simultaneously, he lectured at the School of Pedagogy at New York University, and served as a delegate on several occasions to meetings in Europe. He held several offices in the American Physical Education Association and for two years edited its *Review,* the forerunner of the current *Journal of Physical Education, Recreation, and Dance.*

A list of dates and accomplishments in this five years in New York is amazing. The list reads as follows:

- 1900–1902—Editor of *Physical Education Review.*
- 1903—First head of New York City Schools Physical Education Department.
- Developed the first physical education achievement tests (which according to Spalding was a throwing, running, and jumping pentathlon developed to offset the overwhelming popularity of basketball!).
- Initiated the Public School Athletic League of New York.
- 1904—Helped found the Academy of Physical Education, the forerunner of the American Academy of Physical Education.
- Following the term of Dr. Sargent, elected president of the American Physical Education Association.
- Proposed a cash award for the author of the best article on physical education. (Incidentally, in 1918, the New York Society propsoed changing it to the Gulick Medallion and commissioned R. Tait McKenzie to cast the die. The first Luther H. Gulick award was given posthumously in 1923 to Luther H. Gulick and it was accepted by his widow, Charlotte.)
- 1905—Taught the first course in Philosophy of Play (New York University).[1]

---

[1]USC claimed to have offered the first course in the Sociology Of Play (See Neumeyer).

The period in which Gulick lived was one of great social change. The Industrial Revolution of the late 1800s, economic difficulties in Europe, and a liberal immigration system brought thousands of people to the United States seeking employment, freedom, fame, and fortune. Forced to live in crowded city conditions, working long hours under undesirable conditions, ignorant of the English language and American customs, the immigrants became a concern of those who involved themselves in the areas of human services. Out of a need for safe play areas for the children in cities grew the playground and with it came the development of the Playground Movement, a social movement that swept from Boston to New York to Chicago and into all major cities.

In 1906, Gulick's interest in children's play and the universal need for recreation drew him into the founding period of the Playground Association of America, with Dr. Henry Curtis of Boston. Gulick was elected president of the organization and remained on the board of directors for many years. In 1907, he published a book entitled *Physical Education* which is credited with being the first book on the philosophy and principles of physical education. The book contains much about the need for children to play and the value of safe play.

Dr. Gulick met Jane Addams, the social welfare philanthropist and the founder of the famous Hull House, at a conference in Chicago in 1907. They discussed the merits of small city parks and playgrounds in crowded areas versus summer vacation camps for families and children. Gulick felt that both were important and should be promoted but that the camps must wait if funding was scarce. After this meeting, Miss Addams used her influence to get small parks and playgrounds established in Chicago and delayed her interest in social welfare camps for several years. How much Gulick influenced Miss Addams is conjecture, but the cooperation between the two is worth noting. The effervescent personality of Luther Gulick and the graciousness of Miss Addams must have been an interesting contrast.

A representative of the newly founded Russell Sage Foundation in New York who attended that same conference was so impressed with Dr. Gulick that he recommended the Foundation employ him. On December 1, 1908, Gulick joined the Foundation staff, having resigned from the New York Public Schools. In his position as head of the Child Hygiene Department at Russell Sage Foundation, Gulick found new contacts, new resources, new challenges, and increasingly heavy demands on his time and strength. The records show that in a single year he:

> served on eighteen committees, ten of which involved work aside from attendance at meetings; had responsibilities connected with three international congresses and several local undertakings; prepared seven plans of major scope on varied topics for as many agencies; made fifty-two public addresses, and published fifteen articles. (Butler, 1965:63)

He was closely allied with reform movements, innovative programs in youth, community service, education, and social welfare. He served as a link, a spark, a catalyst, and a dynamic moving spirit. His organizational connections were legion for he had the reputation of bringing a new organization into being every other weekend. He is said to have stated about himself, "I lay eggs for others to hatch." (Eells, 1986:19)

The year 1907 had seen the closing of the Gales Ferry Camp in Connecticut. Evidently, the coming of the railroad in 1899 disturbed the peace of the campsite and the Gulicks moved to South Casco, Maine. Dr. George Meylan, Medical Director and Head of the Physical Training Department at Columbia University, had made a deep impression on Gulick and the two had become friends. Both men were active in the physical education movement, with broad contacts in allied fields. Meylan was an ardent and vocal advocate of camping because of his rewarding experiences on trips and in organized camping programs in the Bangor, Maine and Boston YMCAs. He had known first hand the vital role camping could play in reaching boys and had himself been influenced by the Reverend George Hinckley and his Good Will Farms in Maine.

In 1907, Meylan had established White Mountain Camp for Boys on the Lake Sebago property. Gulick must have been influenced by Meylan's belief in camping, for in 1907 he made arrangements to purchase the adjoining property on the lake and, at the end of the Gales Ferry season, moved his family and the Gulick interests to that site.

Required public education with an emphasis on a standard curriculum and the three Rs created doubt in the minds of many educators. The Progressive Education Movement was made up of people who were determined that education should be more complete and should teach practical application of necessary social skills such as banking, gardening, manual labor, and socialization. One solution was the establishment of the private camps which could teach all the topics the directors felt might be missing in the stringent but stagnating curricula of the day. It was inevitable that the Gulicks join the movement.

The new girls' camp in Maine concentrated the Gulicks attention on the needs of girls in the rapidly changing social scene with new attitudes toward women, the home, and the rearing and educating of children. Different experiences and opportunities were needed for girls if they were to be a part of the new and splendid social world which Luther Gulick envisioned. Camp offered one way in which the Gulicks might work out some solution to these problems and they were ready to tackle the tasks. The entire Gulick family was involved in the preparation for the 1911 camp and its operation. Charlotte had chosen WOHELO as the camp name with the triangle of Work, Health, and Love as its symbol. A program of Indian lore and ceremonials was written in consultation with Ernest

Thompson Seton, the founder of the Woodcraft Indians and one of the organizers of the American Boy Scout Movement. It is interesting that the now called "Gulick camps" in Maine are still directed by descendents of Luther and Charlotte Gulick and to this day retain the Indian ceremonials as part of the program.

It was about the time of the founding of the camp that Charlotte Gulick took a special course with the psychologist G. Stanley Hall (proponent of the recapitulation theory of play) and subsequently wrote and published one of the first articles on sex hygiene. Both Charlotte and Luther were in demand as authors and frequently published articles in current periodicals. Charlotte's book *Emergencies,* one of five volumes on hygiene, was published by her sister-in-law, Frances. The entire series was edited by Luther and was long a standard work in the field of health. Luther's association with Dr. Hall resulted in more than a psychological approach to sex hygiene, for Hall became a frequent visitor to the Gulick home in New York. He must have made a great impression on Luther, who referred to the behavior of the children at camp as being part of normal developmental stages similar to those described by Hall.

Gulick, however, was not a blind follower. After analyzing the recapitulation theory which maintained that children relived the "cultural epochs of the past" in their play, he wrote in opposition to the theory in the posthumously published *A Philosophy of Play:* "No theory could well have been elaborated that was farther from the observed facts of human life than the culture-epoch theory." (Gulick, 1920:145)

In 1909, Gulick had been working with James West, Dan Beard, and Ernest Thompson Seton among others on a national organization for boys which eventually resulted in the incorporation of the Boy Scouts of America in February of 1910. From many requests for a similar organization for girls, Gulick organized a widely representative committee of prestigious men and women to study the problem.

People reading of the formation of the Campfire Girls generally are informed that the organization grew out of the minds of several people. Some accounts credit Luther Gulick with the idea and the inception of the organization. Gulick's brother, Reverend Edward Gulick, and his wife had moved to Vermont where they associated with Mrs. Gulick's sister-in-law, Mrs. Charles Farnsworth, the director of Camp Hanoum. Mrs. Farnsworth was involved in the planning of a pageant to help the six villages of the town of Thetford celebrate its 150th anniversary. To write and direct the material, she brought in William Chauncy Langdon from the department of the Russell Sage Foundation headed by Luther Gulick. Langdon had a background of working with the YMCA when Gulick, Ernest Thompson Seton, Dan Beard, Jacob Riis and others were considering propagating the Boy Scout Movement. While working on the Thetford Pageant, Langdon planned to end the final scene with a group of Boy Scouts, much to the dismay of the girls from the nearby summer camps and homes. Empathetic to the desires of the girls, Langdon and Mrs. Farnsworth convinced Gulick to work on an association for girls.

"You develop a new organization every fortnight anyhow, Luther," Langdon supposedly said. "You might as well work this one in on the weekend." Gulick acquiesced and, with at least 25 others, spent parts of 1910 and 1911 bringing the idea to fruition. So it was Langdon, influenced by Gulick, who wrote the name, ranks, and much of the council fire ceremony of the Campfire Girls. The Alhoa and Hanoum Camps in Vermont and Wohelo in Maine all contributed to the Campfire organization. The Indian lore and names came from Gulick's Camp Sebago and the Wo-He-Lo slogan was Charlotte Gulick's "Work, Health, and Love" from the Sebago Camp in Maine.

Ill health forced Dr. Gulick to take six months leave from the Russell Sage Foundation with a consequent setback to the work he was doing, but Camp Fire Girls (the original spelling) was incorporated in 1911 with Dr. Gulick as president and by 1914, he was made Executive Director.

When Gulick returned to the Russell Sage Foundation late in 1911, he was urged by his doctor to limit his activities but was unable to do so. When the United States entered World War I in 1917, Gulick resigned his position with the Campfire Girls and the Russell Sage Foundation to go overseas with Charlotte on behalf of the International YMCA to study and report on the condition of the American troops and their needs. His doctor had advised against this, yet Gulick not only completed his assignment but also started work on his own recommendations. Hundreds of men and women were recruited to serve in France as YMCA recreation workers.

The couple returned to Camp Sebago-Wohelo in the spring of 1918 and Gulick passed away on August 13, just at the close of camp. Dr. Sargent wrote of his death:

> . . . he lay . . . in just such a setting as he would have asked for life's closing scenes, and so symbolic of his life's work. He had made full and complete arrangements for the water carnival of sports that was to take place on the morrow. Boats, canoes, diving floats, and judges' barges were all in readiness, and the camp girls with their bronzed skins and bright colored bathing suits were eager for the water sports and contests. He started something and got everybody interested in it and then retired. (Sargent, 1918:9)

In the words of Charlotte Gulick, "He died as he wanted to. He felt that he had finished the things he had undertaken; that things were well started." (1918)

Gulick was not popular with everyone. In 1918, he alienated the proponents of the newly introduced Ling System of Swedish gymnastics by refusing to recognize it, saying it had too much attention to detail and too much patience for what it was worth. The following year, he became more positive and expounded on the superiority of the athlete over the gymnast, describing the gymnast as over-developed, muscular, of great shoulders and chest, weak legs, and heavy carriage while the athlete was erect, graceful, fleet, and with splendid endurance.

Gulick was a pragmatic man, ahead of his time in ideas, but impulsive and impatient. He had the capability of developing ideas into institutions but it is the impulsiveness that antagonized others. Dorgan (1934) and McCurdy (1936) each relate how he tried to teach his wife to drive by jumping out of a moving automobile and leaving her inside to fend for herself. It was behavior of this type that caused rifts between him and his co-workers. In spite of this, he brought out the best in people and was able to promote their ideas. He was an innovator, not an administrator or builder.

Bombastic, opinionated, and impulsive though he was, Gulick is credited with founding or assisted in the founding of:

- The New York University Summer School of Physical Education.
- The Department of School Hygiene of the New York Academy of Medicine.
- The American School Hygiene Association.
- The American Folk Dance Society.
- An early camp director's association.
- The Athletic League of North America—a first organization linking the U.S. to Canada.

He edited 5 magazines, wrote 217 articles in 50 periodicals and 8 handbooks, and wrote 9 pamphlets and 14 texts.

Upon his death, a symposium dedicated to Gulick was held with Dr. Dudley Sargent presiding. At that time, Joseph Lee, now known as the "Father of the American Playground," wrote:

Gulick's informal and wholly improper methods of presiding at the 1907 convention in Chicago put life and originality even into official dealings. He was fertile in ideas and [knew] just what should be done and how and what would bring results. Personally, I never saw him without receiving some new and valuable suggestion and usually felt myself about three laps behind him in the development of recreational aims. I think his great characteristics as a leader was his faith that the things were possible; that there was a way of doing the thing that would get the result you wanted and a way of saying it that would get heard. As a result what he said was listened to and the things he started came to pass. (1918:422)

Sargent wrote of Gulick:

Seemingly he would no sooner start one enterprise and get his friends interested in it than he would almost immediately drop it and take up something that furnished more excitement for his playful impulses. To some he typified 'the rolling stone that gathers no moss,' but to me he seemed more like the big rolling snow ball that accumulates more and more as it rolls.

Dr. Gulick was not so much an originator or inventor as he was an educational engineer and health promoter. He was not a visionary or impractical schemer as some thought, but he saw visions, even as a youth of nineteen, of greater possibilities for physical education in America than any other man whom I have met. (1918:7)

So we see a man who influenced many phases of recreation and physical education. His interests included the rich, the poor, the young and the young adult. Why didn't Gulick get involved with the elderly? Probably because he never lived to be an elderly person. His work was always in the present. Had he lived as long as his wife, Charlotte, or son, John Halsey Gulick, perhaps he would have founded the first senior citizen's club, professional organization, or training school for older workers. That is, of course, conjecture; still one cannot help but wonder what Gulick might have accomplished had he lived into his sixties or seventies.

His name has been mentioned in introductory recreation and leisure services textbooks for over 50 years and he is described as a pioneer, leader, and/or effective advocate in the play and recreation movement. Many of his ideas, expressed through his book, A Philosophy of Play, are appropriate today. Some of the most relevant are:

• Education falls short if it equips us only for work.
• Character is formed predominantly during leisure hours.
• Children should be included in all family conferences.
• To make a person well, you must make him happy.
• Exercise without the play drive is useless.
• Camps properly run are a laboratory for life.
• Schools should be kept open to serve all people around the clock.
• Play is an attitude. What is play to me may be drudgery to you.

What messages can one take from this person? Probably one can be inspired by this man who shared his ideas, and inspired and motivated others with no thought to his own immortality. He said he laid eggs for others to hatch. He exemplifies what William James meant when he said "The great use of life is to spend it for something which outlasts it." Certainly the recreation field can emulate his contributions by sharing with others and drawing together recreation, physical education, and youth services as he did. Gulick may be a common connection for all, but he certainly was an uncommon man.

PARTIAL LIST OF GULICK'S PUBLICATIONS

The Camp Fire Girls Lend a Helping Hand. (1914). *The Red Cross Magazine*.

and Patton G. (1912). The Way of Summer Camps for Boys and Girls. *Good Housekeeping, v. 54*.

A Philosophy of Play. (1920). New York: Association Press.

REFERENCES

Butler, G.D. (1949). *Introduction to Community Recreation*. New York: McGraw Hill Book Company, Inc.

Butler, G.D. (1965). *Pioneers in Recreation*. Minneapolis: Burgess Publishing Co.

Dorgan, E.J. (1934). *Luther Halsey Gulick, 1865–1918*. Unpublished doctoral dissertation. Teachers College, Columbia University, Cont. to Ed. no. 635.

Eells, E.P. (1986). *Eleanors Eells' History of Organized Camping: The First 100 Years*. Martinsville, IN: American Camping Association.

Gulick, C.V. (1918, October). Letter. *American Physical Education Review*.

Lee, J. (1918). Dr. Luther Halsey Gulick 1865–1918: A Symposium. *American Physical Education Review*.

McCurdy, J.H. (1936, July). Luther Halsey Gulick. *Recreation*, p. 297.

Nash, J.B. (1960, April). Luther H. Gulick. *Journal of Health, Physical Education, and Recreation*.

Sargent, D.A. (1918, October). The Life and Work of Dr. Gulick, in Dr. Luther Gulick 1865–1918: A Symposium. *American Physical Education Review*.

Sargent, P. (1924). *A Handbook of Summer Camps*. (1st ed.) Boston: Wright and Potter Printing Company.

Sargent, P. (1935). The Pioneer Camps. *A Handbook of Summer Camps*. (12th ed.) Boston: Write and Potter.

Spalding. (1894). *Sports Book* (Publisher Unknown).

11

STEPHEN TYNG MATHER

1867–1930

By Ronald Simpson
Ithaca College

AAHPERD Archives

"*Our job in the Park Service is to keep the national parks as close to what God made them as possible. . . .*"

Shankland, 1970:35

By the time Stephen Tyng was born in California on Independence Day 1867, the Mather name was established in American history. The first Mather to settle in America in 1635 was the Reverend Richard Mather, who had five sons. One son, Increase, together with his son, Cotton, became famous preachers in New England. The religious heritage of the Mather family was carried on by Stephen's father, Joseph Mather who left New England for California where his only son Stephen, was born in San Francisco.

Stephen developed a great affection for his native state. He often retreated from the city to visit rural areas, and he particularly enjoyed camping in the Sierra foothills. His affinity for the outdoors was reinforced by his later development with the Sierra Club, which nurtured his interests in moun-taineering and molded his conservationist attitude.

After his graduation from the University of California, Berkeley in 1887, Stephen left California to be close to his ailing mother in the east. There he worked five years as a reporter for the *New York Sun*. In 1892, he married Jane Floy and returned to California to begin two decades of work as an executive in the borax mining business. The mining industry rewarded Stephen with substantial wealth, and given his record of achievements, he probably could have continued on as a successful businessman were it not for a series of events that occurred in 1914.

In that year Stephen wrote a letter to the Secretary of Interior, Franklin Lane, deploring the conditions he found while vacationing in some of the national parks. Lane responded with a challenge, "Dear Steve: If you don't like the way the national parks are run, why don't you come down to Washington and run them yourself?" (Albright & Cahn, 1985:16). The Secretary's challenge enticed Mather to visit Washington and, after receiv-ing assurance from Lane that he could run the parks with a relatively free hand, Stephen accepted the position as chief assistant to the Secretary for one year. Little did he realize that he would remain at the helm of the National Park Service (NPS) until shortly before his death in 1930.

During the years that Mather guided the NPS, his contributions were numerous, far reaching, and enduring. When Stephen arrived in Wash-ington to begin his public career, the Interior Department claimed respon-sibility for 13 national parks and 18 national monuments. Each of the existing national parks had been created by separate law and was admin-istered as a separate unit. Management of the parks was accomplished by a loose organizational coalition of the Departments of Interior, War, and Agriculture. The management problem was further compounded by a political spoils system which had created a pool of park superintendents and their subordinates who were seldom well prepared for their respon-sibilities. Thus, Mather inherited an expanding park empire in need of dramatic overhaul.

Upon settling into his position, Mather discovered a host of park matters that needed urgent attention. The agenda of items which he set forth to accomplish was impressive:

1. Get Congress interested enough in the national parks (a) to make vast increases in their appropriations and (b) to authorize a bureau of national parks;
2. To authorize a bureau and start it functioning;
3. Get the public excited about the national parks;
4. Make park travel easier by promoting wholesale improvements in hotels, camps, and other concessions and in roads and transportation facilities both inside the national parks and outside;
5. Sell national park integrity to the point where Congress would (a) add to the system all appropriate sites possible, (b) keep out inappropriate sites, (c) keep the established sites safe from invasion, (d) purge the established sites of private holdings. (Shankland. 1970:56).

The agenda Mather proposed was indeed formidable. Moreover, much to his credit, he eventually either accomplished or made significant inroads toward fulfilling all of the tasks.

Establishing a new bureau was of the highest priority to Mather because, "If they [the parks] were ever to get enough money, enough publicity, enough protection, enough partisanship, they had to be administrated by a bureau of their own." (Shankland, 1970:6) Winning congressional approval for a bureau would prove to be a difficult feat because previous attempts to do so had failed and some key congressmen continued to be highly skeptical of the need to create and particularly fund a new Federal agency. Not one to be easily discouraged or intimidated, Mather crusaded vigorously for its establishment.

Mather's first strategy to promote the parks and win approval for the proposed bureau was to hire, primarily with his own money, a former newspaper acquaintance to create favorable publicity. Also at his own expense he organized and personally conducted tours of the parks for influential persons including publishers, authors, editors, railroad executives, and a congressman for the purpose of getting the "powers that be" to actually see what was needed and learn firsthand of the issues surrounding the parks. These personally-conducted tours resulted in a flood of articles featuring the parks which appeared in such prestigious magazines as National Geographic and Saturday Evening Post as well as several prominent newspapers. As public awareness and grass roots support for the parks increased so did the pressure on Congress to come to their aid. Consequently, after some compromise, President Wilson approved the bill establishing the new bureau in August 1916. The legislation creating it (Public Law No. 235, 64th Congress) was only two pages in length and relatively free of rules and regulations. It simply provided for the creation of a bureau "to promote and regulate the use of federal areas known as national parks . . . and to conserve the scenery and the national and historical objects and the wildlife therein and to provide for the enjoyment of the future generations."

With the new bureau in place, Mather set about developing management policies and practices that would allow the national parks to become a smoothly running and well coordinated system. He did his best to keep bureau decisions free of political influence as he "would no more have asked a job applicant his politics than he would have asked his views on infant baptism." (Shankland, 1970: 218) Unhampered by restrictive personnel policies, Mather moved quickly to replace underqualified political appointees in the field with highly qualified appointees of his own choosing. That three of the four directors of the NPS who succeeded Mather were men whom he had personally influenced to join the bureau reflects how well he chose these newcomers.

Mather also focused special attention on upgrading the status of "park ranger." While constrained by budgetary limitations to pay rangers small salaries, he did whatever he could to increase their dedication and ability to serve park visitors. He frequently toured the parks to build *esprit de corps* and to speak the "Park Service gospel, that those entrusted with the care of our nation's great parks are members of an elite corps." (Albright and Cahn, 1985: 141) Mather's special vision for the rangers contributed greatly to building the ranger mystique, and he made it a point to proudly wear the ranger uniform whenever he visited the parks.

Mather also guided the establishment of new divisions within the bureau: Engineering Division (1917), Landscape Engineering Division (1918), Educational Division (1925), Forestry Division (1927), and Wildlife Division (1929). The Landscape Engineering Division reviewed all proposed development plans to ensure the optimal preservation of natural scenery in construction projects. His obsession to maintain their aesthetic quality and rid the parks of eyesores led Mather on one occasion to personally light the dynamite fuse that destroyed a sawmill in Glacier National Park after its owners had ignored his repeated warnings to dismantle it!

In the early years of the bureau, when Congress was reluctant to provide more than minimal financial support for its operation, Mather generously subsidized funds from his own money.

The Mather achievement was necessarily the achievement of a wealthy man. The big gesture, the princely gift that was the rich soil out of which the National Park Service grew. Even small gifts made a difference in the thin years of getting started . . . Mather went so far back then as to buy revolvers for the Yosemite rangers when the government failed to and for years never turned in an expense account, traveling on his own money and government transportation requests. (Shankland, 1970: 294)

Some other examples of how Mather, as a financial angel, contributed to the parks included: the purchase of the scenic Tioga road into Yosemite, the purchase of private tracts of land in Sequoia and land for the park headquarters in Glacier, the construction of the Ranger Clubhouse in Yosemite, and the subsidization of funds to save starving elk in Yellowstone. His own contributions were exceeded many times over by monies from both organizations and individuals that he solicited for park expansion and improvement projects. Probably his greatest benefactor was John D. Rockefeller Jr., who was persuaded on numerous occasions to donate millions of dollars toward such projects as: the development of onsite park museums, roadside improvements, and the acquisition of land in Yosemite, Yellowstone, Grand Teton, Great Smoky Mountains, Redwood, and Acadia national parks.

In order to obtain greater public support and increase government funding of the parks, Mather orchestrated a massive promotion campaign aimed at increasing park visitation. Between 1917 and 1919, hundreds of articles were published on national park subjects. In addition, thousands of inexpensive booklets entitled *Glimpses of our National Parks* were produced for mass distribution, and thousands of feet of motion picture film were sent free of charge to organizations. Marketing efforts were also boosted by the *National Parks Portfolio*, a "luxury picture-book designed by Mather to reach a hand-picked elite, capable, they hoped, of passing the habit of park travel down from above." (Shankland, 1970: 97)

Mather also worked closely with railroad owners to promote park usage since trains were the primary mode of transportation to the parks in their formative years. He encouraged the railroads to offer affordable package tours and to improve visitor services. The improvement of services and living conditions was a high priority since many parks had either no concessions or concessions that were poorly operated or inadequate. Mather had suggested that, "scenery is a hollow enjoyment to a tourist who sets out in the morning after an inadequate breakfast and a fitful sleep on an impossible bed." (Shankland, 1970:134) Gradually Mather was able to generate greater investments in park concessions largely through his management philosophy of "allowing a reasonable return on investment" and his policy of "regulated monopolies." Thus, under his guiding hand, park concessions were recognized, improved, and expanded.

The development programs initiated by Mather attracted increased numbers of tourists, many of whom arrived at the parks in automobiles. To accommodate and visually excite the motorists, Mather endorsed plans that would enable them to see some of the best of each park from their vehicles.

> Even though Mather himself preferred to see the parks on foot or horseback, he felt each park should have one good highway—but no more than one— that could allow people to get deep enough, or through, the park so they could have at least a taste of wilderness. (Albright and Cahn, 1985: 195)

Inside the parks, Mather initiated roadside improvements that enhanced their scenic beauty, and outside the parks he influenced the states to improve access roadways. He also inspired the establishment of the National Park-to-Park Highway Association, which eventually planned a 3,500-mile loop connecting many of the Western parks.

The development of programs and facilities that would make the visitor's stay in the parks more enjoyable and educational was also a Mather goal. To advance these ends, he approved plans to establish park museums, instituted an interpretive program, and implemented campground entertainment programs that "tickled audiences a good part of the summer." (Shankland, 1970:263)

In relation to land acquisition and park expansion, Mather succeeded in enlarging some parks and adding others to the system, including Bryce Canyon, Grand Canyon, Hawaii, Lafayette (now Acadia), Lassen, Mount McKinley, and Zion. Because of his special interest in establishing more parks in the East, the groundwork was laid during Mather's administration for the eventual incorporation of the Great Smoky Mountains, Shenandoah, and Mammoth Cave national parks. In addition, 12 national monuments were added and the total acreage of national parks and monuments increased from 4,751,992 acres to 8,273,170 acres during the Mather years.

Organized attempts to adopt sites into the system that were either too full of private holdings, duplicative of existing parks, or just not good enough were persistantly resisted by Mather. He held firmly to high standards concerning which lands should qualify as national parks. He particularly considered private holdings in national parks a serious threat because they "increased the forest fire hazard, complicated wildlife protection and often introduced a discordant commercialism." (Shankland, 1970:180) While he succeeded in buying out many private holdings in existing parks, change was slow because of scarce funds and escalating land costs.

Frustration was no stranger to Mather as he often experienced it in his efforts to revise and expand the boundaries of some parks. He eventually obtained some boundary line concessions despite vigorous opposition to any shrinkage of adjacent national forest lands by special interest groups related to grazing, logging, mining, and irrigation. Also, such groups occasionally forced Mather into defensive maneuvers as they contended for the right to convert or use national park land for their purposes. Typical of these attacks on park territory was proposed legislation in 1920 which would have permitted the leasing of public waters to national parks for power uses. In this instance Mather fought and won the battle to exempt existing parks from lease agreements. A year earlier in his 1919 annual report to the secretary of the interior, he stated in reference to a reclamation project for Yellowstone:

> The nation has wisely set apart a few national parks where a state of nature is to be preserved. If the lakes and forests of these parks cannot be spared from the hands of commercialization, what hope can there be for the preservation of any scenic features of the mountains in the interest of posterity? (Albright and Cahn, 1985:105)

Mather's dedication to preserve valuable lands in their natural state extended far beyond his work with the NPS and into other organizations with similar goals. He instigated the National Park Association which was founded to save the trees of the State of Washington and to establish a state park system. He also set in motion a movement to organize state parks which he chaired from 1928 until 1930. The Save-the-Redwoods League, which intervened to prevent tracts of northern California's redwoods from falling victim to the lumberman's axe, was also inspired and founded largely through Mather's concern.

In conclusion, it should be recognized that the contributions described above provide only a partial account of Mather's accomplishments. It should also be noted that many of these accomplishments did not come about simply through the efforts of one man, but were often the result of partnerships and alliances in which Mather played a significant role.

> The partnership of Franklin Lane, Stephen Mather and Horace Albright was one of those happy circumstances in which a blend of energies and foresight created an institution exceeding hopes and expectations. They seemed to work in a charged atmosphere in which ideals were transformed quickly into reality. (MacKintosh, 1985:18)

In retrospect it would seem that Mather, as a catalyst, was the ideal person to lead the NPS through its difficult formative years. With vision and enthusiasm he tirelessly labored to protect and preserve the nation's greatest natural treasurers and to carry on the mission of the NPS. Stephen Tyng Mather was indeed a faithful steward over the lands entrusted to him. As inscribed on many plaques placed throughout the national parks in his honor, "There shall never come an end to the good he has done."

REFERENCES

Albright, H. M. & Cahn, R. (1985) The Birth of the National Park Service: The Founding Years 1913–33. Salt Lake City: Howe Brothers.

MacKintosh, B. (1985). The National Parks: Shaping the System. Washington, D.C.: National Park Service.

National Park Service (1986). National Park Service Administration History: A guide. Washington, D.C.: Author.

Shankland, R. (1970). Steve Mather of the National Parks (3rd ed.). New York: Alfred A. Knopf.

12

HENRY STODDARD CURTIS

1870–1954

By Carlton Yoshioka
Arizona State University

"*The greatest need of American life today is some common meeting ground for the people where business might be forgotten, friendships formed, and cooperations established. The playground seems to have great possibilities in this direction. It is already the social center for the children, and it is coming to be so more and more for adults.*"

1923e:434

Henry Curtis was a nationally known and recognized authority on recreation and playgrounds, and considered one of the pioneers of the recreation movement in America. He was born on a Michigan farm in 1870 and died in 1954 at the age of 83 at the home of his son, Dr. Henry S. Curtis, Jr., in Aurora, Ohio. He devoted much of his life to those individuals who lacked the opportunity to experience organized recreation and leisure.

Curtis attended Olivet College in Michigan and went on to graduate from Yale University. In 1898, he obtained a Ph.D. from Clark University. Curtis studied the play activities of children under the direction of G. Stanley Hall. After graduation, he took a summer position as assistant director of a playground in New York City under the direction of Superintendent Seth T. Stewart. Curtis was quickly promoted to director of a playground in the New York City playground system.

In the summer of 1902, Curtis traveled and investigated playgrounds in Germany and England. This information on German playgrounds would serve as a model for the early playground proposals of the Playground Association of America (PAA). In 1905, he became the supervisor of the East Side School system in New York City. The next year he assumed the position of Supervisor of Playgrounds in the District of Columbia.

For the next several years, Curtis would devote much of his efforts to organizing and developing the PAA. Curtis, with Luther Gulick, provided leadership for the PAA until Joseph Lee and Howard Braucher took over command in 1910. At this point Curtis had written about 12 articles on the topic of play and recreation.

During this period, Curtis lectured and acted as a consultant to groups throughout America on the problem of recreation and play. Extensive investigations were also performed on every major playground that existed during the period. This information would provide material for many of his 90 or more forthcoming publications.

In 1918, Curtis acted as an athletic director and lectured in American camps in France during World War I. After that experience, Curtis became the director of Hygiene and Physical Training for the State of Missouri. In the 1930s, he was on the faculty at the University of Michigan as director of a recreation survey project. He later taught recreation courses at Cornell, Columbia, and Harvard. In his later years, Curtis addressed the leisure problems of the aged.

The National Recreation Association summarized his distinguished career in a Resolution of the Board of Directors by stating:

Dr. Curtis' service in the national recreation movement covered a broad range of interests over a long span of years. He worked vigorously and persistently for play for children, for recreation for rural Americans, and for recreation for our older citizens. His service has left its definite imprint on the recreation movement and will be long remembered. (*In Memorium*, 1954:118)

Henry Curtis' contributions to the park, recreation, and leisure movement spanned 50 years with over 100 articles in a variety of professional and scientific journals. His first article appeared in *Harper's* in 1902 titled "Vacation Schools and Playgrounds." This initiated Curtis' effort to promote and develop the play movement in the United States. For the next 50 years, Curtis devoted numerous books and articles to "show the place of school playgrounds, of the municipal playgrounds, the parks, and various commercial forms of recreation . . . in correcting the evils of institutional life more than any other single agency." (Curtis, 1917:v)

Urbanization and the problems of the new industrial society disrupted the traditional patterns of leisure and relaxation for most Americans. City governments were unable as a result of corruption and inadequate organizational and administrative structures to provide proper recreational facilities and programs for their residents. (Patton, 1940; Perry, 1921) People in crowded cities provided the basis for progressive urban reformers and educators to unite under a new movement to improve the quality of everyone's life. The concern for adequate play space for urban children resulted in 14 cities sponsoring playground programs in 1900, which increased by 1906 to 41 cities. (Dickason, 1985)

Within this period of social change and awareness, Curtis graduated from Yale University and studied at Clark University under a well known educational psychologist, G. Stanley Hall. Curtis graduated from Clark University with a Ph.D. in 1898. He developed expertise and interest related to children and their instinctive desire for play.

What started as an attempt to develop training programs for playground leaders led Dr. Luther Gulick and Dr. Henry Curtis to organize a movement to create a national association of playgrounds. In April of 1906, the Playground Association of America (PAA) conducted the opening conference and elected Luther Gulick president, President Theodore Roosevelt, honorary president, Jacob Riis, honorary vice president, and Henry Curtis, secretary. Curtis, at the opening session on April 12, 1906, stated that the purpose of the Association was to:

. . . collect and distribute knowledge of and promote interest in playgrounds throughout the country. It shall also seek to further the establishment of playgrounds and athletic fields in all communities, and directed play in connection with the schools. (*Recreation*, 1907:13)

From 1906 to 1910, the PAA, under the leadership of Gulick and Curtis, experienced growth and expanded influence in the play movement. The 1907 PAA Congress in Chicago had 200 delegates from 30 cities in attendance. One of the participants was a representative of the Russell

Sage Foundation. He subsequently committed $20,000 of foundation money to assist the PAA. This support provided some financial stability and enlarged the efforts of Gulick and Curtis. The 1908 PAA Congress in New York City drew 408 delegates from 31 cities and an additional 397 registered visitors. Now the PAA included officers, Board of Directors and a council of over 130 people. In addition 29 local affiliated playground associations and a dozen national study and advisory groups were associated with the PAA. (*Playgrounds: Proceedings and Yearbook,* 1909)

Despite these outward signs of progress, 1909 was significant for the PAA and its leadership. Growth pains and internal controversy surrounding Gulick (questionable financial obligations connected with the Sage Foundation) and Curtis (personally antagonizing important supporters of the PAA) resulted in restructuring of the PAA leadership. Joseph Lee and Howard Braucher (PAA's first professional executive secretary) assumed the leadership of the PAA in 1910 and filled the positions for the next 40 years. After being passed over for the full time executive position, Curtis agreed to assume a much lesser position as the honorary second vice president. Gulick and Curtis are still recognized as the cofounders of the PAA and the general organized play movement. (Steiner, 1933; Brightbill, 1961; LaGasse and Cook, 1965)

The original progressive educators of the PAA believed that the most appropriate arena to meet the association's goals would require the administration of playground programs through municipal boards of education. Indeed, the keynote speaker at the 1907 PAA Congress in Chicago was the then U.S. Commissioner of Education, Elmer E. Brown. (Knapp and Hartsoe, 1979) Curtis, Gulick, and Stewart decided to implement the PAA's model city playground plan by using Washington D.C. as the demonstration site. Curtis created a detailed inventory and map using school districts with at least one acre of land for each 2,000 children (Curtis, 1908). However, the efforts of Curtis to promote playgrounds through school associations and municipalities lacked federal funding. It was also not the primary emphasis of the PAA and its new leadership. (Butler, 1965)

The efforts of the PAA and Curtis to foster and enhance the use of playgrounds resulted in numerous professional publications. The first book of the Playground and Recreation Association of America (the PRAA name change reflected the broadening role of the PAA) was *The Normal Course in Play* (1909d). Curtis, pursuing his own interests, visited and lectured in normal schools throughout the country on the professional value of playgrounds. Several publications by Curtis discussing the educational relationship of play and recreation appeared in the *Educational Review, School and Society, National Education Association Journal,* and *Education.* This perspective on education through play would dominate the post-PAA writings and activities of Curtis. At the end of his career, Curtis continued to write articles such as "Education for Leisure" in *School and Study* (1945a) and "Nature University" in *Recreation* (1945b).

The association also attempted to educate the industrial sector to the benefits of recreation and play programs for workers and their families. This area of industrial recreation was not seriously pursued by the PRAA until the 1940s. Curtis did recommend that the PRAA initiate a study of recreation in industry prior to 1909. (Knapp and Hartsoe, 1979)

Curtis and others from the PAA also stressed the wider use of schools through the social center approach. This "community movement" viewed the neighborhood and community as a natural social unit. Community activities, particularly recreation, were seen to be best organized by social centers operating within each neighborhood. This also reinforced the belief that the provision of recreation should be under the control of school boards (Doell and Fitzgerald, 1965). According to Curtis, "The social center is a place for sociability or social endeavor . . . The social center is to be the focus of community interest, whether these interests be social, educational, political or business." (Curtis, 1915a:495)

Curtis devoted considerable attention to the absence of social programs for the residents of rural America. Drawing from his personal experiences as a child on a Michigan farm, Curtis attempted to address the problems of isolation, loneliness, and general dissatisfaction of rural families. Curtis and the PRAA extended the concept of urban playground and recreation to the rural areas. Many of the basic urban recreation programs were adaptable to rural settings through organized agrarian social institutions such as churches, schools, granges, and youth organizations like the Boy Scouts and Girl Scouts. The PRAA went so far as to employ a special field secretary in rural New England to develop rural recreation. (Knapp and Hartsoe, 1979)

Curtis wrote a book, *Play and Recreation for the Open Country* (1914b) and several articles ("The Organizer of Rural Recreation," 1912b; "Rural Church as a Social Center," 1913f; "Education Extension Through the Rural Social Center," 1914a) on the problem of rural recreation in America. Curtis concluded that:

> The social center would appear from this study to be crucial to the larger education of the farmer and his wife, to breaking the isolation of the farmer and providing it with needed recreation and social life, and to the organization of the farm community for various cooperative business and civic enterprises. (Curtis, 1914e:759)

LIST OF CURTIS'S PUBLICATIONS

Vacation Schools and Playgrounds. (1902, June). *Harper's, 105*, pp. 22–29.

Play Movement in Germany. (1905, January) *Chautaguan, 40*, pp. 445–452.

Central Games Committee of Germany. (1906, July 7). *Charities, 16*, pp. 433–434.

Playground Progress and Tendencies, 1907. (1907, August 3). *Charities, 18*, pp. 495–499.

Washington Sites Available For Playgrounds. (1908, March 7). *Charities, 19*, pp. 1699–1703.

Congress and the District of Columbia. (1909a, August 28). *Survey, 22*, pp. 725–728.

Growth, Present Extent and Prospects of the Playground Movement in America. (1909b, September). *American City, 1*, pp. 27–33.

Relation of Playgrounds to Other Social Movements. (1909c, May 15). *Survey, 22*, pp. 251–253.

The Normal Course of Play. (1909d, October). *Recreation, 3*, pp. 20–22.

Athletics in the Playground. (1910a, July). *American City, 3*, pp. 21–25.

Public Provision and Responsibility for Playgrounds. (1910b, March). *Annals of the American Academy of Political and Social Science, 35*, pp. 334–344.

Four Recent Methods of Social Advance. (1911a, July). *American City, 5*, pp. 8–10.

Need of a Comprehensive Playground System. (1911b, December) *American City, 5*, pp. 338–340.

Neighbor Center. (1912a, July-August). *American City, 7*, pp. 14–17.

The Organizer of Rural Recreation. (1912b, November). *Recreation, 6*, pp. 282–285.

Reorganized School Playground. (1912c). *U.S. Bureau Education Bulletin, 16*, pp. 1–23.

School Camp. (1912d, July 20). *Survey, 28*, pp. 564–566.

Does Public Recreation Pay? (1913a, February). *American City, 8*, pp. 144–148.

New Games For People. (1913b, May). *Recreation, 7*, pp. 66–73.

Playground Attendance and the Playground Director. (1913c, August). *American City, 9*, pp. 126–131.

Playground Equipment. (1913d). *Playground, 7*, pp. 301–329.

Reorganized School Playground. (1913e). *U.S. Education Bulletin, 40*, pp. 1–28.

Rural Church as a Social Center. (1913f, October). *Education, 34*, pp. 111–118.

Rural Social Center. (1913g, July). *American Journal of Sociology, 19*, pp. 79–90.

School Center. (1913h, April 19). *Survey, 30*, pp. 89–91.

Education Extension Through the Rural Social Center. (1914a, January). *Education, 34,* pp. 283–294.

Physical Training in the Normal School. (1914b, October). *Education, 35,* pp. 82–90.

Play and Physical Development. (1914c, May 9). *Survey, 32,* pp. 174–175.

Play and Recreation for the Open Country. (1914d). Boston: Ginn and Company.

Playground Survey. (1914e, May). *American Journal of Sociology, 19,* pp. 792–812.

Public Improvement and Assessments. (1914f, August). *American City, 11,* pp. 118–119.

Boy Scouts. (1915a, December). *Education Review, 50,* pp. 495–508.

Closing Days on Summer Playgrounds. (1915b, January). *Recreation, 8,* pp. 357–359.

Education Through Play. (1915c). New York: MacMillan Company.

Nature Of The Playground. (1915d, February). *American City, 12,* pp. 135–141.

Ideal of the Play Movement. (1916a, June). *American City, 14,* pp. 574–575.

Practical Conduct for Play. (1916b). New York: MacMillan Company.

Play Movement and Its Significance. (1917). New York: MacMillan Company.

Continuation School for Teachers. (1918a, September). *Education Review, 56,* pp. 108–116.

Education Campaign for Playgrounds. (1918b, July). *American City, 19,* pp. 52–53.

Pedagogy versus Matrimony. (1918c, July 20). *School and Society, 8,* pp. 79–82.

Recreation For Teachers. (1918d). New York: MacMillan Company.

Continuation School for Teachers. (1921a, February 26). *School and Society, 13,* pp. 263–266.

Summer Resort as a Playground. (1921b, April). *Playground, 15,* pp. 55–56.

Teacher's Clubhouse. (1921c, April 2). *School and Society, 13,* p. 415.

School Grounds and Play. (1921d). *U.S. Bureau Education Bulletin, 45,* pp. 1–31.

Nature Study: The Foundation of an Education. (1922, April). *Education Review, 63,* pp. 307–314.

Education for Parenthood. (1923a, September 1). *School and Society, 18,* pp. 257–259.

Financing Child Welfare Movements. (1923b, April). *American City, 28,* pp. 399–401.

Fresh Air or Gymnasium. (1923c, December). *National Education Association Journal, 12,* p. 416.

Motorized Playground. (1923d, August). *Playground, 17,* pp. 264–266.

Portrait. (1923e, November) *Playground, 17*, p. 434.

School-house on Wheels. (1923f, August). *Recreation Review, 68*, p. 186.

At the Devil's Booth Are All Things Sold. (1924a, August 23). *School and Society, 20*, p. 248.

Movie University. (1924b, November). *Playground, 18*, pp. 482–483.

New State Program in Physical Education for Missouri. (1924c, October). *School Life, 10*, pp. 36–37.

Renaissance of Drama. (1924d, May 3). *School and Society, 19*, pp. 513–516.

Physical Education as Teacher Training. (1924e, December). *National Education Association Journal, 13*, pp. 32–35.

Physical Education, Rural and City Aspects. (1925a, May). *Playground, 19*, pp. 106–108.

Relative Values of Physical Activities in High School. (1925b, May). *School Life, 10*, pp. 161–163.

State M in Missouri. (1925c, October). *Playground, 19*, pp. 401–402).

High School Athletics for the Benefit of the Individual. (1926a, May). *School Life, 11*, p. 169.

Sportsmanship in School Athletics. (1926b, November). *School and Society, 12*, p. 48.

Where Are We Going? (1926c, December). *Playground, 20*, p. 511.

Can America Afford an Adequate System of Playgrounds? (1927a, July). *American City, 37*, pp. 65–67.

Two Thousand Counties Need Parks. (1927b, April). *American City, 36*, pp. 503–506.

Leadership, Equipment, Objectives, Activities Determine Success. (1928a, January). *School Life, 13*, pp. 96–97.

Training of Games. (1928b, October). *Playground, 22*, p. 385.

School Grounds Bear an Important Part in the School Program. (1928c, June). *School Life, 13*, p. 200.

Pros and Cons of Interschool Athletics. (1929, February). *National Education Association Journal, 18*, pp. 49–50.

In The Canal Zone. (1930, September). *Playground, 24*, pp. 235–237.

How It Began. (1931a, May): *Recreation, 25*, p. 71.

If Education Were A Business. (1932a, August 13). *School and Society, 36*, pp. 209–210.

Universities and Democracy. (1932b, May 7). *School and Society, 35*, p. 625.

County Grounds for Recreation. (1934a, June). *Recreation, 28*, pp. 153–155.

County Parks and Rural Life. (1934b, April). *National Education Association Journal, 23*, pp. 112–113.

Education and Business. (1934c, September 8). *School and Society, 40*, p. 327.

New Deal and the Schools. (1934d, April 28). *School and Society, 39*, pp. 544–545.

Parks For Every County. (1934e, February). *Survey, 70*, p. 40.

Playgrounds and Public Forests from Farms. (1934f, March). *American City, 49*, pp. 50–51.

There is Hope Even for the County. (1934g, September). *American City, 49*, pp. 74–75.

Dammed River May Make A Resort. (1935a, March). *American City, 50*, pp. 57–58.

Farm Woodlot as a Playground. (1935b, March). *Recreation, 28*, pp. 582–585.

Planning The Summer Vacation. (1935c, August). *Recreation, 29*, pp. 239–244.

Needed: A Common Tongue. (1935d, March). *Education, 55*, pp. 436–439.

School Camp. (1935e, April). *National Education Association Journal, 24*, pp. 113–116.

Creed for the Improvement of Rivers. (1936a, July). *American City, 51*, p. 52.

Recreation Possibilities of a Typical Small River Valley. (1936b, June). *American City, 51*, p. 97.

Traveller's Guide. (1936c, February). *Education, 56*, pp. 362–365.

Plan for the Improvement of Huron Valley. (1937a, September). *Recreation, 31*, pp. 377–381.

Trails. (1938, April). *Recreation, 32*, p. 26.

Park of the Future. (1940, October). *Recreation, 34*, p. 434.

Can Schools Train in Honesty? (1943a, October 2). *School and Society, 58*, pp. 261–262.

Education For Permanent Peace. (1943b, July 17). *School and Society, 58*, pp. 33–35.

Wanted: An International Conference on Post-War Education. (1944, February 19). *School and Society, 59*, pp. 140–142.

Education for Leisure. (1945a, April 28). *School and Society, 61*, pp. 282–283.

Nature University. (1945b, January). *Recreation, 38*, pp. 541–542.

Squirrel Adventures. (1945c, February). *Nature Magazine, 37*, p. 105.

The Other Half of the Playground Movement. (1947, August). *Recreation, 41*, pp. 247–248.

Home of Retired Teachers. (1952a, November). *National Education Association Journal, 41*, pp. 530–533.

Why Retire at Sixty-Five? (1952b, April). *Harper's, 20*, pp. 92–94.

References

Brightbill, C. (1961). *Man and Leisure*. Englewood Cliffs, N.J.: Prentice-Hall.

Butler, G. (1965). *Pioneers in Public Recreation*. Minneapolis, Minnesota: Burgess Publishing Company.

Doell, C. and Fitzgerald, G. (1965). *A Brief History of Parks and Recreation in the United States*. National Recreation Association.

Dulles, F. A. (1965). *History of Recreation: Americans Learn To Play*. 2d. New York: Appleton, Century and Crofts.

Dickason, J. (1985). 1906: A Pivotal Year for the Playground Profession. *Parks and Recreation, 20(8)*, pp. 40–45.

In Memorium. (1954, March). *Recreation, 47*, p. 183.

Knapp. R. and Hartsoe, C. (1979). *Play for America*. Arlington, VA: National Recreation and Park Association.

LaGasse, A. and Cook, W. (1965). *History of Parks and Recreation*. Arlington, VA: National Recreation and Park Association.

Patton, C. (1940). *The Battle for Municipal Reform: Mobilization and Attack, 1875–1900*. Washington, D.C.: American Council on Public Affairs.

Perry, C. (1921). *Ten Years of the Community Center Movement*. New York: Russell Sage Foundation.

Playgrounds: Proceedings and Yearbook, Volume II. (1909). Playground Association of America.

Recreation. (1907, June). *1*, pp. 13–15.

Steiner, J. (1933). *Americans at Play*. New York: MacGraw-Hill.

CLARK HETHERINGTON

1870–1942

By Kathleen A. Cordes
Whittier College

AAHPERD Archives

"**E**very recreation worker out in the field who has lifted up his eyes to the harvest has realized the abounding opportunities for service through which the ordinary routine of games and dances cannot touch."

1909:35

Clark Wilson Hetherington was a pioneer in leisure and recreation. He authored numerous articles and was the leader in preparing *The Normal Course of Play* (1909). Known as "the modern philosopher of physical education," he spent a lifetime analyzing and communicating the fundamentals of education and play. Demonstrating the importance of play as an educational tool, he introduced recreation courses to the curriculum in normal schools, colleges, and universities. Hetherington was prominent and influential in shaping the Playground Association of America, and his vigorous work as a member of the Board of Directors helped to determine the philosophy and methods of the new organization which precipitated the rapid increase of city programs.

Born in Lanesboro, Minnesota in 1870, he moved to California by the age of four. In his younger years, he worked as a cowboy, a dentist's assistant, warehouse clerk, businessman, and an architectural apprentice. A finished athlete skilled in gymnastics and acrobatics, he had his own show in a handmade gymnasium where he imitated circus performers. By the age of 21, he enrolled as a member of the first class to enter Stanford University. Here, he began a fruitful association with Dr. Thomas D. Wood in the study of natural activities in the general physical education program rather than the formal exercises of the European gymnastics systems. To help defray his costs while earning his degree, he was employed by Wood as a gymnasium instructor. He participated in track and was an expert at the art of club swinging. After graduation he served as an assistant in the University Physical Training Department at Stanford. (Hackensmith, 1966:389; Weston, 1964:159)

Upon graduation in 1895 and for the next two years, Hetherington secured a position as the director of Physical Training at the State Reform School in Whittier, California, where he verified that wholesome play and recreation was fundamental to the healthy development of the individual. His studies included psychological experimentation with various aspects of play and athletics, and his detailed data on the background of 480 of the boys inspired him to write that "eighty per cent of the inmates were in the institutions because of the neglect of their play impulses." He later wrote "Social workers agree that the bad boy is largely the product of restricted or misdirected play energies. Juvenile deliquency diminishes in the districts where playgrounds are established." (Hetherington, 1910: 629–635) His program of organized play had a profound effect on the character of the boys and on the institution. The Board of Trustees recommended that a gymnasium be provided at the earliest possible date and found that the activities were "beneficial to their moral and physical development." This was the first time that such a program was implemented in a reform school in California, and one of the first gymnastic and athletic programs in a penal institution in the United States. (Butler, 1965: 17–18; Hackensmith, 1966: 389–390, Weston, 1964: 159)

This early experience helped to mold Hetherington's educational philosophy which centered on the positive impact of recreational programs on the development of youth when conducted under trained leadership. As a Fellow and Assistant in Psychology, Hetherington continued to study individual differences and character training under Dr. G. Stanley Hall in the field of experimental psychology at Clark University in Worcester, Massachusetts. Like Wood, Hall inspired Hetherington's mission that physical education should focus on natural play activities. Soon Hetherington developed and pursued an interest in child study. (Butler, 1965: 18; Zeigler, 1988: 212) Later his career included positions as director and founder of the Department of Physical Education and director of Athletics at the University of Missouri (1900–1910), director at the University of Wisconsin (1913–1917), California State Supervisor of Physical Education (1918–1921), and faculty member of Wellesley College, Columbia University, New York University, and Stanford University.

While at the University of Missouri, he cultivated the development of playgrounds and recreational opportunities throughout the state. He devoted energy to the establishment of intercollegiate athletics as a controlled educational activity, and supported sport and recreational programs for women and all students. Hetherington helped to organize the National Amateur Athletic Federation, served as a founder in 1907 of the Athletic Research Society, and had a vital role in elevating the standards of amateurism in the United States.

In his publication, "The Foundation of Amateurism," (1909), he described amateurism as an attitude of the mind. Finding that play and amateur educational athletics should share the same purpose (i.e., personal pleasure), he focused sharp criticism on organized athletics for spectator amusement and external reward. His paper addressed amateurism among children, youth, and college students. He expounded that, "Educators dealing with play must realize the folly of leaving children and youth to their own devices in play. They must have proper opportunities, stimuli, examples, sympathy, and guidance." He discovered among college students a tendency of the ambitious to withdraw from athletic participation when a disproportionate amount of time must be surrendered to athletic endeavors. He wrote, "A custom that either discourages general culture or the education contained in athletics must be condemned." Administrators were called upon to teach the public that professional athletics are for the pleasure of spectators and that amateur athletics are for the pleasure and benefit of participants. (Hetherington, 1909: 556–568)

By 1906, Hetherington was appointed chair of the committee charged with the preparation of *The Normal Course in Play* for the Playground

Association of America. The report submitted at the Recreation Congress in 1909 was published in the *Congress Proceedings*. A landmark in educational philosophy, the document influenced the development of the recreation movement and offered valuable information to the public sector. Hetherington believed that all teachers, regardless of specialization, would benefit from leadership training in recreation. The report served as a professional guide for teachers and students in normal schools, for playground directors, and for temporary employees of playground associations and summer schools. The document defined and set standards for training, and establishing duties, and provided appropriate qualifications for leaders of various positions. Additionally, it presented information on the nature and function of play; theories of play; social conditions of the neighborhood; hygiene and first aid; the playground movement; the practical conduct of playgrounds; and the organization and administration of playgrounds. Dr. Hetherington was credited with the final development and basic philosophy underlying the report. The committee agreed that "the position of playground supervisor may be no less important than that of the superintendent of schools and that a playground system needs to be run with definite objectives just as a school system." (Butler, 1965: 10–21) By 1925, Hetherington's book was revised to include arts and crafts, music, and drama for contemporary community and adult recreation centers.

During the middle of his tenure at the University of Missouri, he was granted a year's leave to study biological psychology at the University of Zurich in Switzerland. In 1910, the Joseph Fels Endowment Fund provided Hetherington a grant of $5,000 per year for two years to continue his work in the promotion of recreation and educational athletics. He conducted recreation and physical education surveys and visited and studied institutions in 300 cities in 35 states. Many of these institutions adopted his *Normal Course of Play* as a guide to training recreation leadership. During this period, he helped to start a number of local and state physical education associations. (Butler, 1965: 17–21; Lee, 1983: 208–209)

Speaking at the National Education Association meeting in 1910, Hetherington, as president of the Physical Education Department of the National Education Association, defined the role of physical education in the new century by pointing out that education was not exclusively aimed at the mind or at the body, but rather at the integration of all human potential. He described physical education or "fundmental education" as fundamental to the education process. His publication, *Fundamental Education*, describes his philosophy of "the new physical education" with the "emphasis on education, and understanding that it is physical only in the sense that the activity of the whole organism is the educational agent and not the mind alone." (Hetherington, 1910: 629–635) The function of play activ-

120   PIONEERS IN LEISURE AND RECREATION

ities in the educational process involved four objectives: organic education for vital vigor, neuromuscular education for power and skill; social
education for character and spiritual development; and intellectual education acquired through free play or development of social thinking.
Hetherington sold physical education to general education.

In 1922, Hetherington published his book *School Program in Physical
Education*, which further defined the new physical education. In sharp
contrast to earlier programs of formal gymnastics in which the body was
developed as an end in itself, the new physical education concept evolved
into present-day programs of physical education. Physical education,
thus, offered a vital contribution to the education process, educational
values capable of revolutionizing the mental, physical, and emotional,
and social aspects of an individual. Playing skills, developed through
sports, games, and recreational activities, enabled a more natural and
useful benefit for everyday life as well as a carryover to leisure time.

The Child Demonstration Play School, implemented at the University
of California, Berkeley, was Hetherington's ideal that play is the business
of the child. Hetherington started and conducted the school for four years,
then his wife, Daisy, directed the school until 1934. It served as a combined play center and school which focused on the children and their
activities. The outdoor center combined play with the social purpose of
education, and established the need in the school setting for leadership
in play from infancy to maturity. Through the school, he sought to demonstrate the importance of leadership in play. He worked to convince the
public that recreation was essential and deserved government support.
The uniqueness of the Play School attracted widespread interest, and
influenced Hetherington to later urge New York University to establish a
summer camp and physical education school at Lake Sebago. (Butler,
1965: 21–22)

California was the second state to establish the post of a state supervisor
of physical education. Hetherington accepted the position, and soon
proposed a program of natural recreation activities as outlined in his new
physical education program. He introduced the revised curriculum in a
guide for teachers and administrators in his *Manual in Physical Education
for the Public Schools of the State of California*, issued by The State Board
of Education in 1918. Topics in the manual included principles in organization and leadership, natural activities, drills and exercises, athletic
activities, values, and methods by age. The syllabus was intended as a
daily guide for all teachers and directors throughout the school system
with no other course of study needed. He proposed that "the activities
bring teacher into touch with the joyous side of child life, and by giving
the natural leadership so much craved by children the problems of dis-
cipline are practically eliminated." (Hetherington, 1918: 10) Hethering-

ton's manual was widely praised, and adopted as a model for many states. In 1921, he returned to teaching at Teachers College, Columbia University and to do educational research. The following year, 1922, he was offered the directorship of the new Department of Physical Education at New York University. Soon he convinced the University to sponsor a summer camp with recreational and outdoor living facilities to be used as a training center for physical education and recreation leaders. He organized the undergraduate and graduate curriculum. In his address in 1924 to the Society of Directors of Physical Education in Colleges, he stressed his concerns that institutions would simply list their undergraduate courses as graduate courses. It was in the graduate program that Hetherington believed that the student could be exposed to opportunities for specialization provided that the undergraduate curriculum was well-planned and organized. He also maintained that the professional program should provide a broader content than was prevalent. He encouraged course work in other areas of the curriculum such as biology, chemistry, and psychology. Such inclusion, he felt, would increase the status of the profession. (Hetherington, 1925: 5; Zeigler, 1975: 279)

At a meeting of the National Recreational Congress in 1922, Hetherington suggested to Blanche M. Trilling, chair of the Committee on Women's Athletics, that women physical educators should immediately organize a national women's athletic association. In response to the NRC resolution voicing opposition to status of athletic competition for girls, a women's division of the National Amateur Athletic Federation was formed. (Hackensmith, 1966: 430) Earlier in his career, Hetherington introduced play days and recreation for girls in the Missouri high schools as a substitute for interscholastic athletics. (Butler, 1965: 23)

Impressed with Hetherington's understanding of the recreational interests of people and the relationship of recreation and education, Howard Braucher arranged for a three-year foundation grant so that Hetherington could devote a portion of his time to writing. Ill health, administrative pressures, and worry over his incomplete writing projects prompted his resignation from New York University in 1928, despite the offer to take a leave of absence. Joining the staff at Stanford University, he hoped to find conditions more suitable for writing. His plans to publish a series of books were, however, never realized. Health problems and his high standards of perfection made the task an impossibility. Always seeking to express himself better, he refused to consider any of his manuscripts as finished. (Lee, 1983: 210; Butler, 1965: 24–25)

The list of Hetherington's achievements is exhausting. He was an organizer and founder of the Pacific Coast Physical Education Association, the Midwest Physical Education Association, the Joint Committee of the NEA and the AMA on Health Problems in Education, the National Amateur

Athletic Federation, and the Athletic Research Society. He was among the five who founded the American Academy of Physical Education which was based on an earlier organization of prominent male leaders of which Hetherington had been a member. Throughout the organizational period, he acted as chairman. Hetherington also shared in the foundation of The Boy Scouts of America and served on its National Council for several years. He participated as a member of the Board of Directors of the Playground Association of America. A member of the Council of the American Physical Education Association for several years, he actively influenced its policies and was among those recognized for outstanding leadership at its first Honor Award Ceremony. He was the recipient of the Posse Medal for distinguished service to physical education. The University of Southern California conferred upon him the honorary degree of Doctor of Pedagogy while the American Academy of Physical Education has established the Hetherington Award in his honor.

When Hetherington's wife of 38 years died in 1940, his health began to fail rapidly, although his sense of service continued to his last days. Before his death he wrote the article, "Are They Fit for Combat?" in order to help in the nation's war effort. In this last article, he recommended correct physical fitness programs with professionally-trained observers who could recognize mental cases. He suggested that a placement service be formed for potential work candidates. Other qualified men might be released from their jobs for combat duty. (Butler, 1965: 25)

As a child and young man, Clark Hetherington continuously fought tuberculosis. Plagued with ill health much of his life, he overcame his frailties by becoming a skillful gymnast in his younger years and by hiking later in life. A monumental figure in the recreative aspect of the physical education program in America, he was clearly ahead of his time. His thinking laid the base for an integrated philosophy and curriculum in physical education and led to its acceptance in general education. He promoted intramural programs for all students, and sportsmanship and ethics in intercollegiate athletics. He supported women's programs in health, hygiene, and physical activities, and developed training programs for recreation. He worked for the natural play of children, playgrounds, and summer camps. He served as a founder and chairman of numerous associations, and as an administrator, teacher, and author he influenced scores of leaders and students. Hetherington served to remove the barriers that prevented physical education and recreation from achieving full integration into the developmental process of the individual. He contributed generously and ceaselessly to educational and social institutions of the United States. To paraphrase his own words, he had lifted up his eyes to the harvest and had realized the abounding opportunities for service.

PARTIAL LIST OF HETHERINGTON'S PUBLICATIONS

Analysis of Problems in College Athletics. (1970). *American Physical Education Reviews, 12.*

The Normal Course of Play. (1909) New York: Playground Association of America.

The Foundation of Amateurism. (1909, November). *American Physical Education Review.*

Report of the Committee on Amateur Law to the Intercollegiate Athletic Association. (1910, December). *American Physical Education Review, 15.*

The Demonstration Play School of 1913. (1914). Berkeley, California: University of California Press.

Manual in Physical Education in the Public Schools in the State of California. (1918). California State Department of Education.

Professional Training Course in Physical Education. (1920, May). American Physical Education Review, 25.

School Program in Physical Education. (1922). Yonkers-on-Hudson, New York: World Book Co.

Graduate Work in Physical Education. (1925, April/May). *American Physical Education Review.*

REFERENCES

Butler, George. (1965). *Pioneers in Public Recreation.* Minneapolis, Minnesota: Burgess Publishing Co.

Hackensmith, C.W. (1966). *History of Physical Education.* New York: Harper and Row, Publishers.

Hetherington, Clark. (1910, December). Fundamental Education. *American Physical Education Review, 15.*

Lee, Mabel. (1983). *A History of Physical Education and Sports in the U.S.A.* New York: John Wiley and Sons.

Weston, Arthur. (1964). *The Making of American Physical Education.* New York: Appleton-Century-Crofts.

Zeigler, Earl. (1975). *A History of Physical Education and Sport in the United States and Canada.* Champaign, Illinois: Stipes Publishing Co.

Zeigler, Earl. (1988). *History of Physical Education and Sport,* revised edition. Champaign, Illinois: Stipes Publishing Co.

JOHAN HUIZINGA

1872–1945

By Hilmi Ibrahim
Whittier College

"For many years the conviction has grown upon me that civilization arises and unfolds in and as play. Traces of such opinion are to be found in my writings ever since 1903."

1950: ix

Johan Huizinga was the son of a professor of Medicine at the University of Groningen, the Netherlands. He completed his university education in literature and language. He began to teach secondary school in Harleem in 1897 and to lecture on India at the University of Amsterdam in 1903. He was appointed instructor in history at the University of Groningen in 1905 where he stayed until 1915. He moved to the University of Leiden and became its Rector until it was closed by the Nazi occupation in 1941. His work as a historian of genius did not emerge until 1919 when he wrote *The Waning of the Middle Ages, Thought and Art in France and The Netherlands in the Fourteenth and Fifteenth Centuries,* which appeared in English five years later. He showed no interest in matters of state, refuted the socio-economic approach of Marx, and rejected the Freudian method of historical analysis. Instead, he placed a great emphasis on the historian's ability to intuitively grasp an age or ages.

In his book, *Homò Ludens: A Study of the Play Element in Culture,* which is hailed as a classic, Huizinga placed a great emphasis on mass culture and symbolism. Here he assumed the role of a cultural critic more than a historian (Pois, 1983:261–263), although a generation later he might have become a sociologist. (Colie, 1968, p. 534)

Huizinga believed that play is older than culture. His proof is that animals, who are devoid of culture, play as did early man. In play, there is something "at play" which transcends the immediate needs of life. Play, then, is manipulation not only of objects, but also images and imagination. This is observed in the archetypal activities of human society.

There is a lot of play in language, for "behind every abstract expression there lies the boldest of metaphors, and every metaphor is a play upon words." (pg. 4) In myth, a "fanciful spirit is playing on the borderline between jest and earnest." (pg. 5) In ritual, "which serves to guarantee the well-being of the world, [there exists] a spirit of pure play truly understood." (pg. 4)

But what is play? Huizinga listed the following characters of play. (pg. 7)

First and foremost, play is a voluntary activity.

Secondly, play makes us step out of real life into a temporary sphere of activity with a disposition all its own.

Thirdly, play is characterized by its secludedness. It takes place within certain limits of time and place and it contains its own course and meaning.

Play creates order, particularly in the field of aesthetics, which is reflected in rhythm and harmony.

Play also creates tension, uncertainty, and a striving to decide the issue.

Play has rules that are absolutely binding and allow no doubt.

In the second chapter entitled "The Play Concept As Expressed In Language," Huizinga suggested that "all people play and play remarkably alike; but their languages differ widely in their conception of play." (pg. 28) For example, the Ancient Greeks used the suffix *inda* merely to give any word the connotation of playing at something. Sanskrit has at least four verbal roots for the concept of play. There is no grouping of all the activities one may consider play in Chinese expressions. In Japanese, a very definite word exists for play in general, also for recreation, amusement, and passing time. In Arabic, the word for play also connotes laughter and mocking, as well as playing a musical instrument. Originally, the Germanic expression for play meant a lively rhythmical movement. Latin has only one word to cover the whole field of play: *ludus*.

In the third chapter, "Play And Contest As Civilizing Functions," Huizinga advocated that the idea of winning is closely connected with play. Winning is very much related to exhibition. These do not proceed from culture, but rather preface it. The evidence comes to us again from animals, where rams butt their heads, wolves hold reception, woodcocks perform dances, crows hold flying matches, and egrets decorate their nests. No wonder then that the words "prize," "price," and "praise" are so closely related. The player receives his winning, a prize; the merchant, a price; and the actor gets praise. Anthropology shows us that social life in early societies depended to a great degree upon antagonism. Competition between two halves of one tribe is very common. This is witnessed in the *potlatch* of the American Indians, *Almufakhara* of Arab tribes, and the *Jul-feast* of the Nordic people.

Huizinga believes that there is a relationship between law and play. This is particularly true in ancient cultures where the legal system settled disputes by the outcome of a contest. "For example, it was an old Germanic legal custom to establish the "marke" or boundary of a village or a piece of land by running a race or throwing an axe." (pg. 82) "In Abyssinia, betting on the sentence was a constant practice in the course of a legal session." (pg. 84)

There is an element of play in war. Young dogs and small boys fight for the fun of it. The medieval tournament was regarded as a sham fight. Animals fight, but do not kill each other. The olympic games started as a substitute for war. In many cultures, before the battle begins, the bravest challenges the other side and a single combat will take the place of the battle itself. Trial by battle in civil suits took place in the Court of Common Pleas in Westminster in 1571. "The whole ceremony much resembled athletic entertainment at a village sports." (pg. 94)

In Chapter Six, "Playing And Knowing," Huizinga advocates that man learned to settle his disputes through agon (contest) rather than through war. Contests take many forms among which are oracles and riddles. He believed that "competitions in esoteric knowledge are deeply rooted in ritual and form an essential part of it." (pg. 105) Examples come to us from Vedic lore and Greek tradition. He concluded that the riddle was originally a sacred game and as civilization develops, it branched out into two directions: mystic philosophy on the one hand and recreation on the other.

Huizinga suggested that in highly organized societies, religion, science, law, and politics gradually lose their touch with play. (pg. 119) But poetry (and literature) remain fixed in the play sphere where they were born. *Poiesis* is a play function which proceeds within the playground of the mind. "Poetry as a social game of little or no aesthetic purport is to be found everywhere and in the greatest variety of forms." (pg. 124) A good example of the fusion of play and poetry is the traditional method of reciting the Finnish *Kalevala;* also in the drumming/singing contests of the Eskimos. Poetry everywhere precedes prose, for a pre-literate or bookless society finds it easier to memorize its text in this way. No wonder then, that there is a threefold connection between myth, poetry, and play.

In Chapter Eight, Huizinga advocates that play is an important element of mythopoiesis. Personification, to him, is both a play function and a supremely important habit of mind. He believed that play "has been present before human culture or human speech existed, hence the ground on which personification and imagination work was a datum from the remote past forward." (pg. 141) Today, drama remains linked to play. Language itself reflects the bond, particularly Latin and German, where dramatic performance is "played." In drama, the player withdraws "from the ordinary world by the mask he wears." (pg. 145)

At the center of the circle that Huizinga used to describe his idea of play, there stands the Greek sophist. "Two main factors of social play in archaic society are present in him: glorious exhibitionism and agonistic aspiration." (pg. 145) His business was to exhibit his vast knowledge and defeat his rival in public contest. For the Greek, the treasures of the mind were the fruit of his leisure (*schole*). Games, or *jeux d'esprit,* designed to catch people by trick questions, held an important place in Greek conversation. Sophistry became a game of wits, vascillating between solemn ritual and playful rivalry. And sophists laid the foundation for the Hellenic idea of education and culture, *schole,* which at first meant leisure, and later came to mean school.

In Chapter Ten, Huizinga suggested that there is much of play in the Arts, be they "musical" arts or plastic arts. By musical arts, he meant those activities that the Greeks believed to be related to the Muses, such as music, dancing, singing, drama, and exhibition. These types of activities are closely related to ritual, for "all ritual is sung, danced, or played." (pg. 158) The element of play in plastic art is known to everyone "who, pencil in hand, had ever had to attend a tedious board meeting . . . barely conscious of what we are doing, we play with lines and planes, curves and masses." (pg. 168)

Huizinga indicated in Chapter Eleven that although all civilizations were affected by the sphere of play, medieval life was brimful of play, "full of pagan elements that had lost their sacred significance and had been transformed into jesting and bafoonery, or the solemn and pompous play of chivalry, the sophisticated play of courtly love, etc." (pg. 179) And if the play element is discerned in the later period known as Baroque, the ensuing period known as Rococo "has so many associations with play and playfulness that it might almost be a definition of it." (pg. 186) The play quality of the 18th Century goes deeper for it "imbued the literary and scientific controversies which formed so large a part of the higher occupations and amusements of the international elite that waged them." (pg. 187)

In the closing chapter of *Homo Ludens*, Huizinga concluded that the 19th Century had lost many of the play elements that so characterized the former era. "More and more the sad conclusion forces itself upon [him] that the play element in culture has been on the wane ever since the 18th Century, when it was in full flower." (pg. 206) He used sport as an example of such decline. He advocated that with the increasing systemization and regimentation of sport, something of the pure play quality is lost. Sport has become a thing *sui generis;* neither play nor earnest.

Pois commented (1983) that the uniqueness of *Homo Ludens* is not only in its contents, but in the effective fusion of the concerns of both Marxists and Freudians. This is not surprising as Huizinga was a great admirer of Max Weber. Both Huizinga and Weber were committed to the study of contemporary and historical societies and the role of the irrational in human affairs.

Colie (1964) believed that *Homo Ludens* was Huizinga's most extraordinary and original book. It is more or less a meta-social approach to the human race. He saw the task of the cultural historian to be the interpretation of societies. Huizinga's work forced historians to pay attention to the nonpolitical/social forms of human life.

Thomas Rayan (1986) believed that Huizinga's description of the shift towards over-seriousness was fatal. He pointed out that not only sport, but all other aspects of recreation will suffer from the same fate of the demise of the spirit of play to the chagrin of many professional organizations, including the American Alliance for Health, Physical Education, Recreation, And Dance. The Alliance's "New Physical Education" is designed to turn the tide and bring the spirit of play back.

Others (Briggs, 1981) believed that *Homo Ludens* must be reckoned a stimulating failure. Although the idea of isolating and analyzing the play element in culture was a brilliant one, the execution was too eclectic and haphazard. Huizinga should have benefited from anthropology. Yet *Homo Ludens* remains a tribute to Johan Huizinga's spirit of intellectual adventure.

PARTIAL LIST OF HUIZINGA'S PUBLICATIONS

(In English)

The Waning of the Middle Ages: A Study in the Forms of Life, Thought and Art in France and the Netherlands in the 14th and 15th Centuries. (1954). (Originally in Dutch, 1919). London: Arnolds, 1924; Garden City: Doubleday.

America: A Dutch Historian's Vision From Afar. (1972). (Originally in Dutch, 1927). New York: Harper.

Erasmus. (1924). (Originally in Dutch, 1924). London & New York: Scribner.

In The Shadow of Tomorrow: A Diagnosis of the Spiritual Distemper of Our Times. (1938). (Originally in Dutch, 1935). London: Heinemann, 1938; New York: Norton.

Homo Ludens: A Study of the Play Element in Culture. (1955). (Originally in Dutch, 1938). London: Routledge, 1949; New York: Beacon.

Dutch Civilization in the Seventeenth Century. (1968). (Originally in Dutch, 1941). London: Collins.

History And Ideas. (1959). New York: Meridian Books.

REFERENCES

Briggs, R. (1981). Huizinga, Johan. In Justin Wintle's *Makers of Modern Culture.* New York: Facts On File, Inc.

Colie, R. L. (1964). Johan Huizinga and the Task of Cultural History. *American Historical Review 63:* 607–630.

Colie, R. L. (1968). Huizinga, Johan. In David L. Sills (editor) *International Encyclopedia of Social Science.* New York: MacMillan.

Parkinson, C. Northcote. (1970, June 6). "Game Points." *Spectator.*

Pois, R. (1983). Huizinga, Johan. In Elizabeth Devine, et al, (editors) *Thinkers of the Twentieth Century.* Detroit: Gale Research.

Raban, J. (1970, June 5). Conservative Cosmologies. *New Statesman.*

Rayan, T. (1986, July–August). Whatever Happened to "Play" in Sports? *New Catholic World,* 169–170.

15

HARRY A. OVERSTREET

1875–1970

By Hilmi Ibrahim
Whittier College

" We have to an extent, grown work-wise. In the future we shall grow leisure-wise. "

1934:9

Philosopher, author, and educator, Harry A. Overstreet devoted a good part of his professional life to the problem of adult education. He was born on October 27, 1875, to a Missourian father who served in the Civil War and as a compositor on the *San Francisco Bulletin*. His mother was born in Germany and came to California as a young girl. Overstreet entered the University of California at Berkeley as a member of the class of 1898. He was attracted to the writings of Herbert Spenser, Waldo Emerson, and Charles Darwin, but his social consciousness was affected by the sights of drunks brought to the city jail near his home and by street corner orators. (*Current Biographies:* 433)

Due to financial difficulties, he was not able to obtain his B.A. until 1899, and with election to Phi Beta Kappa, along with a grant, he went to Oxford where he obtained a B.S. in 1901.

Upon his return to the United States, he was appointed an instructor in philosophy at Berkeley and became an associate professor in 1911. That same year he accepted a full professorship and chairmanship of the depart-ment of Philosophy at the College of the City of New York.

He was interested in industrial disputes and decided that firsthand experiences would be best to grasp the real cause of conflict between capital and labor. He became convinced that the conflict was between the unintelligent and the intelligent and that the solution could be found in education, not only of the young, but of everyone from the cradle to the grave.

Harry Overstreet wrote many monographs and articles on adult edu-cation. He first book-length work, *Influencing Human Behavior*, appeared in 1925 and had 26 printings. This was followed by *About Ourselves: Psychology For Normal People* in 1927, which had 25 printings. His third and fourth books, *The Ending Quest* and *We Move In New Directions*, respectively, were not as successful as his first two. His fifth book, *A Guide to Civilized Leisure* reflected some of his concerns about America.

He saw two threats to the American way of life: the threat from without and the threat from within. The book was originally titled *A Guide To Civilized Loafing*. (W.W. Norton, Philadelphia, 1934) He deleted the last chapter in *Loafing*, entitled "Leftovers" and added two to *Leisure*, "Leisure and Unemployment" and "Leisure and Youth." In 1939, *Let Me Think* dealt with the management of the mind, and 1940 saw *Leaders For Adult Education* (with Mrs. Overstreet) appear. His eighth book, *Our Free Minds*, (1941) did not reach the zenith that his ninth book, *The Mature Mind*, (1949) reached. It was the nonfiction best-seller in 1950 and had 18 printings. Seven more books were authored by the Overstreets, five of which were politically oriented.

In the opening pages of his fifth book, *A Guide to Civilized Leisure*, Overstreet quoted Maxim Gorky's remark upon his visit to Coney Island.

Gorky's friends had taken him to the huge amusement park where people were swarming on a Sunday afternoon. His friends "took him through crowded concessions . . . underground and overground . . . through bewildered mazes . . . and museums of freaks." At the end of what seemed to be a perfect day, they asked him how he liked the park. After a moment of silence, Gorky simply said "what a sad people you must be!" (pg.17)

Overstreet was concerned with what he called the new leisure. To him, Gorky was not deceived by the fanfare and frenzy of Coney Island attendants. He believed that Gorky viewed their activities as a psychiatrist might view high excitement in a manic-depressive patient. Overstreet asserted that Gorky saw people who were weekday-driven, suppressed and subdued, breaking into a delirium of release. To him, Gorky saw Coney Island not as a joyous place, but as an echo of sick souls.

Overstreet suggested that two requirements must be met before civilized loafing, as he initially called it, may take place. Work must be man's first necessity. Secondly, man's environment, both physical and social, must be improved. While all work and no play makes Jack a dull boy, dull work and dull homes make Jack a foolish and pathetic boy in his play.

Leisure, then, faces a dilemma. Either its projects must wait until the reconstruction of man's social and work environment takes place, or leisure projects will come in as an apologetic second. Overstreet advocated that leisure could be used effectively in the remodeling of the human condition in *A Guide To Civilized Leisure*. (1934b)

Overstreet considered the book a frontier adventure in that it was a scouting out of the possibilities that lay dormant in life, and was an examination of the kind of activities to be discovered and enjoyed in liberated hours. He believed that the hours that make us happiest, make us wise as well. He felt that there is a new opportunity for Americans to do as they please and ventured to call it "civilized leisure" to contrast with the more or less barbaric forms of leisure: the leisure of the privileged class who are exempt from toil and that of the indigent class who are either voluntarily or involuntarily workless. His is the leisure of a maturing society which was beginning to consider the rights and possibilities of all its members. (Overstreet, 1934a:12)

To achieve the mature, civilized leisure, he advocated a number of possibilities. First is the fun of handling materials; be it soil, wood, stone, or metal. "Our selfhood is far more than that which lies within the boundaries of our bodies . . . it can realize itself through the mechanism we devise; it can gain wide mastery and create great joy by assembling physical things into wholes that give comfort and delight." (Overstreet, 1934b:42–43)

Secondly, in our liberated hours we can pursue the activities that bring us to union with one another. There we shall dance together, act our play together, and play our instruments together. These are the authentic ways of social life. (Overstreet, 1934b:58)

A third pleasure which passes into our leisure life is mastery and skill in physical performance. No one enjoys being an oaf in anything. The clumsy handed as well as the clumsy minded carry a profound sorrow in their souls. The human race has tried hard throughout the last few centuries to make the inward beautiful, but had left the outward lagging behind. Our mighty minds are laboring within stunted bodies. The new leisure is an opportunity to correct the unbalance. (Overstreet, 1934b:76)

The new leisure also allows one to be alone, to take stock of oneself and the world. Overstreet suggested that as America grew wiser, Americans would see the value of retreats if and when they dissociate monasteries from religious creed. He believed that in the Protestant fervor, the baby was cast out with the bath water. He praised the national government for its wisdom in providing national parks. In solitude one can adventure with thought. Thought has the power of "Open Sesame"—unlocking possibilities that lie hidden from us. Also we can have companionship without physical presence. We carry with us Plato, Buddha, or Kahlil Gibran. (Overstreet, 1934b:91)

Overstreet suggested that Americans should utilize the resources at their command, organize things such as sunlight, clean air, warm soil, running water, and the call of birds. Also, there are man-made things such as stories, books, and paintings. (Overstreet, 1934b:109–110)

Humans can go wandering, whether it is with their bodies or their imaginations. Humans can use the bicycle, the car, the train, the boat, or the airplane to travel. Overstreet warned that "if an ass were to go traveling, he will not come back a horse." (1934b:143) A good traveler is one who is also a good home dweller.

In his review of Loafing, Laird (1934) noted that Overstreet suggested over 700 ways to spend leisure moments. Other than the above-mentioned activities, he pointed out flower arrangement, politics, service, and just fooling around, which is the title of Chapter Fourteen. Chapter Fifteen is entitled "Leftovers" and was dropped from the second printing.

Leisure came out during the Depression years and Overstreet started the chapter on "Leisure and Unemployment" by asserting that leisure that is made compulsory by the partial breakdown of an economic system can hardly be called civilized, for its is a carryover from barbarism when man was unable to control the forces of his existence. (1934b:217) He suggested that unemployment would be an opportunity for one to test his interests and abilities. In the meantime, the society must cater to three basic needs of the unemployed:

1. A physical set-up to keep the unemployed off the pavements while standing, waiting in vain. Places where the umemployed could find physical recreation should be provided. (pg. 229)

2. Social companionship designed to keep the unemployed from feeling like outcasts. Meeting places are particularly needed for women, the homeless, and workers. (pg. 230)

3. The unemployed must be given the sense that they can still contribute to society. (pg. 231)

In the sixteenth chapter, "Leisure and Youth," in *Leisure*, Overstreet lamented that the annual per capita expenditure in New York City for the cost of crime was $7.76, while the annual per capita cost for recreation was $0.22. He considered this an unthinking cruelty to youngsters who are forced to play in crowded streets. Automobiles turn the corner, honk their horns, and kids scatter to the curb. An adult voice screams "Out of the road. Life is real, life is earnest, and your play is not its goal." (pg. 236)

Overstreet believed that Americans were standing on the threshold of a new era of liberation and that "crime will disappear when work is ordered in justice and when play is the free release of our imaginative energy." (pg. 245)

For adults, mastery of time is important, for in "large measure, it takes on the complexion of ourselves. We can lengthen it or shorten it, fill it or empty it, make it into a being of terror or into a rhythm of delight." (pg. 164)

Overstreet suggested the following:

Life, as we know, can be very little more than a succession of moments. It is then like a string of beads—one after another. In such life one is simply in the flux of time, carried along, with ones head scarcely above the surface of the flow. But there can be another kind of life, one, paradoxically, in which we are both in time and out of time. When, for example, one meditates, one casts backward and forward over the stream of time. One looks down, as it were, upon the flowing river, and for the time being one exists in a kind of movelessness of contemplation.

It is this ability to lift oneself out of the stream of time that is a peculiarly powerful way of life. Every thinker achieves this power. Instead of being merely swept along from one moment to another, he moves back and forth among the moments, selecting from among them with a nice discrimination what is significant for his purpose. The past becomes living as it yields up phases that are valuable to him. Thus he is able, at will, to lengthen the brief present moment of his existence by incorporating into it innumerable moments that have gone before. And he can lengthen out his brief present into the future by projecting what he has recovered from the past into what he contemplates for the future. (pgs. 165–166)

In one review, Overstreet's contribution to leisure was hailed by some critics as potent for benefit now as it might be in some future time of larger leisure. (*New York Times*, 1934) The reviewer also stated that Mr. Overstreet wrote well and persuasively, with wisdom and understanding.

D.A. Laird wrote that Overstreet began to show full stature in *Loafing*, which "is not only his best production but also a sorely needed book. It is a book of the spirit of civilization, not a book of hobbies." (1934:704) On the other hand, Karl Brown wrote that he "hesitates to characterize Professor Overstreet's little volume as sophomoric, (in light of his past accomplishments) . . . all he has managed to say is that intelligent loafing is good stuff. (1934:47a)

PARTIAL LIST OF OVERSTREET'S PUBLICATIONS

A Guide To Civilized Loafing (1934a). New York: W.W. Norton.

A Guide To Civilized Leisure (1934b) New York: W.W. Norton.

REFERENCES

Brown, K. (1934, June). A Guide To Civilized Loafing: A Review. *Library Journal* 59,p. 479.

Current Biographies (1950). Overtreet, Harry Allen. pp. 433–435.

International Who's Who (1950).

Laird, D. A. (1934, May 19). A Guide To Civilized Loafing. *Saturday Review of Literature, 10,* p. 704.

Staff (1934, May 6). *New York Times.* "A Guide To Civilized Loafing," May 6, 1934, 12.

Who's Who In America (1950–1951).

Who's Who In American Education (1947–1948).

Who's Who In Philosophy (1942).

16

LEBERT HOWARD WEIR

1878–1949

By Janet R. Maclean
Indiana University

Courtesy National Recreation and Park Association Archives

"Man is essentially an outdoor animal."

Skelton, 1967:10

Ever on the move, geographically and creatively, Lebert Weir might well have been called, "The Man With the Suitcase." Within that suitcase were his inspiration, knowledge, and imagination which allowed him to make numerous contributions to the progress of the park and recreation movement.

The second of three sons born to Benjamin and Barbra Weir, Lebert was born September 20, 1878, in a small log house on a farm near Scottsburg, Indiana. Though the parents were humble pioneers, all three sons distinguished themselves: William, the oldest, in education as president of Pacific University and Rollins College; James, the youngest, in science with a doctorate from the University of Munich; and Lebert, in recreation, with 39 years of distinguished service at the National Recreation Association.

Lebert attended "Broady," the little red brick school in which he taught after his graduation from the new Scottsburg High School. Shy and nonathletic, he spent his time reading. As a former classmate remarked, "Even before high school, Lebert studied Latin and algebra and could quote long passages from *Plutarch's Lives.* His college major was history at Indiana University from which he graduated in 1903. His senior academic requirements were finished by the end of the winter term, so he spent the spring semester as a special student at Stanford. Weir's leadership abilities manifested themselves early, as he served as president of the University YMCA, as a member of the Board of Managers for the Arbutus yearbook, and as a Sigma Nu officer.

In spite of being successful in his teaching position at Broady, Weir chose, as his first job after college, social work with the Juvenile Court in Cincinnati. It was during this period that he convinced himself and others that creative use of leisure could have definitive influence on a city's capability for reducing juvenile delinquency costs. His work gained national prominence as he strove to make the work of the court *preventive,* as well as *remedial.* In his words,

"I resolved, when the opportunity came, to give the remainder of my life to working with citizens and public officials, for the definitive purpose of publicly providing those things which would make it easier for the young people to do right than to do wrong, while at the same time living their normal, natural lives fully and joyously. (Skelton, 1967:121)

And so it was that Lebert Weir became the prime advocate for the raison d'etre of recreation in the 20th century.

His work at Cincinnati drew the attention of Howard Braucher, then executive director of the American Playground and Recreation Association. Braucher invited Weir to try his philosophy on a national scale with the Association. He became the first paid field secretary and worked tirelessly for the national organization until his death in 1949.

On the road, as usual, in 1949, attending the annual conference of the American Institute for Park Executives, Weir was stricken with a heart attack, transferred to Indianapolis, and died seven weeks later. The many tributes which poured into his family and to the National Recreation Association had a similar focus—a reference to the man whose first love was the trees which surrounded his homes. "I am reminded of the face of a great tree," said Josephine Blackstock. (Skelton, 1967: 142) "What a vast void it leaves in many lives and in the field in which he towered like the timeless redwood giant," wrote Faust. (Skelton, 1967: 142)

Tall, blue-eyed, distinguished, sporting a plaid tie to honor his Scottish ancestry, Lebert Weir, as Skelton indicated, was "a big man—big in body, big in mind, and big in soul. He was a handsome physical specimen, six feet three inches tall, slender, straight as an arrow. His spirit and his intellect drew people to him in a magnetic way. He was a man ahead of his time but marvelously adapted to the needs of his day." (Skelton, 1967: 289)

Warm and sensitive, Weir had two primary passions: a love of people and love of the land. He was a son of the soil with tremendous energy, firm convictions, and an uncanny ability to interpret to people from all walks of life the need for giving all ages and all capabilities the opportunity to *live*, truly live, as well as to work. Most who knew him agreed that, for the first decades of the 20th century, Weir had greater influence on the growth of the park and recreation movement than did any other man.

Starting from the philosophy premise that "Man is essentially an outdoor animal," Lebert Weir advocated reservation and preservation of open spaces; active forms of recreation in the scenic parks; nature study; consideration of the special needs of atypical populations; the need for trained volunteers; broadening of leisure opportunities to include creative, intellectual, and artistic, as well as physical avenues, and the necessity for cooperation and coordination of effort among community agencies. (Weir, 1928a:1)

Weir was a visionary in several respects. He admonished Americans to learn to live their lives more leisurely for better health. He prophesied that possession of natural resources might be the determining factor in political attitudes of nations toward each other. He observed that the basis of some of our national economic, social, and political difficulties might stem from the manner in which natural resources and leisure have been mismanaged. He was ahead of his time, prophetic in his vision.

During the NRA years of crisis, Weir crossed the United States and Europe with his suitcase of energy and ideas and made his mark on almost every state. He served communities, states, and nations with his perceptive surveys of the needs of individual situations. He lectured at universities to instill in faculty and students the need for and the worth of the recreation function and the value of professional preparation in this exciting field. He did field work in the Midwest, the Pacific Coast, New England, and the Southwest. He taught at the National Recreation Association School with his *Parks* manual as his text. He helped plan the future of parks and recreation in areas as diverse as the Chicago Park District, Canada, the Virgin Islands, and Germany.

His professional contributions are detailed in Skelton's doctoral dissertation (1967) from Indiana University and are briefly summarized thus:

1. Weir was instrumental in unifying the once separate professional entities of parks and recreation. He articulated their need for each other with perhaps greater influence and clarity than anyone in his time.

2. As a born salesman and a persuasive speaker, he promoted the need for, or expansion of, park and recreation facilities and broad programs to include interests which involved physical activity; manual, creative and constructive challenges; environmental concerns; and linguistic, rhythmic, dramatic, social, civic, and religious outlets.

3. He was a gold mine of information on legal matters and a forceful advocate for park and recreation legislation in several states.

4. Weir's emphasis on trained leadership, both for professionals and for volunteers, had a profound influence on the universities in which he articulated the wisdom of the development of professional curricula.

5. His ability to forcefully interpret the worth and the influence of creative leisure opportunities was an inspiration and a springboard from which many municipal and state programs were realized.

6. He was a spirited advocate of preservation and conservation of natural resources long before that advocacy became a popular national issue.

Weir made three major contributions to the literature. (See List of Publications.) Although Weir's publications have had widespread use and success, his numerous magazine articles, speeches, and the many community surveys written during his years with NRA are of equal importance. Each contains the all important interpretive message of the dynamic impact of recreation on human dignity and on individual and societal welfare as well as the carefully researched data which pertained to the local concerns.

Lebert Weir was well respected among his colleagues. Here is just a sample of the evidence of their affection, devotion, and admiration: (Skelton, 1967)

"Weir, in his day, was the number one recreation person in the United States . . . Someone else might have had more name, but Weir had greater influence than any other man in recreation. (pg. 204)

"His whole life was given to rendering service." (pg. 144)

"I can see why both recreation and park people wanted to claim him as their own." (pg. 157)

"Weir was a strong advocate of agencies working together." (pg. 128)

"Weir was strong for activities for all ages, from the cradle to the grave." (pg. 160)

"He used to preach the necessity for coordination and cooperation of all community agencies." (pg. 168)

"Weir's emphasis on training is still a fetish with me." (pg. 181)

"His work and many contributions will influence the direction of recreation in the world for years to come." (pg. 203)

"He was the best informed all-around man in parks and recreation. You could ask Weir anything connected with parks and recreation, and he'd pull an answer out of some cubby-hole in his mind. If you followed it, you'd find out it was accurate." (pg. 241)

"He had the most remarkable ability to summarize. He had an analytical mind and a beautiful way of expressing himself. He was a gentleman of the highest order." (pg. 244)

"He peddled more inspiration than anybody in the business by far." (pg. 250)

"I always thought that Mr. Weir got a bit more out of life than the rest of us because he was so much on speaking terms with every shrub and tree." (pg. 269)

"It goes without saying that Lebert Weir's name has been deeply engraved in the park and recreation movement. He was a leader in every sense. His courage, vision, and personality contributed immeasurably to the development of the parks and recreation field and the professional growth of his associates." (pg. 203)

"Because Lebert believed in a guy, the balance would swing right and that man would achieve his finest. Weir believed in people. There was a spiritual leavening that Lebert did with all he touched. He would envelope people with affection and respect. He gave the best that he had and lifted people up spiritually and held them aloft while he pointed out what, in the fog and mist, they had missed or forgotten—the heights which they had seen at dawn and tried to scale but had become discouraged and sunk by the wayside or slowed down. Along would come this great mountain top guy and enfold them in his faith and in his belief in their essential greatness. That would lift them, and he would point to the heights that they had seen at dawn. That was Lebert. That was his greatest contribution. We have no way of measuring the hundreds of people, directly and indirectly, who have been lifted up and put on the way again by Lebert Weir." (pg. 253)

Last, but certainly not least, is the tribute which Conrad Wirth wrote in 1967, as the foreword to Skelton's dissertation:

"It was apparent to everyone who knew him that Lebert Weir had a profound understanding and love of people, and his care for their welfare was most directly expressed in his work directed toward the establishment, preservation, and extension of parks, outdoor recreation, and areas of natural environment . . . His concepts were greatly in advance of his times and are only now becoming realities. Only now has what he so strongly advocated and strove for—the opportunity for all to enjoy and be restored through a natural outdoor environment—become a matter of national inquiry and concern. Lebert Weir's personal qualities of kindness, thoughtfulness, patience, and care were uniquely deep and were extended to everyone he met. He was, indeed, a man among man." (pg. 111)

Although this writer did not know Lebert Weir personally, the wealth of evidence which surfaced during preparation of this biography prompts her to reiterate, "He was a man among men." He was, indeed.

PARTIAL LIST OF WEIR'S PUBLICATIONS

Street Play and Juvenile Delinquency. (1906, May). *The University Settlement Review, 1,* pp. 25–28.

The Cincinnati Juvenile Court Conference. (1909, December). *The Juvenile Court Record.* Chicago.

Playgrounds and Juvenile Delinquency. (1910a, May). *The Playground, 4,* pp. 37–40.

A Probation Officer in Rural Communities. (1910b, August). *Rural Manhood,* pp. 10–12

and Durham, Stella Walker. (1914). *A Practical Recreation Manual for Schools.* Department of Education, State Printing Department, Salem, Oregon.

Plans and Suggestions upon the Development and Organization of a System of Public Recreation for the City of Eveleth. (1915a). Minnesota: National Recreation Association.

Survey of Minneapolis. (1915b). Minnesota: National Recreation Association.

Report Upon the Properties, Development of Properties, Social Uses of Properties of the Louisville Park and Recreation System and Upon the Organization and Management of the Louisville Park Department. (1916). National Recreation Association.

Vocational Recreation in Indiana. (1917). (1916 Bul., Vol. 3, No. 2). Bloomington: The Extension Division of Indiana University.

Camping Out—A Manual on Organizational Camping (Ed.). (1924). New York: The Macmillan Co.

Eighteen Years' Progress in Community Recreation. (1925a, August). *The Playground, 19*, pp. 265–267.

Recreation Survey in Buffalo. (1925b). Published as a joint enterprise of Department of Parks and Public Buildings and City Planning Committee of the Council, Buffalo City Planning Association, Inc.

Local Park Achievements in the U.S. (1928a, March). *The Playground, 21*, p. 627.

Parks: A Manual of Municipal and County Parks. (1928b). New York: A.S. Barnes and Co., 2 vols.

Public Recreation in the City of Houston, Texas. (1928c). Parks and Recreation Department.

Survey Report of Oklahoma City, Oklahoma. (1931). National Recreation Association.

Land and Water in the Recreation Program. (1933a, August). *Recreation, 27*, pp. 211–214.

Recreation Services of Chicago Park District. (1933b). National Recreation Association.

Report on Public Recreation in Washington, D.C., and Environs. (1934). National Recreation Association.

Report of a Study of Public Recreation in the City of Providence, Rhode Island. (1934–1935). National Recreation Association.

The Government of Parks. (1936a, March). *Parks and Recreation, 19*, pp. 209–212.

The Executive Organization of a Park or Recreation Department. (1936b, April). *Parks and Recreation, 19*, pp. 269–271.

Europe at Play. (1937a). New York: A. S. Barnes and Co.

Government and Administration of Parks and Recreation in Philadelphia. (1937b). National Recreation Association.

Public Recreation Abroad. (1938a, January). *Parks and Recreation, 21*, pp. 181–184.

Restore Harmony Between Man and Nature. (1938b, November). *Parks and Recreation, 22*, p. 130.

Why Do We Want Parks? (1939a, November). *Parks and Recreation, 23*, pp. 91–95.

How Shall We Play? (1939b, November). *Parks and Recreation, 23*, pp. 91–95.

Park and Their Use. *Parks and Recreation, 24*, pp. 399–402, May 1941; *24*, pp. 448–451, June 1941; *24*, pp. 497–500, June 1941.

Recreation Survey of Minneapolis, Minnesota. (1944). Minneapolis: Board of Park Commissioners.

What's Ahead for Recreation? (1946a, March, April). *Parks and Recreation, 29*, pp. 68–72.

Notes and Comments on Public Recreation in Duluth, Minnesota. (1946b, July). National Recreation Association.

Historical Background of Recreation Movement in America. (1946c, July–August). *Parks and Recreation, 29,* pp. 238–243.

Notes and Observations on Public Recreation in Cleveland, Ohio. (1948a). National Recreation Association.

Report Concerning Parks and Recreation, Alton, Illinois. (1948b). National Recreation Association.

REFERENCE

Skelton, D. (1967). *Leibert Weir.* (Doctoral dissertation, Indiana University.)

17

HOWARD S. BRAUCHER

1881–1949

By William DeGroot and
E.A. Scholer
University of New Mexico

Courtesy Dr. E.A. Scholar, University of New Mexico

"**M**an reveals himself most fully in his worship and his play."

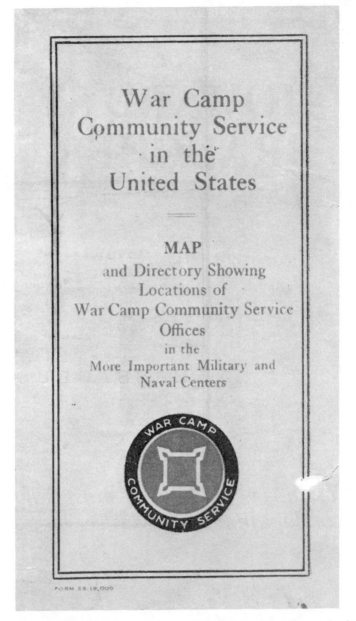

The PRA, under Braucher's leadership, organized the War Camp Community Services (WCCS) and in approximately two years raised over 2 million dollars to aid communities in the development of recreation programs.

Courtesy National Recreation and Park Association Archives

Howard S. Braucher, son of Solomon A. and Emma A. Braucher, was born in Royalton, New York on July 19, 1881. After graduation from Lockport High School, Lockport, New York, Braucher attended Cornell University on a State Scholarship. During his undergraduate years, he was active in the University Christian Association and served as president of the organization. In addition to his interests and endeavors on behalf of the Christian Association, he also took time to participate in debate and sports, such as cross country and rowing. He was elected to Phi Beta Kappa upon receipt of the Bachelor of Arts degree in 1903.

He continued his education, doing advance study at several institutions in New York, including the Union Theological Seminary, New York School of Philanthropy, and Teachers College, Columbia University. During this period he worked at the Madison Square Church House of the Convenant. In 1931, for his outstanding contributions to the park and recreation field, he was awarded the honorary degree, Master of Physical Education, by International Y.M.C.A. College, presently known as Springfield College, Springfield, Massachusetts.

On January 18, 1912, Braucher married Edna Vaughn Fisher of Denver, Colorado. He met his bride-to-be at the 3rd Playground Association of America Congress in Pittsburgh, Pennsylvania, where she delivered a paper on storytelling and also directed a pageant as a part of the Congress Program. The Brauchers had two children, a daughter, Jane, and son, Robert. In addition to his commitments and contributions to the recreation and park movement, Braucher continued during his lifetime to maintain a deep interest, as well as active membership, in many national, state, and local organizations that directly or indirectly relate to this profession. Braucher was the recipient of numerous awards and citations for outstanding service, such as the Silver Buffalo Award from the Boy Scouts of America, the Citation and Medallion of the National 4H Club, and the Special Service Award from The Society of Recreation Workers of America, whose name later was changed to the American Recreation Society. This national professional organization awarded Howard Braucher its prestigious Fellow of the Society Award in 1948, prior to his death.

Howard Braucher began his professional career in 1905 as secretary of the Association Charities of Portland, Maine, a position he held for four years. In addition, he was also the secretary of the Maine Conference on Charities and Corrections. It was during this early period that his interest in recreation began, as a direct result of his volunteer involvement in the recreation centers of the city as well as from a fact-finding trip he made to visit recreation programs in cities throughout the United States. (Butler, 1965:96)

Braucher, the first choice of the Playground Association of America's Board of Directors was approached, and subsequently agreed to serve as the first full time executive secretary of the Association, beginning in September 1909. He brought to the fledgling Association an interest, not only in recreation, but in social work as well. According to Knapp and Hartsoe, religion was a leading motive of Braucher's entire life—"the work of the Playground Association of America was for him a spiritual movement and when recruiting prospective staff members, he was always careful to consider their basic motives in life. He saw recreation and religion as two of the major areas of living and sought to maintain a close relationship between them." (1979:36)

Braucher's interests, as contrasted to those of the PAA president, Joseph Lee, were of the sociological and psychological and not the biological aspects of play and recreation. As Knapp and Hartsoe stated, "To him recreation was an answer to materialism and the work ethic, two factors detrimental to the quality of American life." (1979:37) At that early period he firmly believed that Americans would need to make wise use of leisure that would result from technological development and in the reduction of hours that previously had been devoted to work. He was an early advocate of a definition of recreation that not only incorporated activity during leisure, but also indicated that it was an attitude or a way of life.

Braucher was so convinced that local government should be the principal provider of organized recreation programs that he could not conceive of a federal organization or agency that would ever impose rules and regulations on local government which would curtail local government's freedom to plan, and develop programs, areas, and facilities to meet specific needs. This belief, would in the future, bring him into conflict with members of the American Recreation Society, an organization he helped establish.

When he accepted the invitation to become the executive secretary of the PAA, he did so with the stipulation that the Association assume a national leadership role in the provision of recreation opportunities to all, regardless of age, color, creed, or religion. This philosophy was, at his insistence, incorporated in the general purpose of the Association and reflected in the change of the Association's name in 1911 to the Playground and Recreation Association of America. (Butler, 1965:96)

Braucher's philosophy, paralleling that of Joseph Lee's, was that PRAA resources and strength should be used to implement a national movement rather than one of a self-perpetuating organization. Thus the public relations of the Association, internal and external, were directed to the perpetuation of the importance of recreation rather than the work of the Association.

According to Butler, (1965:96), Braucher visualized recreation as permeating all phases of life, work, worship, education, and leisure and insisted that it acquire a distinct and separate movement and not be subordinate to another field as some leaders proposed.

Braucher was an early advocate of the use of parks for recreation and not just for aesthetic purposes. He further felt that professionals should be employed to enhance the recreation opportunities and experiences of the public. He early recognized the relationships between planning and recreation and pointed out that city planners were among the first professional groups to recognize recreation as a basic human need that needed consideration and inclusion in total planning. (Butler, 1965:97)

As a stalwart advocate of qualified individuals working in the field, Braucher worked diligently for the selection and training of such capable persons and also to protect them from political influences.

With the involvement of the United States in World War I and the subsequent draft, cities and towns adjacent to military installations underwent a rapid change as the numbers of military personnel impacted their community recreation programs. The PRAA, under the leadership of Braucher, organized the War Camp Community Services (WCCS) and in approximately two years raised over 2 million dollars to aid communities in the development of recreation programs, which included a wide variety of activities and services.

An important element of the WCCS was Braucher's insistence that it include coordination of programs and facilities for black servicemen. Such programs did not exist in most communities. Braucher did not attempt to fight local segregation and racial laws, but he was instrumental in working with local black leaders to establish programs and facilities, equal to, if not better than, those for whites. (Knapp and Hartsoe, 1979:70)

The Service, disbanded after the War, received praise not only from the military but also from civilians and returning servicemen. One well known park worker of that period, Allen T. Burns, was profuse in his praise of Braucher and the War Camp Community Service. He stated, "Mr. Braucher and the War Camp Community Service was the greatest service he, Braucher, had ever rendered. It had a wider influence on public opinion in reference to recreation than anything he ever did." (Butler, 1965:100)

In 1918, Braucher was instrumental in initiating an experimental program for workers in war industries that included activities related to civic involvement, education, and recreation. This was a forerunner of the present employee recreation programs in industry today.

Since the WCCS had been successful, Braucher in 1919 established the Community Service or CS as an independent corporation, and planned that it would take over the assets of the PRAA, but backers of the Association convinced Braucher and Joseph Lee to combine the two organizations instead. The growth of the CS and the fund raising to cover expenses failed to reach the potential envisioned by Braucher. Thus, in 1922, the CS became a department of the PRAA.

The poor physical condition of American youth and their ability to qualify for military service prompted the U.S. Commissioner of Education to call a conference to establish steps to correct this situation. The PRAA was required to accept the responsibility for establishing such a program. Under Braucher's guidance, the national Physical Education Service (PES) was established for developing a nationwide campaign to promote legislation establishing physical education as a compulsory subject in school curriculums. A direct result of this endeavor by the PES was the rapid growth of physical education in the United States during this period. Clark Hetherington praised the part played by Braucher when he stated, "Howard S. Braucher gave one of his many exhibitions of genius and devotion when he established the National Physical Education Service." (Butler, 1965:100)

In 1926, Braucher was instrumental in establishing the National Recreation School to train recreation professionals. He strongly believed this one-year graduate school, of which he served as president, was one of the Association's most significant accomplishments.

Braucher was quick to perceive the need for the Association to cooperate with state and federal agencies as these groups began establishing recreation services. He assigned Association field staff the responsibility to assist state authorities in developing intra-agency committees, which served as clearinghouses for cooperation and coordination between agencies. He was to initiate the same type of service on the federal level after World War II, when he assigned a PRAA staff member to serve on the interagency committee for recreation. He recognized the need for recreation training in rural areas in cooperation with the Department of Agriculture Extension Service, and he established a rural recreation training program for volunteers under the direction of the Association's field staff.

Building on the services to blacks that began the program during World War I, he established a Bureau of Colored Work in the PRAA in 1920 and hired Ernest T. Atwell, son of the prominent Harlem clergyman, to the head of the Bureau. Braucher was realistic in his appraisal of the segregationist attitude of the public and felt that separate-but-equal facilities and programs were better than none.

During the mid 1920s, the PRAA actively joined in the efforts of the National Conference on Outdoor Recreation, although Braucher and Lee both felt this new organization was a threat to the PRAA. The Association did, however, take an active role in the Conference by lending staff and conducting specific research projects. In this latter instance, the PRAA, in cooperation with the American Institute of Park Executives, conducted a comprehensive survey of acreage and administration of municipal and county parks. This was the beginning of Braucher's effort to expand the PRAA's involvement in research and publications. In late 1925, Braucher urged the PRAA to establish a research department in the Association.

Braucher had assumed the editorship of the PRAA magazine, *The Playground*, later to be called *Recreation*, when he was named secretary of the PRAA, and he held this position until his death. His editorials reiterated his conviction that things of the spirit exceeded in value material possessions. He stated, "It is far greater importance to man that he have [sic] a share in life, liberty and happiness than that he have [sic] a share in the machinery of production." (Butler, 1965:104) Braucher's editorials were very persuasive and truly expressed the significance of recreation for everyone. Selections of his writings were compiled and published in a volume entitled *A Treasury of Living*, by the National Recreation Association on the Fifteenth Anniversary of the Association. Braucher's writings were very well received and had a definite impact on the overall recreation movement.

In the late '20s Braucher was finally able to engage the services of a female field secretary responsible for women's sports and athletics and to employ a staff member as a music expert. Both positions emphasized his philosophy that recreation was broad and there was a need for competent, qualified personnel to educate for recreation.

The 1930s brought significantly more leisure for which Braucher and Lee had urged the nation to prepare. The PRAA undertook several steps to meet the challenges posed by this increased leisure, and to offset the public view of the PRAA as a "playground" child-centered group. The first step was the long-needed name change to the National Recreation Association (NRA). To examine the domestic alternatives which the NRA could adopt to help Americans utilize the abundance of leisure of the early 1930s, Braucher initiated a survey of leisure activities and preferences of 5,000 citizens which was completed by the NRA in 1934. (Knapp and Hartsoe, 1979:104)

As Joseph Lee's health gradually failed, Braucher found himself increasingly at the helm of the NRA. Braucher's personality, which was shy and retiring, combined with his management style, which was office bound and aloof, would have to be characterized as a liability in public relations and image building. On the other hand, he had in place an able, experienced staff of professionals who, in some cases, had served almost as long as Braucher. (Butler, 1965:107. Knapp and Hartsoe, 1979:107)

During the Depression, Braucher became a trusted associate of Harry Hopkins of the Works Progress Administration (WPA) and Aubrey Williams of National Youth Administration (NYA). He directed the NRA to align itself with these agencies to provide recreation services as part of the federal work relief program. Braucher's advice to utilize relief personnel to conduct recreation activities and develop recreation facilities resulted in a tremendous increase in recreation resources throughout the country and in the public's appreciation of the importance of recreation services. He further cooperated with the WPA and NYA by allowing the National School to conduct onsite four-week institutes in which thousands of workers on the relief programs experienced intensive training in recreational leadership, music, arts and crafts, and dramatics. (Butler, 1965:101)

The Depression provided the impetus for the expansion of park systems in many states, under the direction of the National Park Service, which secured funds from the Civilian Conservation Corps. Braucher assigned James B. Williams, one of the most experienced staff members, to the National Park Service as a consultant to advise and cooperate on a variety of research projects. This spirit of cooperation was also evident in the loaning of additional professional staff to assist and advise federal, state, and local housing authorities on recreation programs under consideration in Washington, D.C. and in areas around the United States. (Butler, 1965:101)

In 1932, Braucher was the catalyst who brought together representatives of several organizations and formed what eventually became the National Education and Recreation Council. This Council promoted recreation opportunities for unemployed youth and adults.

He served as the chairman (1922–1940) of the National Social Work Council. This council essentially operated as a clearinghouse for planning and problem-solving. In 1937, he recognized the need to develop a formal organization to serve the increasing numbers of recreational workers in a professional manner. The Society of Recreation Workers, later titled the American Recreation Society (ARS), was established separately from the NRA. However it's purpose was to enhance professional recreational leadership to the mutual benefit of both organizations. Braucher's assistance was recognized by his continued appointment as an ex officio member of the society's executive committee over a period of many years. (Butler, 1965:103).

Braucher's commitment to leadership training continued through 1935 with the on-going programs of the National Recreation School and then shifted into the NRA with the initiation of the apprentice fellowship training plan. (Knapp and Hartsoe, 1979:1)

A major issue which Braucher was unable to resolve during his professional career was the relationship of the federal government to municipal recreation. This issue was a point of contention between the ARS and the NRA. It was fueled by the New Deal movement in which federal resources were made available to support public education, welfare, and recreation services cut back during the Depression, and caused Braucher and others of the NRA concern about federal control over the operations of the NRA.

The decade of the '30s came to a close with Braucher realizing that the NRA needed to drastically improve its position of leadership and control in order to keep pace with the general rise of public recreation and the resultant influx of private and federal agencies into its primary domain.

The 1940s opened with gloomy prospects of global war and a diminishing fund-raising ability of the NRA. Braucher steadfastly refused to seek federal assistance and additional funds were sought from corporate philanthropy. Due to the lack of other able leadership, the NRA board of directors selected Braucher as president of the Association in June, 1941. This action, in effect, formalized Braucher's leadership role as he had been the guiding force behind the NRA for several years.

As the nation began to mobilize its war effort, Braucher's concern was to avoid a duplication of the jealousies and problems experienced by the recreation effort during World War I. Unfortunately, his attempt to coordinate defense recreation met with mixed success. He tried to consolidate the various religious organizations which were intent on providing defense recreation programs after the WWI model. This resulted in the formation of the National United Welfare Committee (NUWC) which eventually evolved into the United Services Organizations (USO) and became an independent recreation delivery agency to servicemens clubs throughout the U.S. In the meantime, President Roosevelt appointed the Federal Security Agency (FSA) to coordinate all Health, Welfare, and related defense activities, including recreation. Braucher realized the future of the NRA was in a precarious position and opted to coordinate with the FSA. He loaned NRA staff members to the FSA Recreation Division on a temporary basis to assist in data collection and organizing local defense recreation committees. Eventually the FSA Recreation Division assumed the overall supervision of local defense recreation programs and coordinated the local committees with other national agencies and the USO. (Knapp and Hartsoe, 1979:132) Throughout World War II, Braucher attempted to position the NRA into a high priority coordinating agency. He had several battles with those who supported the "New Deal" and federal control over public recreation. Braucher and his staff were severely tested by the proposed legislation to establish a national advisory board of public and private recreation authorities which would eventually evolve into the Federal Bureau of Recreation. The legislation, supported by the American Recreation Society (ARS), was only the tip of the iceberg regarding the philosophical conflict of control over public recreation and between Braucher and the ARS. (Knapp and Hartsoe, 1979:132)

In 1943, Braucher stated, "Very complete decentralization in recreation will help us to keep what is most characteristic of us as a people. Recreation should always remain rooted in the community." (Sessoms, 1943:30)

Braucher's solution to the encroachment of the federal agencies was to arrange for formation of the Interagency Committee which could coordinate the emerging and existing recreation organizations. This action temporarily blocked the need for a new federal agency, but forced Braucher to step up his opposition to the emerging role of the ARS in the promotion of a federal agency for recreation.

During this period, Braucher, in addition to facing budget constraints, was unsuccessful in recruiting young, able replacements for the NRA staff or finding someone fit to assume his leadership position.

Braucher, in 1947, suffered a serious illness that confined him to bed for many months. He refused to retire, and when able was back to work trying to resolve the problems facing the NRA. The strenuous self-imposed work schedule and the complexities and demands of serving as the executive secretary, as well as president, of the NRA, caused his health to break again. He died May 22, 1949 in New York City. He left a written legacy to his wife that was published in the National Recreation and Park Association tribute to him:

> The principal legacy I leave my wife is the memory of the happiness we have both had in sharing each other's lives and the knowledge that I have sought to know and follow truth without reference to personal gain or loss.

PARTIAL LIST OF BRAUCHER'S PUBLICATIONS

A Treasure For Living. (1950). New York: National Recreation Association.

REFERENCES

Butler, G. D. (1965). *Pioneers in Public Recreation.* Minneapolis, MN.: Burgess Publishing Co.

Knapp, R. F., and Hartsoe, C. E. (1979). *Play for America.* Arlington, VA.: National Recreation and Park Association.

Sessoms, H. D. (1943). "Editorial." *Quarterly.* New York: Society of Recreation.

Sessoms, H. D. (1984). *Leisure Services* (6th ed.). Englewood Cliffs, NJ.: Prentice Hall, Inc.

Solomon, E. (1988). Personal letter.

Sutherland, W. (1988). Personal letter.

Tait, W. (1988). Personal letter.

18

KURT HAHN

1886–1974

By Alan Ewert
Pacific Crest Outward Bound

" . . . he will know how to tap his hidden resources."

1942:2

Amid the bleakest moments of the Battle of the Atlantic during World War II, Great Britain was recording a strange and deadly paradox. The survivors of torpedoed ships were, most often, the captains, first mates, chief petty officers, and chief engineers. They were not the younger, more physically-fit seamen. This was occurring in spite of the fact that the younger crewmen had the same survival equipment, along with more strength and vigor. In light of this situation, Lawrence Holt, a partner in Alfred Holt and Company (a large merchant-shipping enterprise) (Miner and Boldt, 1981:32), became convinced that some "thing" kept the older sailors alive during the lifeboat ordeal and this had to be transferred to the younger sailors in order to keep them from giving up and dying. Whatever that "thing" was, Holt was sure that a survival-training experience was the way to have it instilled in others. (Kalisch, 1979)

To accomplish this task, Holt decided to team up with a relatively obscure educator, Kurt Hahn, who was trying to establish a "Country Badge Scheme," an ambitious national plan for fostering physical fitness, enterprise, tenacity, and compassion for others. Together, they established the first Outward Bound school at Aberdovey, Wales in 1941. "Outward Bound," a nautical term implying a ship leaving the safety of the homeport and heading toward the unknown, was first and foremost a survival-training experience in boat-handling skills, physical fitness, and the development of an attitude to "arm the cadet against the enemies within—fear, defeatism, apathy, and selfishness." (Price, 1970:81–82)

This training experience developed into the Outward Bound movement that now encompasses over 30 schools worldwide. It is the largest and most well-respected adventure education system in the world, and serves thousands of participants every year. As James (1980:20) points out, Outward Bound was founded to teach the young the tenacity and strength of the old. That lesson is now as necessary for Americans in the 1980s as it was to the British during the 1940s. The following section describes the life and contributions of Kurt Hahn and the development of the educational movement he is most widely noted for—Outward Bound.

> To those who seek to adopt Hahn's precept, one would like to stress that behind all his practices there was a passionate concern that youngsters should not only survive the experiences but that they should emerge strengthened.
>
> Jim Hogan
> First Warden
> Aberdovey Outward Bound School

Despite popular belief, the concept of an educational movement such as Outward Bound did not originate in the 20th century or with any one individual. Rather, the concept of combining physical, spiritual, and cognitive growth for the betterment of the individual and society had its foundation in Plato's *Republic*, Books II and III. It was here that the idea of cultivating civic-minded leaders in remote areas, within a small group context, and with an emphasis on physical challenge, was first formally brought forth. In addition, the idea of the betterment of the individual for the improvement of society, an underlying theme of Plato's "principle of perfection," e.g., a human being cannot achieve perfection without becoming part of a perfect society, was first synthesized.

Long after Plato, other thinkers and educators emerged and promoted the idea of personal and societal excellence. Goethe with his "Pedagogical Province," Rousseau and his emphasis on Nature as an educational tool, or William James and his "Moral Equivalent of War," as well as others, helped lay the foundational thinking around which Kurt Hahn developed the Outward Bound model. Ultimately, Hahn sought to create an educational institution that accomplished a number of specific goals, including impelling youth into experience rather than forcing them to accept an opinion; a cultivation of an enterprising curiosity; reasonable self-denial; solving real life problems; a dedication to community service; adventure and risk; and a compassion for humanity. Hahn's concept of risk was social risk; the need to define oneself as an autonomous person in morally confusing times. (James, 1980:9) To Hahn, challenge meant seeking self-knowledge with which a person can "hold his own." These ideas were not mere academic exercises, however, as Hahn intended to create long-term changes in the English and German schooling systems, and adherence to these values often led to threats on life.

Hahn, the eldest of three sons, was born into a cultured Jewish family in Berlin in 1886. Interested in teaching at an early age, young Kurt would lead the local young people on long hikes over rough terrain or read to them tales of heroic adventure. With an interest in understanding the old in order to help the young, Hahn eventually studied at Oxford. It was while at Oxford that Hahn conceived the idea of developing an educational environment that would become a countervailing force against the decline of personal courage and action; as a force against the growing presence of "spectatoritis."

As is often the case with people who have a vision of society, Hahn experienced a personal catastrophe at the age of nineteen. He suffered a severe case of sunstroke while rowing. The injury forced him to spend a year in a darkened room, and periodically cast him back into darkness throughout his life. It was during this time of seclusion that he integrated the teachings of Plato into his growing belief that education should combine thought with action.

During the First World War, Hahn held a minor foreign office post with Germany and at the war's end became assistant to Prince Max of Baden, Germany's last imperial chancellor. In 1920, Prince Max founded the coeducational boarding school, Salem (a.k.a. salaam or peace school), with Hahn as its headmaster. Hahn immediately became both a taskmaster and champion of youth. At the foundation of Hahn's philosophy was a belief that "the well-meaning educator who flatters and humors the young not only does a disservice to the community, but also damages the individual by depriving him of opportunities of self-discovery." (McLachlan, 1979:8)

While at Salem, Hahn inculcated his beliefs into the *Seven Laws of Salem*. These "laws" describe his educational methods:

- Provide opportunities for self discovery;
- Create opportunities in which individuals can experience success and failure;
- Create situations whereby the students can serve the "common good";
- Provide periods of reflection and silence;
- Develop and train for individual creativity and imagination;
- Keep competition as a positive force, not an all encompassing one;
- Develop a mix of privileged and under-privileged students.

From these convictions developed the principles of his later accomplishments: The Salem school, Gordonstoun, and Aberdovey (in Great Britain), the worldwide Outward Bound movement, and the Atlantic College (a college system developed toward the end of Hahn's life and renamed the United World College).

Hahn believed in the efficiency of these methods in producing the type of citizen necessary in the 20th century. Writing in 1941, he said:

> He [the student] will have a trained heart and a trained nervous system which will stand him in good stead in fever, exposure and shock; he will have acquired spring and powers of acceleration; he will have built up stamina and know-how to tap his hidden resources. He will have trained his tenacity and patience, his initiative and forethought, his power of observation and his power of care. He will have developed steadfastness and he will be able to say "no" to the whims of the moment . . . The average boy when first confronted with these tests will nearly always find some which look forbidding, almost hopelessly out of his reach, . . . but once he has started training he will be gripped by magic—a very simple magic, the magic of the puzzle . . . and he will struggle on against odds until one day he is winning through in spite of some disability. There always is some disability; but in the end he will triumph, turning defeat into victory, thus overcoming his own defeatism." (Hahn, 1944:2)

As profound and needed as these viewpoints were, the development of autonomous individualism collided head-on with the emerging statism of Hitler. For while Nazism engendered the beliefs in action and physical challenge, the concepts of justice and compassion for others were serious points of departure between Hahn and the Brown Shirts. In 1933, Hahn was arrested and only released in exile to Britain after requests by the British Prime Minister.

By 1934, Hahn, guided by his underlying philosophy of "your disability is your opportunity," converted a decaying castle at Gordonstoun, and opened a school with the first class composed of 21 boys—one of whom would later marry the future Queen Elizabeth II, Prince Phillip. Seven years later, during World War II, Gordonstoun became the model for the emergence of Outward Bound. In Hahn's view, Outward Bound was a counterforce to the adverse effects of modern society:

> There can be no doubt that the young of today have to be protected against certain effects inherent in present day civilization. Five social diseases surround them, even in early childhood. There is the decline in fitness due to modern methods of locomotion; the decline in initiative due to the widespread disease of "spectatoritis"; the decline in care and skill due to the weakened tradition of craftsmanship; the decline in self-discipline due to the ever-present availability of tranquilizers and stimulants; the decline in compassion, which William Temple called 'spiritual death.'
>
> Kurt Hahn in *Phillip* 1987

Since its inception, Outward Bound has strived to provide education *through* the outdoors rather than *for* the outdoors. Borrowing from Tennyson, "to serve, to strive, and not to yield" has become the motto of Outward Bound. From its beginnings with Kurt Hahn's Gordonstoun in 1941, there are now over 30 Outward Bound schools throughout the world, with schools on 5 continents: Europe, Africa, Asia, Australia, and North America. Drawing on Hahn's inspiration, the first Outward Bound school was established in Colorado in 1962. There are currently seven Outward Bound centers within the United States including Colorado, New York City, Pacific Crest, Voyageur, Hurricane Island, North Carolina, and Thompson Island (Boston Harbor). Along with the traditional teenage population, Outward Bound now offers courses for a variety of participants including battered women, people with specific health problems such as cancer, adults in transition, people over 50 years old, people with disabilities, and corporate managers.

Built around Hahn's philosophy, Outward Bound's theoretical and philosophical base emphasizes the following beliefs:

• That man is a part of Nature and should live in harmony with it;
• Man is primarily a social being;
• Man's nature is basically good;
• Man's definition of himself can best be defined by his behavior.

Hahn believed that "Outward Bound could only ignite; it is for others to keep the flame alive." What Kurt Hahn's philosophy and educational beliefs do, primarily through Outward Bound and the hundreds of organizations that have developed from it, is provide society with an acceptable experiential training setting and legitimate pursuit of adventure.

PARTIAL LIST OF HAHN'S PUBLICATIONS

Outward Bound—Address at the Conference at Harrogate, England. May 9, 1965.

Origins of the Outward Bound Trust. (1965). In D. James (Ed.) *Outward Bound.* London: Routledge and Kegan Paul Ltd.

The Seven Laws of Salem, 1930. Ten Years of Gordonstoun: An Account and An Appeal. (1944). Welshpool, Wales: Country Times Printers.

Active Service by the Young. (1965, November 9). (Memorandum). New York.

REFERENCES

Hahn, K. (1941, November). "The Country Badge: Its Why and Wherefore." *Journal of Physical Education and School Hygiene,* v. 10.

James, T. (1980). *Education at the Edge.* Denver, CO: Colorado Outward Bound.

Kalisch, K. (1979). *The Role of the Instructor in the Outward Bound Educational Process.* Three Lakes, WI: Wheaton College.

McLachlan, D. (1979). "Hahn." In H. Rohrs and H. Tunstall-Behrens (Eds.) *Kurt Hahn.* London: Routledge and Kegan Paul, p. 8.

Miner, J and J. Boldt (1981). *Outward Bound USA.* New York: William Morrow and Company, Inc.

Price, T. (1970). "Some aspects of character-building." In H. Rohrs and H. Tunstall-Behrens, (Eds.), *Kurt Hahn.* (pp. 81–82). London: Routledge and Kegan Paul.

Prince Phillip (1987) Kurt Hahn Award Address. Denver, CO: Colorado Ballroom of the Denver Marriott Hotel. Saturday, Oct. 24, 1987.

19

JAY BRYAN NASH

1886-1965

By Jane E. Kaufman
University Of Northern Colorado

AAHPERD Archives

"The concepts of freedom and choice are closely associated with those of democracy and leisure. Democracy assumes freedom; freedom assumes choice. But to be able to choose, man must have a trained intellect and be disciplined in choices pertinent not only to the good of himself but to the good of all."

1953a:37

Jay Bryan Nash 1926.
From AAHPERD Archives

Jay Bryan Nash was born to William and Harriet Nash, and raised in the rural community of New Baltimore, Ohio. He was the youngest of four children and, like his brother and sisters, worked hard on the family farm assisting his parents and maternal grandparents with chores. Little time for play and recreation were left, although Nash recalled:

I remember the wagonhouse [workshop] where I could make my own coaster [wheels on planks or a small wagon], bows and arrows for hunting . . . skating on a small pond . . . going (sometimes barefoot) to milk the cows on cold, frosty mornings with a faithful dog at my side . . .

(Jessup, 1967:67)

After graduation from the New Baltimore Elementary School, Jay B. Nash attended Marlboro High School in Stark County, Ohio, horseback riding the three miles to and from school. At the completion of high school in 1904, Nash became a one-room schoolhouse teacher in Hogback Corners, Ohio, teaching all grades and subjects, including an element of physical education during recess periods. It is surmised that from this experience Nash realized the value of play in the education of the child. (Jessup, 1967)

Nash taught for two years and then entered a preparatory academy in Oberlin, Ohio. Preparation for his university entrance requirements began and he later enrolled in Oberlin College. At Oberlin, Nash pursued the liberal arts during his first two years and then studied sociology and economics. Jessup (1967) suggested that this combination of academic study (i.e., examination of "societal forces in education and recreation") had a great influence on Nash's future contributions to the recreation and physical education profession.

While at Oberlin, Nash participated in a variety of extracurricular activities such as the college newspaper, varsity football, and public speaking. For example, one summer, Nash was a salesperson for *The Book of Knowledge,* and bicycled through southern Ohio selling his wares. Perhaps most influential to his future career were the summers of 1910 and 1911 when Nash worked as a playground supervisor in Pittsburgh, Pennsylvania.

Upon graduation from Oberlin College in 1911, Nash accepted a high school teaching position at Pacific Grove High School in California. Although Nash was not teaching physical education, he soon realized a need to expand the existing physical education program. With monentary assistance from the school board and physical assistance from volunteer high school boys, Nash provided leadership for the refurbishing of the gymnasium. Upon its completion, Nash volunteered after school hours and evenings to conduct special physical activity classes for children and high school youth. (Jessup, 1967)

Word of Nash's activities spread, and he was offered a new position as director of Physical Training and Athletics in the neighboring high school of Fremont. According to Jessup, the program was "a heavy athletic program, which gave considerable participation to the few highly skilled but left the general student body devoid of opportunities to learn and participate in physical activities." (1967:92) However, one of Nash's first curricular reforms was to initiate a new program in which all students were required to participate in a program of physical activity. This educational program consisted of three components: health, physical education, and recreation. Also, a controlled program of interscholastic competition and recreational play for the entire student body was included. It is at this juncture that Nash conceptualized his philosophy regarding "spectatoritis." In a report about competition, he stated:

> The cooperation of the boys, their parents, the Board of Education and all concerned seems to point to a great future for this line of extensive athletics. It is no longer the case of the strong playing and getting stronger and the weak looking on and getting weaker, but it is the case of all getting stronger. (Jessup, 1967:100)

After three years at Fremont High School, Nash accepted a new position in Oakland, California as assistant superintendent of Recreation and assistant director of Physical Education. This joint appointment between the Board of Education and the Board of Recreation was one of the first in the nation, (Fulk, 1922) and helped make Oakland a premier city in the field of recreation (Jessup, 1967).

Also during this period, Nash and his recreation supervisor, George Dickie, realized the need for the young children to have an opportunity to participate in play experiences. In 1916, they issued the Bulletin on Backyard Playgrounds which recommended utilizing open space behind homes for meeting the play needs of the small child. (Jessup, 1967)

Following the retirement of Dickie, Nash was first appointed acting, and then full Superintendent of Recreation and Director of Physical Education. Under Nash's administration, the playground program expanded, and Nash continued to develop his conceptualizations of play and recreation. Through graduate studies at the School of Directed Activities at the University of California at Berkeley, Nash further refined his beliefs. His play philosophies evolved into a curriculum and are evident in his coauthored work, "Organization of Playground Activities" in Syllabus.

In mid-1918, Nash accepted an additional position as assistant state supervisor for Physical Education. Besides providing general consultation in physical education, his duties included visiting schools, conducting teacher training, holding educational forums, and publishing special bulletins. Nash also was responsible for teaching at the University Extension

Division of the University of California where he chose to instruct the course "Play Activities for Children." (Jessup, 1967)

In 1919, Nash resigned his position with the State and resumed full-time work with his Oakland position. While joint use/cooperative playground programs (i.e., between municipal, community, and educational facilities) continued to receive commendations for progressiveness in Oakland, Nash embarked on other innovative projects. Jessup (1967) reported that the development of evening recreation centers, municipal costume rooms, archery programs, municipal golf courses, industrial recreation programs, municipal and family camps, and support of the Boy Scout and Camp Fire movements were Nash's priorities.

The camp concept was extremely successful, with the establishment of the Oakland Recreation Camp in the Stanislaus National Forest and the Oakland Feather River Camp in the Plumas National Forest. Both camps operated under a cooperative system whereby residents were required to assist in camp chores and assume responsibility for different camp functions. These camps were noted by Nash as providing him with an experience in which he derived "the most pleasure." (Jessup, 1967:133)

During the mid-twenties, Nash faced a dilemma: to stay in public recreation or to move into a realm of higher education. Nash chose to accept an appointment at New York University. Besides assisting Clark Hetherington, NYU Physical Education Department Chair, in the establishment of a sound curriculum in the Department, Nash had a heavy teaching load, instructing courses such as "Recreation in Industrial Institutions," "Administration of Public Recreation," and "Nature and Function of Play." (Jessup, 1967:162)

Additionally, Nash continued his own higher education, completing a Master's degree at NYU in 1927. Two years later he finished requirements for a Doctor of Philosophy degree. Also during this busy period in Nash's life, he wrote his first book, *The Organization and Administration of Playgrounds and Recreation.* Nash went on to become a prolific writer, writing or contributing to over 20 books and 100 articles during his career.

Nash played a major role in the establishment of a camp affiliated with NYU. In the summer of 1927, the first session of the camp was held. Located in Palisades Interstate Park, the camp was based on Nash's philosophy and focused on living; learning where the concept of education and recreation could be jointly implemented. Additionally, in 1944, the camp implemented another of Nash ideas: equal rights. This made NYU camp facilities and programs racially integrated.

Due to the deteriorating health of Clark Hetherington, Nash became acting administrative head of the Department of Physical Education in 1928 and was officially named to the chair position in 1930. He remained in this post until his retirement from NYU in 1953.

Under Nash's leadership, the physical education curriculum continued to be refined, making it one of the strongest in the country. Jay Nash also seized the opportunity to expand the department seeking interdisciplinary collaboration. The curriculum progressed toward the development of nonteaching programs, providing the initial impetus for the creation of curricula in nursing education, physiotherapy, and recreation. (Jessup, 1967)

Further momentum for the development of recreation professional preparation programs occurred as a result of the 1930s Depression. Under the auspices of Nash, the recreation staffing needs in the voluntary and public sectors were met by initiating a concentration of courses in recreation administration. Further curricular expansion occurred in 1936 when Nash created an undergraduate program in recreation leadership. In future years, Nash also was credited with the establishment of a graduate program for the preparation of Boy's Club administrative executives, specialization in camping administration and outdoor education and a course in the area of hospital recreation. However, it was not until the end of World War II that the innovation of departmental subdivisions (i.e., health, physical education, recreation, and safety) was initiated, each with a designated curriculum and department head.

In 1933, Nash requested and received a leave of absence from his administrative/teaching position. He was appointed director of Indian Emergency Conservation Work. The aim of the project was to establish work camps similar to those operated by the Works Progress Administration (WPA), on Indian lands. The focus of the project was the development of forest conservation, reforestation, and control of soil erosion programs. Apparently, Nash was successful in his role with this project and, was personally influenced by the culture of the Native Americans. (Jessup, 1967)

Besides providing leadership within his department at NYU, Jay Nash was active universitywide and nationally. Most noteworthy was his activity in developing roots of professional organizations such as the Playground and Recreation Association, the American Physical Education Association and the National Education Association. Throughout his illustrious career, Nash held numerous professional offices including president of the Western District Association and Eastern District Association of the American Physical Education Association; president of the Department of School Health and Physical Education of NEA; secretary of the American Academy of Physical Education; chairman of the First World Seminar for Physical Education, Health, Recreation and Youth Work; and president of the American Association for Health, Physical Education and Recreation, to name a few.

One of Nash's most outstanding talents in which he gained notoriety was that of public speaker. Influences during his boyhood years by Russell Conwell's Chautauqua lecture, "Acres of Diamonds," and later in life by John Dewey and William H. Kirkpatrick, Nash's career was filled with opportunities to expound his own philosophy. Frequently, this conveyed the virtues of physical activity, the need for the carryover of such activities throughout life, and the problems associated with idleness. Additionally, Nash advocated adequate facilities for leisure pursuits including playgrounds and open space. (Jessup, 1967)

After Jay Nash's retirement from NYU in 1953, he accepted a Fullbright professorship in India. According to Jessup, Nash "traveled through virtually every part of the country teaching; conducting seminars; consulting with government officials, educational leaders from high schools, colleges, and universities; giving addresses to various professional and lay groups; and advising the Ministry of Education on their various problems on health, physical education, and recreation." (1967:34)

For the next two years after his India journey, Nash held the position of Dean of the College of Recreation, Physical and Health Education, and Athletics at Brigham Young University. His main tasks were to evaluate and reconstruct all aspects of the curriculum.

Following the BYU position, Jay Nash accepted employment as executive secretary of the New York State Association for Health, Physical Education, and Recreation. Although he resigned this position in 1963 to work at Montclair State College in New Jersey, he was asked to return until a new secretary could be appointed. Two years later, on September 20, 1965, Jay B. Nash suffered a fatal heart attack.

Jay Bryan Nash was a philosopher in the true sense of the word. Throughout his life, Nash evoked in others the desire to think and challenge—to question the society in which they lived. His work was not only a major influence on individuals but also on the fields of physical education, recreation, health, camping, and outdoor education.

In the area of play and recreation, perhaps one of Nash's most noteworthy accomplishments was to put the "playground within the reach of every child." (Jessup, 1967:139). This effort was promoted through innovations such as cooperative use of facilities by municipal recreation departments and boards of education. The importance of play in Nash's philosophy is best summarized in this quote taken from the Oakland Recreation Department *Bulletin:*

Play, which is the serious occupation of child life, is the outcropping of the natural instincts of the child. It is more than instincts of the child. It is more than exercise—it is education itself. Play is the child's expression of life and is impelled by the all-powerful element of interest. (Jessup, 1967:139)

Another noteworthy contribution of Nash was the conceptualization of worthy use of leisure time. Nash asserted that happiness and the desire for life resulted from active participation not "spectatoritis"—the passive observation of leisure pursuits.

Nash had a tremendous impact on the promotion of camping and outdoor education. This was evident in the establishment of the California family and municipal camps and in the New York University Camp. Additionally, Nash was active with the Boy Scouts and promoted camping for girls through his active membership with Camp Fire, Inc. Nash viewed the out-of-doors as a means to promote democratic living, and he utilized this milieu in the training of thousands of students.

Jay Nash was also a leader in the development of the social aspects of physical education. His writings and teaching advocated physical fitness and also the necessity for sportsmanship, character, citizenship, and loyalty. According to Jessup, Nash "probably far more than any other leader in the profession, emphasized the cultural and recreative aspects of physical education." (1967:323) Nash put this philosophy into practice through his leadership roles in the formation and development of numerous professional organizations.

To say that Jay B. Nash was a leader in the profession does not do justice to his widespread influence. Perhaps, his most lasting contribution has been the impact he has had on those studying within the fields of health, physical education, recreation, camping, and outdoor education. The philosophy of Jay Nash is a part of all of them, and it will continually live through his disciples.

PARTIAL LIST OF NASH'S PUBLICATIONS

Teacher's Golden Opportunity. (1920, December). *Normal Instructor,* pp. 8–10.

Presidential Address. (1921a). *American Physical Education Review, 26,* pp. 55–56.

The Summer Playground. (1921b, June). *Normal Instructor and Primary Plans,* pp. 11–13.

Office Administration and Personal Efficiency As Seen By A Superintendent of Recreation. (1924, March). *The Playground,* pp. 6–8.

Six Bits Apiece, Please! (1926, January). *The Survey.*

The Organization and Administration of Playgrounds and Recreation. (1927). New York: Barnes and Company.

Physical Education Should Train the Impulses. (1928a). *The Pentathlon, 1,* pp. 6–7.

Athletics For Girls. (1928b). *The North American Review,* pp. 99–104.

Leadership—The Hope Of Physical Education. (1929a). *The Virginia Teacher, 10,* pp. 141–142.

What Does The Education System of a Modern Democracy Expect From Physical Education? (1929b). *Mind and Body, 35,* pp. 118–124.

The Great Whats. (1929c). *Redbook,* pp. 44–45.

Symposium on Physical Education and Health. (1930a). New York: New York University Press.

The Administration of Physical Education and Health in the Light of General Education. (1930b). *The Journal of Health and Physical Education, 1,* pp. 9–12.

Interpretation of Physical Education to School Officials. (1930c, April). *New Jersey Journal of Education,* pp. 6–8.

A Modern Public School Physical Education Program. (1930d, October). *Michigan Journal of Physical Education,* pp. 36–41.

Interpretations of Physical Education. (1931a). New York: A.S. Barnes and Company.

The Administration of Physical Education. (1931b). New York: A.S. Barnes and Company.

Contributions of Physical Education to Mental Morality. (1931c). *National Education Association Proceedings,* p. 543.

Standards of Play and Recreation Administration. (1931d). *National Municipal League Review Supplement, 20.*

Playgrounds and Recreation. (1931c). *Public Management,* pp. 15–16.

Report of the Committee on High School Administrative Standards for the Directors of Physical Education. (1932). *Research Quarterly, 14,* pp. 127–130.

The Role of Physical Education in Character Education. (1933a). *The Journal of Health and Physical Education, 4,* pp. 28–29, 69.

Concerning the Idea That Health Can Be Taught. (1933b, January). *Clearing House,* pp. 278–280.

Why Send a Girl To Camp? Campfire Opportunities That No Girl Should Be Denied. (1933c, April). *The Guardian,* p. 304.

Eternal Youth. (1934a). *The Journal of Health and Physical Education, 5,* p. 25.

Physical Activities and Education. (1934b, January). *Michigan Journal of Physical Education,* pp. 39–42.

Leisure Time Recreation. (1934c, January). *New Jersey Municipalities,* pp. 11–14.

Scientific Foundations of Physical Education. (1935a). *Mind and Body, 41,* pp. 289–297.

Franklin: Philosopher of Capitalism: Why We Never Developed a Recreational Philosophy. (1935b). *Common Sense, 4,* pp. 20–22.

When To School. (1935c, October). *Journal of Exceptional Children,* pp. 44–46.

You Must Relax—But How? (1935d). *The Journal of Health and Physical Education*, 6, pp. 10–13.

Guiding Youth in Health. (1935c, June). *The Digest*, pp. 15–16.

Ourselves and the Greeks. (1936, May). *The New York Times*.

Healths and Health. (1937, February). *The Education Digest*, pp. 27–29.

The Physical Education Director. (1938a, June). *The School Executive*, p. 458.

After School Play. (1938b). *The School Parent*, 5, pp. 3, 9.

Spectatoritis. (1938c). New York: Barnes and Company.

Teachable Moments: A New Approach to Health. (1938d). New York: Barnes and Company.

Busy-ness, Interest and Health. (1938c). *Journal of Health and Physical Education*, 9, p. 25.

Camp's Unique Contribution to the Philosophy of Living. (1938f). *The Guardian*, p. 7.

Concerning Camp—Some Philosophical Points. (1938g). *Camping Magazine*, 10, pp. 3, 38.

Improvements of Recreation Facilities. (1938h, September). *The Annals of the American Academy of Political and Social Sciences*, pp. 1–10.

Hygiene Teaching—A Worship of Non-Essentials. (1939a, December). *The School*, pp. 305–307.

Can a Baby Run an Athlete Ragged? (1939b). *This Week*, pp. 8–9.

Youth Caught Between Millstones. (1939c). *Youth Leader's Digest*, 11, p.p. 330–334.

Has Education The Answer? (1939d). *The Journal of Health and Physical Education*, 10, pp. 443–446.

A Plan for National Preparedness Through Health, Physical Education, and Recreation in Schools and Camps. (1940a). *The Journal of Health in Schools and Camps*, 11, pp. 28–32.

The Nature and Scope of Teacher Education for Recreational Leadership. (1940b, March). *Black and Gold*, pp. 13–18.

Recreation as a Foundation for Democracy. (1940c, March). *The American Citizen*, pp. 7–12.

Leisure Time Education and the Democratic Pattern. (1940d). *Proceedings*, pp. 11–20.

Those First Years. (1940e, November). *Vital Speechs of the Day*, pp. 82–84.

Can Health Be Taught? (1940f). *West Virginia School Journal*, p. 7.

Parents Set The Pattern. (1940g). *National Parent-Teacher*, pp. 28–30.

Lawlessness and Deliquency—What Can Education Do About It? (1940h, November). *Illinois State Normal University*, pp. 26–37.

Fire The Teacher When Children Hate School. (1940i). *Youth Leaders' Digest, 12,* pp.62–65.

Some Community Coordination Problems Relative to Physical Education, Health, and Recreation. (1940j). *New York State Journal of Health and Physical Education and Recreation, 4,* pp. 64–67.

Values of Camping. (1940k). *The Guardian, 14,* pp. 1–2.

I Like Badminton Myself. (1940l, March). *The Badminton Journal,* pp. 4, 13, 17.

Building Morale. (1942a). New York: Barnes and Company.

Let's Build Morale. (1942b). *The Journal of the Florida Education Association,* p. 14.

It's Time The Schools Thought of Physical Fitness. (1942c, April). *Louisiana Schools,* p. 3.

You Can't Build Physical Stamina On A Diet Of Information. (1942d). *The Journal of Teacher Education, 4,* pp. 27–31.

Health and Fitness in Wartime. (1942e). *The Allied Youth, 11,* p. 6.

Athletics Vs. Calisthenics. (1943a). *The Clearing House, 18,* pp. 29–30.

The Camping Technique—An Aid To The War Effort. (1943a). *Progressive Education,* pp. 174–176.

Never Again. (1943c, April). *The Bulletin of the National Association of Secondary School Principals,* pp. 101–104.

What Constitutes Physical Fitness? (1943d, August). *The Nation's Schools,* p. 34.

Something For Which To Keep Fit. (1943e). *The Physical Educator, 3,* p. 44.

The American Academy of Physical Education. (1945a). *The Journal of Health and Physical Education, 6.*

Physical Fitness. (1945b). *Paths to Better Schools,* pp. 46–81.

We Can Build Physical Stamina. (1945c, April). *Educational Record,* pp. 103–106.

Letters To The Editor. (1946a). *Youth Leader's Digest, 8,* p. 205.

Will Technology Set Us Free? (1946b). *Youth Leaders' Digest, 7,* pp. 241–243.

Recreation and Leisure Time—Forward. (1946c). *General Federation Clubwoman,* pp. 19–20.

The Greek's Had A Way. (1946d). *Youth Leaders' Digest, 7,* pp. 241–243.

Hobbies For Happiness. (1946e). *Self, 1,* pp. 9–10.

Camping is the Biting Edge of Education. (1947a). *The Boardman, 4,* p. 12.

Our Work is Here—Our Reward is Ahead of Us. (1947b). *First Year Book,* pp. 12–18.

Tapping the Enthusiasm of Youth. (1947c). *The New Jersey Club Woman, 21,* p. 12.

To Travel Hopefully. (1947d). *Proceedings,* pp. 30–33.

The Contributions of Physical Education to Recreation. (1947e). *Journal of the American Association for Health-Physical Education Research, 22,* pp. 53–56.

Don't Let Democracy Die. (1948a, March). *The Camp Fire Girl,* pp. 7–8.

A Philosophy of Recreation in America. (1948b). *The Journal of Education Sociology, 21,* pp. 259–262.

Health As A Means Of Full Living. (1948c). *The Journal of Education Sociology, 22,* pp. 1–7.

Youth Must Belong. (1948d). *Youth Leaders' Digest, 10,* pp. 124–129.

Physical Education: Interpretations and Objectives. (1948e). New York: Barnes and Company.

The Aristocracy of Virtue. (1949f). *The Journal of the American Association for Health, Physical Education, and Recreation, 20,* pp. 216–217.

Recreation: An Opportunity and a Responsibility. (1950a). *Education, 71,* pp. 69–73.

Take It Easy. (1950b). *Youth Leaders' Digest, 13,* p. 81.

Work Makes Men. (1950c). *Youth Leaders' Digest, 13,* p. 24.

Physical Education and Recreation for Life Adjustment. (1950d). In H.R. Douglass' (Ed.) *Education For Life Adjustment.* New York: The Ronald Press Company, pp. 267–289.

The Role Of Camping in Recreation—Today and Tomorrow. (1950e). *Camping Magazine, 14,* pp. 22–23.

Opportunities in Physical Education, Health, and Recreation. (1950f). New York: Vocational Guidance Manual, Inc.

Why a School Camping Program? (1950g). *The Journal of Educational Sociology, 23,* pp. 500–507.

Why School Camping? (1950h). *Youth Leaders' Digest, 12,* pp. 323–327.

When Philosophers Are Kings. (1951a). *Newsletter of Jersey Association for Health and Physical Education, 24,* pp. 5–7, 23, 33.

The Law of Reach. (1951b). *Youth Leaders' Digest, 13,* p. 321.

The Role Of Recreation In Our Culture. (1951c). *Professional Contributions, 1,* pp. 72–75.

The Adults' World. (1951d). In *Developing Democratic Human Relations Through Health Education, Physical Education and Recreation.*Washington, D.C.: American Association for Health, Physical Education and Recreation, pp. 433–435.

The Public School and Deliquency. (1951e). *Youth Leaders' Digest, 14,* pp. 24–25.

The Need To Enlighten: A Forward. (1951f). *The Journal of Education Sociology, 25,* pp. 433–434. (With M.F. Hanck and M.R. Fields).

Physical Education: Organization and Administration. (1951g). New York: The Ronald Press Company. (With F.J. Munch and J.B. Saurborn).

The Skill Learning Years. (1952). *Youth Leaders' Digest, 15*, p. 111.

Philosophy of Recreation and Leisure. (1953a). St. Louis: Charles V. Mosby.

The Importance of the Skill-Learning Years. (1953b). *Proceedings*, pp. 4–8.

The Belonging Youth Is Loyal. (1955). *The Physical Educator, 12*, pp. 43–45.

Man Will Be Very Much The Same 2,000 Years From Now. (1958, February). *Education*, pp. 7–11.

Kids and Athletics. (1961, October). *Changing Times.*

Opportunities in Physical Education, Health, and Recreation. (1963). New York: Vocational Guidance Manuals.

The Tragedy Of Free Time. (1964a). *Journal of the Canadian Association for Health, Physical Education and Recreation, 30*, pp. 9–10.

Those Hands. (1964b). *Quest*, pp. 53–59.

Recreation: Pertinent Readings. (1965). Dubuque, Iowa: Wm C. Brown Company Publishers.

REFERENCES

Fulk, J. R. (1922). *The Municipalization of Play and Recreation.* Washington D.C.: McGrath Publishing Company and the National Recreation and Park Association.

Jessup, H. (1967). Jay Bryan Nash, His Contribution and Influences In The Fields of Physical Education, Health, Recreation, Camping, and Outdoor Recreation. *Dissertation Abstracts International, 28*, 1282A.

20

ALDO LEOPOLD

1887–1948

S. Elaine Rogers
East Stroudsburg University
and
Phyllis Ford
Michigan State University

"*I am glad that I shall never be young without wild country to be young in. Of what avail are forty freedoms without a blank spot on the map?*"

1949:49

The name of Aldo Leopold may not be as well recognized among park and recreation professionals as it is among foresters, wildlife managers, and wilderness preservation advocates, yet it should be. Leopold is considered by many to be one of the most important conservationists of the 20th century, not only because he, along with others, established early principles and practices for conserving our natural resources, but also because he provided us with a philosophical basis for doing so. He was an early advocate of the idea that our nation's public lands should be managed not only for economic purposes such as timber production but also for public enjoyment through recreation.

While various reports disagree on the date being 1886 or 1887, Susan Flader (1979) and others who have done extensive research into the life of Aldo Leopold, write that he was born in Burlington, Iowa, in 1887. Just five years earlier, Mark Twain had toured the Mississippi River municipalities and found Burlington to be a progressive, flourishing town. This Mississippi River community, the site of Aldo Leopold's early years, afforded him ample opportunities for becoming acquainted with the wildlife he championed the rest of his life.

Aldo was a sandy-haired child with green-blue eyes and the sturdy frame of his father. Even though devoted to his younger sister Marie and brothers Carl, Jr. and Frederic, Aldo's mother Clara saw in Aldo something special. It was known to all the family, who accepted it as a fact of life that Aldo could do no wrong as he was his mother's favorite. There is evidence that Aldo and his brother Carl were especially good pals, setting traps, skinny-dipping, and sliding on the ice near the house. Frederic remembered him later as being a great influence on his own life and credited him with great optimism concerning the potential for educating the general public toward an appreciation of ecological values. While Aldo went on to school and a professional career in conservation, Frederic stayed home to take over the family furniture manufacturing business but became, as an amateur, the world authority on the nesting habits of wood ducks.

Leopold's interest in the natural world was enhanced by the geographical location of his home near the Mississippi River, but the main influence came from his family. Aldo's father, Carl, was an avid waterfowl hunter, and from their father, Aldo, Carl Jr., Frederic, and Marie all learned about the outdoors through many hunting experiences. Their father's approach was to set an example of sportsmanship and to develop in his children a sense of wonder and respect for the land. Long before game laws were written, Carl Sr. decided it was wrong to hunt waterfowl during the nesting season and stopped that practice among all his family. When he was 11, Leopold wrote an essay on the study of birds, with particular reference to the 120 young wrens hatched in his backyard the previous year. In the essay, he listed 39 other species he had seen and gave reasons for the wrens being his favorite. Later in his life, Leopold dedicated his 1933 book, *Game Management,* "To my Father, Carl Leopold, Pioneer in Sportsmanship."

When planning their son's education, Leopold's mother, who had gone east to school, felt her son also should go to an eastern school. At first, however, Aldo was to attend the local high school which had an excellent reputation but which was very crowded. The over-enrollment of students meant double sessions and the necessity to show up only for recitations. Aldo was able to plan his schedule so that all his classes were in the afternoon, allowing him plenty of time in the morning for explorations. He roamed the countryside on a daily basis, collecting information on everything that lived in the area. After two years in Burlington High School where he excelled as a student, particularly in English and biology, Leopold was sent east to the Lawrenceville Prep School in New Jersey.

When Leopold went off to school, his mother, evidently knowing how much she would miss him, requested that he write home as often as possible, "about everything." He did this throughout the next ten years of his life, producing approximately 10,000 pages of letters. Leopold had learned grammar, spelling, and composition in school but, through his mother's encouragement, he learned to write by writing. These letters home contributed to the development of another habit. While at prep school, he began keeping a journal of his observations on nature, a habit that stayed with him throughout his life. Throughout his days at Lawrenceville, Aldo filled his letters and journals with accounts of birds, ponds, fields, animals, and all aspects of the natural life surrounding the campus.

Following his childhood attraction to the romanticism of forestry, Leopold entered Yale University in 1906 where he studied for two years before he was admitted to the Master's degree program in Forestry. The Yale School was the best school for foresters in the country at that time. During his time there he continued to write, both to his family and in his journals, and it is from these accounts that one can learn of Leopold's early dislike for details, laboratories, and finely documented statistical reports. His preference was for the macro aspect of the out-of-doors—not the micro.

Upon completion of his graduate degree in 1909, Leopold was employed by the U.S. Forest Service as forest assistant in the newly formed District III, which was made up of the territories of Arizona and New Mexico. Three years later, he was promoted to supervisor of the Carson National Forest in northern New Mexico. During the same year, New Mexico and Arizona became states.

Leopold married Estella Bergere on October 9, 1912, in Santa Fe and built a home in Tres Piedras, New Mexico, where he was extremely satisfied with both his professional position and his home life. Eventually the couple had five children all of whom built their own distinguished careers as conservationists and scientists.

In 1913, sickness overcame Leopold as the result of overexposure while camping out on an assignment in a remote part of the national forest. He had been called out on a grazing dispute which kept him outdoors for five days during which he endured a two-day storm consisting of hail, rain, sleet, and snow, slept in a soaked bed roll, and was forced to take a long detour toward home. His illness kept him confined for 16 months, during which time he returned to Burlington, Iowa, to recuperate. During this time, he lost his position as forester supervisor. Although a depressing time for Leopold, this was perhaps one of the most influential times of his life. During his recuperative period, he read widely from the works of others who also loved nature and the outdoor life. It is not known exactly what Leopold read, however, Flader (1974) speculates that among his readings were the works of Thoreau that he had received as a wedding gift and the writings of men who had influenced him all his life—Lewis and Clark, Francis Parkman, John Burroughs, and Ernest Thompson Seton.

When he was able to work again, Leopold was assigned to the Office of Grazing at the District III headquarters in Albuquerque. In this capacity, he began organizing local hunters and fishermen into game protective associations. In 1915, he was offered a desk job in Washington, but declined it in favor of staying in the Southwest to fight for game protection. He founded and edited *The Pine Cone*, a quarterly newspaper of the New Mexico Game Protective Association. Through these efforts, Leopold came to see that national forest lands should be used for recreational as well as commercial purposes.

In 1917, the Albuquerque Chamber of Commerce offered him a position at considerably more salary than the Forest Service could offer and Leopold accepted the position in January, 1918. World War I had caused a shift in Forest Service priorities. Many foresters were shipped to Europe to serve with the Army Corps of Engineers in France to provide the technology needed to get lumber for building barracks, trenches, and aircraft. On the homefront, many recreational developments on the National Forests were postponed and the range lands were stocked with more cattle than ever before. When Leopold resigned from the Forest Service in 1918 to assume the position of secretary of the Albuquerque Chamber of Commerce, he did so with the intention of returning to the Forest Service after the war was over. During the war years he still pursued his cause of game protection in the Southwest.

In 1919, Leopold rejoined the Forest Service as assistant district forester in charge of operations. During the next couple of years, Leopold's "interest in game conservation continued, but gradually he recognized that the maintenance and indeed the appeal of hunting and fishing was part of the larger problem of preserving the wilderness conditions in which these activities took place." (Nash, 1973:185) In 1921, in a most significant article published in the *Journal of Forestry*, entitled "The Wilderness and its Place in Forest Recreational Policy," Leopold defined wilderness as "A continuous stretch of country preserved in its natural state, open to lawful hunting and fishing, big enough to absorb a two weeks' pack trip and kept devoid of roads, artificial trails, cottages, or other works of men." (p. 719)

His definition is significant because he did not define wilderness as something to be left alone, but as an area of human activity—a special kind of human activity, that of the pioneering American. In his arguments for the designation of a portion of the Gila National Forest as wilderness area, he called for preservation of a distinctive kind of recreational experience, the pack trip, unique because opportunities for it were disappearing. His argument was based on the need for diversity in recreational and cultural experiences.

In 1924, Leopold left the Southwest that he had come to love so deeply to accept the post of assistant director of the Forest Service's Forest Products Laboratory at Madison, Wisconsin. Before he left, however, the Forest Service accepted his recommendation to designate the Gila region in New Mexico as a wilderness area. For years, Leopold had been reluctant to see the Forest Service set aside so many areas for recreational "improvements" such as homesites, public campgrounds, public and private leased concessions, and sanitary facilities. He believed there should be a balance of recreational opportunities for everyone. The designated wilderness area would provide opportunities for a form of recreation that was very different from the opportunities available to those who sought tourist campgrounds and vacation homes. This novel idea, articulated 40 years before the now famous Wilderness Act, marked Leopold as a "Pioneer of Wilderness."

In his lengthy article entitled "Wilderness as a Form of Land Use," Leopold (1925) began to develop the notion that Americans needed a totally new way of regarding their countryside. Wild natural areas were no longer something to conquer as the pioneers had believed. Leopold began to feel that not only should we set aside large portions of wilderness for posterity but we should also regard all wild natural areas in a new light. He advocated that large and small portions of the wild outdoors of the United States should be allowed to retain the qualities that attracted the pioneers. Successive generations of Americans could then acquire the characteristics of pioneers by experiencing firsthand the conditions that shaped their culture. In this manner, wilderness preservation was to become an American contribution to the culture of the world. He stated his case most eloquently in *A Sand County Almanac:*

To the laborer in the sweat of his labor, the raw stuff on his anvil is an adversary to be conquered. So was the wilderness an adversary to the pioneer. But to the laborer in repose, able for the moment to cast a philosophical eye on his world, that same raw stuff is something to be loved and cherished, because it gives definition and meaning to his life. This is a place for the preservation of some tag-ends of wilderness, as museum pieces, for the edification of those who may one day wish to see, feel, or study the origins of their cultural inheritance. (1949:188)

Leopold dedicated the remainder of his life to preserving the wilderness and developing his ideas on land use into what he later would call a "land ethic." At the Second National Conference on Outdoor Recreation in 1926, Leopold was a speaker, calling wilderness the fundamental recreation resource and urging a national wilderness preservation policy. U.S. Forest Service Chief William B. Greeley publicly endorsed this idea. Influenced by Leopold, Assistant Chief L. F. Kniepp developed an inventory of roadless areas of the United States. Included in the inventory were 74 areas of at least 230,400 acreas each, comprising approximately one-third of the total acreage of the national forests at that time. The inventory was reported at the Third National Conference on Outdoor Recreation in 1928.

With continued prompting from Leopold, the U.S.F.S., in 1929, issued the so-called L-20 Regulations which directed the Forest Service Districts to take steps to preserve undeveloped areas. These regulations were significant because they represented the first steps toward the establishment of a system of officially designated "primitive" areas in the national forests.

In his position in the laboratory at Madison, Leopold found he had little administrative detail to ponder over which gave him more time to write. But he also learned that it was a frustrating position for him. The job entailed the development of products made from wood and Leopold realized that he was in reality a field naturalist, not a chemist. Because of frustration with the laboratory job, he left the Forest Service for good in 1928 to work for the Sporting Arms and Ammunition Manufacturers' Institute for whom he conducted game surveys in the north central states. This game survey work and the subsequent 1933 publication, *Game Management,* established Leopold as one of the country's best authorities on native game. He had laid the groundwork for a new profession and became known as the "Father of Game Management."

In the same year of the publication of this innovative text, he was offered the chair of game management created especially for him at the University of Wisconsin, Madison. Through these same years, Leopold remained deeply concerned as well with the concept of management of all natural resources for enjoyment and renewal through recreation. But Leopold's concept of recreation was not traditional. In later years he was to write,

"Recreation development is a job not of building roads into lovely country, but of building receptivity into the still unlovely human mind." (1949:176)

In 1935, three events took place that impacted heavily on the philosophy of Leopold:

1. With Robert Marshall and others he founded the Wilderness Society.
2. He and his family acquired the "shack," an abandoned farm on the Wisconsin River near Madison, which would later be the inspiration for his book, A Sand County Almanac.
3. He spent three months in Germany studying German forestry and wildlife management methods.

According to Flader,

The year 1935 marked a reorientation in his thinking from a historical and recreational to a predominantly ecological and ethical justification for wilderness. (1974:29)

. . . the impact of the German experience, his redefinition of the wilderness idea and the convergence of observation, activity, and reflection at his sand-country shack signal in important ways the beginning of his mature philosophy. (1974:30)

In 1939, before a joint meeting of the Society of American Foresters and the Ecological Society of America, Leopold presented a paper containing his new ecological viewpoint. The paper is significant because of Leopold's holistic approach to thinking about the land. He restated the purpose of conservation to be the preservation of a healthy total system, rather than merely protecting each separate part, e.g. fauna or flora. In 1940 in his presidential address to the Wildlife Society, Leopold expressed his holistic approach again and presented implications for those who teach outdoor education and recreation. In this address he defined the role of wildlife managers to be that of contributors to the total design of living for the landowner and the general public. But he spoke not only to wildlife managers, recognizing the role of others who influence landowners and/or the general public, among them teachers. He claimed that teachers could demonstrate this new idea of what land is for. He called for a new emphasis on broad public understanding. As a professor himself, he attempted to lead his own students in this new direction. He explained his own objective in teaching: "to teach the student to see the land, to understand what he sees, and enjoy what he understands." (Flader, 1974:33) It is at this point in the development of his philosophy that Leopold gave a new rationale for conservation education: to broaden American thinking of the land from utilitarian to ethical and esthetic.

Nash wrote that "Before Leopold and ecologists, the source of American respect for nature had been more sentimental and spiritual than scientific."

(1973:194) In the 1940s, Leopold contributed his best essays, among them "Odyssey," "Wildlife in American Culture," and "Thinking Like a Mountain." During this period he was involved in recommending new policy directions for a number of professional societies and conservation agencies and groups, among them in the Wilderness Society, Ecological Society of America, Wildlife Society, National Audubon Society, American Ornithologists Union, Society of American Foresters, and American Forestry Association.

The capstone of Leopold's writing, which includes over 350 articles and 3 books, is A Sand County Almanac (1949). It is the most well known and perhaps the most influential of all his writings. The book is the result of a lifetime of observation of nature and the development of ideas concerning the relationship of ecology, esthetics, and ethics. In the preface, he wrote "There are some who can live without wild things, and some who cannot. These essays are the delights and dilemmas of one who cannot. . . . Like winds and sunsets, wild things were taken for granted until progress began to do away with them." (p. viii) The book is divided into three sections. "Part I, A Sand County Almanac," recounts episodes of observation at the "shack" during each of the 12 months of the year. "Part II, Sketches from Here and There," recounts essays written during work or travels in the west, southwest, midwest, Mexico, and Canada, and "Part III, The Upshot," consists of four sections in which the famous land ethic is developed.

In this final section is an essay entitled "Conservation Esthetic," where Leopold divided recreation into five levels of experience, each of which affected the natural resources differently. Collection of physical objects included hunting, fishing, collecting shells, and other natural objects and also photography, an activity that makes no demands on the resources. The recreationist who pursues the feeling of isolation is in the second category and may have considerable impact on the place of solitude, depending upon the numbers of seekers of isolation. Those who seek fresh air and a change of scenery usually make few demands on the resources, consuming very little and causing relatively little damage (except in extreme cases). Perception, the understanding of the ways in which nature operates, makes no demands on the environment and consumes no resources. The final type of recreational use of natural resources, husbandry, is what Leopold considered the most satisfying component of the recreational experience because, instead of diluting the resources, it maintains and enhances them.

The major contribution of Leopold to the recreation movement is thought by some to be the four remarkable essays found in the third section of Sand County Almanac wherein he calls for a fundamental reform in our relationship to the land. The following quotations probably tell most clearly how the land ethic relates to and is of such great significance to the recreation field:

> The outstanding characteristic of perception is that it entails no consumption and no dilution of any resource. (p. 173)
>
> To promote perception is the only truly creative part of recreational engineering. (p. 173)
>
> Recreation, however, is not the outdoors, but our reaction to it. (p. 173).
>
> The only true development in American recreational resources is the development of the perceptive faculty in Americans. (p. 174)
>
> To those devoid of imagination, a blank place on the map is a useless waste; to others, the most valuable part. (p. 176)
>
> A thing is right when it tends to preserve the integrity, stability, and beauty of the biotic community. It is wrong when it tends otherwise. (p. 224)

The land ethic is based on a premise that through the history of civilization, the development of ethics has followed a discernable evolution. First the ten commandments gave us laws of moral behavior. These were followed by the Golden Rule that prescribed behavior toward other individuals. These two sets of ethics were based on the premise that the individual is a member of a community of interdependent humans. Ethics prompt the individual to cooperate within an environment of competition. The land ethic enlarges the boundaries of the community to include the land and everything on it. The land ethic changes the role of the human from a conqueror of the land to a steward of it. It implores us to hold the same respect for the land that we do for the humans on the land. That land is a community is the basic concept of ecology, but that land is to be loved and respected is an extension of ethics. (Leopold, 1949, pp. viii-ix)

Leopold's thinking developed as a result of his experiences with the land. He was a well educated and learned man; however, not all of his learning was derived from books or discussions with others. His learning came primarily from experiences in the outdoors. At critical points in the development of his philosophy, he was involved in some form of outdoor experience. "It was his conviction that ecological perception was a matter of careful observation and critical thinking." (Flader, 1974:35) It may be said that the key to Leopold's success lay in his ability to combine the methods and understanding of a scientist with the ethical and esthetic sensitivity of a romantic. He was able to give a concrete, new meaning to the old idea of the goodness of nature without robbing it of emotional content. In a tribute to him, J. D. Wellman stated, "The chief 20th century prophet of wilderness, Aldo Leopold, began his career as an advocate with attitudes close to (Theodore) Roosevelt's and gradually moved to an intellectual position closer to Muir's." (1987:126)

While helping neighbors fight a brush fire that threatened his Sand County farm, Leopold suffered a heart attack and died on April 21, 1948. Only a week earlier, the Oxford University Press had informed him that they had accepted his book of essays for which he had been seeking a publisher since 1941. It was this book that was published posthumously as *A Sand County Almanac*. The magnitude of Leopold's work may not be known for many years. Leopold, himself, recognized that his ideas might not be adopted overnight. In 1947 he reminded us, "It required 19 centuries to define decent man-to-man conduct and the process is only half done; it may take as long to evolve a code of decency for man-to-land conduct." (p. 49) Leopold was a pioneer of wilderness and the prophet of the new ethic.

PARTIAL LIST OF LEOPOLD'S PUBLICATIONS

Forestry and Game Conservation. (1918). *Journal of Forestry, 16, pp. 404–411.*

Wilderness and its Place in Forest Recreational Policy. (1921) *Journal of Forestry, 19, pp. 718–721.*

Wilderness as a Form of Land Use. (1925). *Journal of Land Use and Public Utility Economics, 1,* pp. 398–404.

Game Management. (1933) New York: Charles Scribner's Sons.

Why the Wilderness Society. (1935, September). *The Living Wilderness.*

Ecological Conscience. (1947) *Bulletin of the Garden Club of America, p. 49.*

A Sand County Almanac. (1949) New York: Oxford University Press.

REFERENCES

Brooks, P. (1980, September). The wilderness ideal: How Aldo Leopold and Bob Marshall articulated the need for preservation. *The Living Wilderness,* pp. 4–12.

Errington, P. L. (1948). In appreciation of Aldo Leopold. *The Journal of Wildlife Management, 4,* pp. 341–350.

Flader, S. L. (1974). *Thinking Like A Mountain: Aldo Leopold and the Evolution of an Ecological Attitude Toward Deer, Wolves, and Forests.* Columbia: University of Missouri Press.

Flader, S. L. (1979, December). Aldo Leopold and the Wilderness Idea. *The Living Wilderness.* pp. 4–8.

Gibbons, B. (1981). Aldo Leopold: A durable scale of values. *National Geographic, 160,* pp. 682–708.

Knudson, D. (1984) *Outdoor Recreation* (rev. ed.). New York: MacMillan Publishing Co.

Mann, R. (1948, July). The Conservation Conscience. *Audubon,* pp. 211–215.

Mann, R. (1948, July). Aldo Leopold: Priest and Prophet. *American Forests,* pp. 23, 42–43.

Meine, C. (1988). *Aldo Leopold: His Life and Work.* Madison: The University of Wisconsin Press.

Nash, R. (1973). *Wilderness and the American Mind.* (rev. ed.). New Haven: Yale University Press.

Nash, R. (1976, June/July). Elder of the tribe: Aldo Leopold. *Backpacker,* pp. 21–22, 66, 68, 71.

Schoenfeld, C. (1978, May). Aldo Leopold Remembered. *Audubon,* pp. 28–37.

Tanner, T. (Ed.). (1987). *Aldo Leopold: The Man and His Legacy.* Ankeny: Soil Conservation Society of America.

Taylor, J. W. (1987, November/December). Aldo Leopold: A Celebration of the Land Ethic. *The Conservationist,* pp. 12–15.

Tindall, B. (1968, October). Aldo Leopold: A Philosophy and a Challenge. *Parks and Recreation,* pp. 28–30.

Wellman, J. D. (1987). *Wildland Recreation Policy: An Introduction.* New York: John Wiley and Sons.

21

GEORGE BUTLER

1894–1985

By Joseph J. Bannon
University of Illinois

AAHPERD Archives

"I have a feeling that you exaggerate my fame. . . ."

Letter to the Author
3/20/83

One of the great privileges of my life was my association with George Butler, who embodied all the qualities that enrich life. I am sure he influenced everyone who came in touch with him. I often heard him tell of recreation experiences with his wife, Becky, and sons, George, Jr. and Bob. He did this with tremendous enthusiasm, and I knew this was a person who truly believed in the experience of leisure. George Butler was a humble man, discouraging all recognition of himself. However, he was recognized by his peers by election to the Academy of Leisure Science. When I told him of this honor, he replied, "There are so many who are more deserving."

George D. Butler died in Sarasota, Florida on May 21, 1985. His ideas and contributions are well known to many of us in the park and recreation profession. Men, women, but especially young people in communities throughout the United States are indebted to him for his contribution to the park and recreation field. He was one of the first to emphasize the importance of parks and recreation in human development. The open-space standards he developed in the 1930s have been used as guidelines by community leaders and educators ever since. The open space where a child plays today is in many cases a result of his foresight and wisdom. In his book, *Introduction to Community Recreation,* he challenged government to accept the responsibility of providing park and recreation programs to its citizens. Through his efforts, many communities in the United States established and organized recreation programs.

In addition, George Butler was one of the pioneers in recreation education. In the 1930s, he became one of the first instructors in the National Recreation School, and was one of the first to recognize the importance of research in the park and recreation profession. He served for 43 years as the director of research for the National Recreation Association (NRA). In cooperation with federal agencies, he directed national studies of municipal parks in 1930, 1935, and 1940, and was responsible for a series of NRA surveys of community recreation. The information in these studies has served as the basis of much of the research that is conducted today.

He is the author of many books. However, the one he was most proud of was *Pioneers in Public Recreation.* This work was an historical synopsis of individuals who contributed most to our profession. It was interesting to note he did not include himself among this group. Those of us who knew him know this was an error.

George Butler gave parks and recreation its finest interpretation. In his practical and common sense way, he taught us the importance recreation plays in maintaining a high level quality of life. George Butler's interests in community affairs were many. A service that was of utmost importance to him was his membership on the Recreation Commission of Leonia,

New Jersey—his hometown. He served on this Board from 1946 to 1962. The gymnasium in the Leonia Recreation Center is named in his honor.

Few people know of the courage George Butler demonstrated as a soldier in World War I. His valor was recognized by his receiving one of France's highest honors—the Croix de Guerre Medal. The inscription on it reads, "George Butler had shown proof of the qualities of courage and endurance while transporting, day and night, over roads under bombardment, the wounded of the 128th Division of the French Army."

George Butler is truly one of the pioneers of the recreation and park movement. He was a great thinker, wise in action, a doer, a giver, and an understanding man. His life's work will survive, and his memory will be long cherished.

In our present society, with its emphasis on social services and the degree of leisure many of us enjoy—or shall enjoy when retired or when the promises of technology increasingly release us from drudgery—it is difficult to comprehend the resistance these two social concepts encountered in the early part of the 19th century. Our Anglican heritage of Puritanism, with its emphasis on the virtue of ceaseless (and sinless) hard work, and the parish poorhouse for those less fortunate than ourselves, were roots to the kinds of barriers the pioneers in recreation and parks encountered. What we now take for granted conceptually—even if we still struggle for funding—are programs and ideas about public recreation and leisure, which are the direct result of the efforts of the earlier proponents of communal recreation and parks. While much has been written about the organizational history of parks and recreation, little was known about the individual pioneers who made parks and recreation an everyday social reality for all of us. That is, until George Butler, himself a pioneer, undertook the task of gathering their biographies into one volume: *Pioneers in Public Recreation* (1965). Although this book was a product of his retirement, he did not include himself among those whom he honored for their contributions to the inception and development of communal parks and recreation. This was not false modesty, or a hope that another would document his contribution, but a lifelong, genuine modesty on his part in the human scene. Whether it was the risks of war, or the more benign challenges of fostering new concepts on his society, George Butler performed excellently, yet systematically declined the limelight.

George Butler worked with many of the pioneers he included in his tribute, though that was not a criterion for selection. Because of his central role on the staff of the National Recreation Association (now NRPA) from 1919–1962, he was perforce a participant or supporter of most of the significant accomplishments of our professional predecessors. As noted by Joseph Prendergast, Executive Director of NRPA at the time George Butler published his tribute to pioneers, "Perhaps not so well known, but familiar to all his fellow workers, are the uncompromising honest and salty good humor that evoke these personalities as three dimensional human beings, rather than cardboard heroes. In these pages they live again through their work." (Foreword, v)

> Joseph Lee; Clark W. Hetherington, Henry S. Curtis; Ernst Hermann; Edward B. DeGroot; George E. Dickie; Luther H. Gulick; Lee F. Hanmer; George E. Johnson; Otto T. Mallery; Virgil K. Brown; Howard S. Braucher; Lebert H. Weir; James E. Rogers; Charles H. English; Arthur Williams; Abbie Condit; Dorothy Enderis; Josephine D. Randall; Clarence E. Brewer; and Ernest T. Attwell. Other Early Pioneers: Ellen M. Tower; Jane Addams; Robert Garrett; Gustavus T. Kirby; Mrs. Willoughby Rodman; Beulah Kennard; Seth T. Stewart; C. B. Raitt; Clarence A. Perry; Thomas S. Settle; Charles F. Weller; and John Bradford. Other Early Leaders: George A. Parker; Theodore Wirth; John McLaren; Stephen T. Mather; James H. McCurdy; William A. Burdick; Jay B. Nash; Peter W. Dykema; Elizabeth Burchanel; Mrs. Eva Whiting White; and John H. Finley.

Not only are individuals acknowledged for their specific contributions, but *Pioneers in Public Recreation,* (1965) also documents the roots of many of the major service and professional organizations that we are familiar with: The American Institute of Park Executives, The American Recreation Society, The National Conference of State Parks, and The National Recreation and Park Association. Those individuals selected by George Butler are generally the men and women who saw a need for these organizations, then founded and directed them. Also, most of the persons selected by George Butler had some connection with NRPA. Again, this was not the basis of his selection, but emerged as he began to refine the list of those on whom he would concentrate. Thus, the story of *Pioneers in Public Recreation,* (1965) serves also as a history of the NRPA, in its 80 years of formal evolution, and more generally as a record of the origins and early development of public recreation in the United States.

With this array of pioneers, George Butler could easily describe the public recreation movement as "one of the outstanding developments of the Twentieth Century." Butler was motivated to write this book because he feared few of those who would succeed these leaders, or benefit from their insightful work, would have ever have heard of them! The same can be argued for this present volume, where George Butler finally receives his rightful prominence. While I knew him personally and worked with him for many years, how many of my students would have known him otherwise, not to mention subsequent generations?

Although George Butler recognized the critical role of group work, legislation, and the value of developments in related professional fields, it is a truism that such composite achievements are never possible without notable individual contributions. For group action to occur in any endeavor, it inevitably requires the "imagination foresight, convictions, and actions of individuals who recognized recreation as a basic need and proceeded to do something about providing it. Public recreation has attained its present form and status largely as the result of the work of individuals who as pioneers prepared the way for others to follow." (Preface, vii)

Much as this present volume is limited to key pioneers, Aristotle to Brightbill—in *Pioneers in Public Recreation*, (1965) George Butler carefully selected those who would appear. He wished to cover the scope of the last century's history of parks and recreation by discussing the contributions of selective, *indicative* pioneers. The "salty good humor" is evidenced by Butler's willingness to discuss a pioneer's shortcomings if these were significant or influenced a contribution.

Of course, everyone involved in the early development of public recreation was a pioneer simply by involvement, much as those who crossed our plains were pioneers. Thus, it became important for Butler's work, and for this present book as well, to establish guidelines for pioneers who were a cut above the rest, or who were indicative of groups of others. Those selected for Butler's book served in public recreation before the end of World War I (which is possibly a simple way of excluding himself since he was serving in the War). Also Butler excluded those whose contributions were more local or regional, with little or no national or international influence. Certainly, Butler's influence has been global. The opening quote to this chapter is in response to my report on the popularity of *Introduction to Community Recreation* (1976) in Cape Town, South Africa!

The easiest pioneers to select, according to Butler, were those whose ideas, actions, or writings brought about distinctive happenings in public recreation, and whose leadership was generally recognized by their contemporaries. Again, this criterion easily includes George Butler among post-World War I pioneers. Since conspicuous achievement was also one of Butler's selection criteria, it is even more amazing that he remains among these pioneers considering his modesty and genuine self-effacement. These, of course, are compensated for by his substantial written works. The most indicative criterion, which portrays Butler fully, was his personal knowledge of the work of most of these 53 pioneers. These were not selected, I might add, because of any personal involvement with their work, since many of them preceded his own appearance in public recreation, but his awareness of these significant contributions and, in many cases, his having had the honor of knowing them. Such scope and breadth of knowledge, without any self-aggrandizement, is truly a Butler trait. He familiarized himself with these notable pioneers through their writings, or more fortuitously through personal association, because of his own position at the center of the early developments of public recreation. Although not included among them in his book, he certainly is with these pioneers in spirit.

Enough progress had been made between the two world wars by the initial group of pioneers that Butler acknowledges as his own contemporaries, for him to publish his 1936, 400-page book on *Playgrounds: Their Administration and Operation*. To Butler, by this time, the "value and need of playgrounds are taken for granted in this volume." The scope of this seminal book offers visionary and practical information ranging from the physical playground, the sorts of leadership required, the activities and programs that can take their place as well as the various administrative and practical problems likely to arise. Although there had been much written prior to his book on the need for playgrounds, and their design and equipment, very little had been published about their administration. In essence, George Butler pioneered one of the first problem-solving or decision-making texts in public recreation.

Playgrounds was directed to playground administrators, playground staff, and to teachers of playground courses in schools and colleges. Thus, everyone likely to be involved in the issue of playground management and effectiveness was considered in this text. By the time this book was published, the playground had rapidly expanded beyond its original goal of being a play area for children, to include youth, as well as adults. Thus, the scope of Butler's discussion was to acknowledge that playgrounds were no longer confined to children. Leisure was not something confined to childhood, nor to time squeezed between chores. Other groups were gaining freedom from stultifying labor, or from a merciless work ethic that scorned play for the working class, especially in large cities. These other groups, too, required play areas for more youthful or adult leisure activities.

Regardless of the expanding demands of these latter groups for broader recreation and park service, Butler limited his book to playgrounds, since these were used by all age groups, even if such areas were incorporated within larger parks. He also excluded from his book consideration of planning, acquiring, organizing, and establishing a playground, or much discussion of specific playground games or rules. Ample literature on these aspects of playground administration already existed in Post Depression America. By honing his subject carefully, Butler emerges as one of the first recreation professionals to concentrate on the administration and management of leisure services more than a half-century ago. Planning, problem-solving, administration, management—catch words today for all of us—began to emerge in these pages as synonyms for the more homey terms Butler was comfortable with: leading/leaders, operating/operators, authorities, conducting, etc. In fact, most of Butler's writing is of a refreshingly earlier style, virtually free of academic jargon and pompous inflation.

In fact, his books, other than their content, would serve as a good example for teaching recreation and park students to write simply, directly, and with feeling.

Butler put it simply: "The function of playground administration is to bring to reality the limitless possibilities which the playground affords for fun and good citizenship." (p. 5) In this handbook, Butler covers various management steps and methods for achieving this broader function. Butler also provides arguments for the necessity of playground leaders, or what we now call facilitators. Although community officials recognized the value of playgrounds—the outcome of the work of earlier pioneers—they still had to be convinced about the value of leaders. In order to make a convincing case, Butler had to also elaborate on leadership skills, apart from those parents or the local police force might have for playground supervision. This case, of course, is very well known to us all, though Butler had to make it, and convincingly, if playground administration was to succeed as a prescribed need.

Butler further made a clear distinction between leadership and supervision of play activities, relieving recreation professionals of the onus of law enforcement when there was considerable political pressure to police children and young adults. Butler realized, as we certainly do, that nothing kills a recreation program quicker than the presence of chaperones or guards, whatever their title. But more specifically than those leaders who influence or guide the young is the manager: the one who plans, works, and provides for areas of play, arranges for equipment and maintenance, prepares the budget, secures funding, selects playground leaders, and supervises the overall program so that more inspirational leadership and guidance can occur. What is especially useful in Butler's discussion is the position descriptions included, ranging from a superintendent of recreation to life guards. I dare say, many of these well-thought-out and concise job responsibilities, as well as his representative examination questions, civil service guidelines, sample job applications, training programs, and staff rating systems formed the basis of many personnel and job recruitment efforts.

In addition to concentrating on the enhancement of leadership abilities among staff, Butler also stressed the value of developing leadership ability in the children who used the playground facility, as well as encouraging a range of volunteer activities for adults to participate more directly in playground management. By concentrating on program planning, and particular programs for various seasons (by week!), the organization and operation of various activities, the array of administrative problems—from personnel to financing, public relations, and operational problems, George Butler very early, and in useful detail, encompassed the full array of responsibility areas encountered by a recreation administrator.

About ten years later, George Butler prepared *Recreation Areas: Their Design and Equipment* (1947) for the National Recreation Association. This volume was an update of previous volumes (1928, 1938) in response to the continued expansion of recreation and park facilities throughout the United States, in large and small communities alike, with the concomitant need for propagating the principles underlying the design and operation of recreation areas. This text, unlike the previous one which focused on administering play areas, concentrates on planning recreation areas, especially play areas and fields. The book offered planning principles, practical suggestions for design of areas, as well as detailed information on facilities, structures, and equipment. The book provided many examples of mostly urban post-war municipal recreation areas, which were well-designed, often elaborate, and extensive, with discussion of how these notable examples could be adapted to smaller communities. This book was a compendium of the information and experience of many recreation workers and planners, which Butler brought together and presented for wider dissemination.

Recreation Areas discusses the types of municipal recreation areas a planner is involved with, their design and construction features, playground apparatus needed, swimming pools, facilities and equipment, buildings, areas for sports and games, the neighborhood or housing project playground, the playfield and athletic field, landscape design and development, and winter use of areas.

For those of us who grew up in cities and smaller towns after World War II, this book illustrates, both literally and figuratively, that what we accepted as our childhood's given right to innovative play areas, was actually the hard work of many foresighted, dedicated individuals. For those of us not so fortunate as to have been raised on farms or in villages, this book provides excellent testimony, as well as practical advice, on how to bring the miraculous wonders of more open, natural spaces to the greater confinements of populated areas. For this effort, alone, we are grateful to George Butler's vision and persistence.

The book for which George Butler is best remembered is *Introduction to Community Recreation*, prepared for the National Recreation and Park Association as were most of his works. It is a comprehensive overview of the nature and significance of community recreation as this evolved into an increasingly important part of American life. Again, Butler's emphasis is on suburban and urban recreation programs and park services, but the material is equally applicable to smaller municipalities, and the focus of the book is on the governmental agencies that provide most community recreation services. However, the value of this important book is that it is also useful for private or voluntary agencies that provide community recreation programs, which makes it invaluable as different government philosophies of social service prevail.

Over a span of twenty-five years, the *Introduction to Community Recreation* went through five editions, not only because of its usefulness, but to keep up with the dramatic expansions in recreation since the end of World War II. The book was written, as well, for the expansive audience: educators and students, park and recreation workers, park and recreation board members, and local officials and community leaders. With typical modesty, Butler attributes the value of his book to the fact that it incorporates "the best thinking of many leaders in the recreation and park movement and describes procedures that have proved most successful." (xiii) He also acknowledges the role of NRPA in contributing to the book's content, and the many recreation examples he uses from a wide range of communities throughout the United States.

Before imparting examples of successful park and recreation programs, Butler concentrates on the more difficult task of defining recreation, or re-creation, to include both play and re-creation of one's energy, spirit, or of childhood's more playful creations. Even more so than education, Butler perceived recreation as applying to all groups, and throughout one's life span.

Once he defines the scope of recreation, Butler also deals with the value and purpose of recreation, its various theoretical underpinnings— from the surplus-energy theory to the catharsis theory to those more broadly based. He admits, as we all do, that the weakest part of recreation and park research has been its theoretical bases. Butler relies more on a more-inclusive explanation of recreation as a form of self-expression, which seeks no reward, and is carried on for its own sake. This dramatically expands recreation beyond play, and beyond activities that are recognizably leisure pursuits, and broadens the definition of recreation to encompass its equally dramatic expansion in American society. "Recreation, then, is more like a tool; it is in tune with nature and therefore is an essential part of living, of direct benefit to the individual. To have value as recreation, activities must be suited as (a person's) physical, mental, and emotional needs." (p. 8) Butler was also alert, and quite early, to the differences between leisure and recreation, a distinction that now forms distinct areas for research and education in our profession.

Butler recognized the broad range of activities that can be considered recreation, from beneficial to harmful. However, only those that are considered by the public to be personally and socially useful, and which can be provided by a community agency, receive his attention. He resolves the various theories and definitions of recreation by considering recreation not as any specific activity, but the result of an activity, and in this text concentrates only on those that are publicly acceptable and fundable.

With this broad yet careful distinction in mind, Butler then discusses the importance of recreation to individuals and communities; the wide array of agencies that provide recreational opportunities, from national to volunteer programs; leadership in community recreation: including recreation and park department personnel, educational programs for park leaders, selecting and maintaining a staff, and the use of volunteers; recreation areas and facilities; municipal recreation planning, including special areas and structures; design and equipment of recreation areas; activities and program planning; operation of areas and facilities; program features and service; and organization and administration problems in community recreation programs.

Thus, over a career that covered nearly half a century, and this book that was rewritten and revised throughout a quarter of a century, there is very little of what concerns our profession today that was not scrutinized and discussed by George Butler. He is not only one of the pioneers in recreation and parks, he fits comfortably and deservedly among its forefathers.

PARTIAL LIST OF BUTLER'S PUBLICATIONS

Play Areas—Their Design and Equipment. (1928).

Playgrounds: Their Administration and Operation. (1936). New York: A. S. Barnes and Company, Inc.

New Play Areas—Their Design and Equipment. (1938).

Recreation Areas: Their Design and Equipment. (1947). New York: A. S. Barnes and Company.

Pioneers in Public Recreation. (1965). Minneapolis: Burgess Publishing Company.

Introduction to Community Recreation. (1976). New York: McGraw-Hill. (Previous editions, 1949, 1959, 1967, 1968).

22

MARTIN NEUMEYER

1892–1978

ESTHER NEUMEYER

1893–1975

By Hilmi Ibrahim
Whittier College

Courtesy Marjorie R. Zickfeld

"*The tone of any society is conditioned by the quality of its leisure whether it be restricted to a few or indulged by the many.*"

1936:12

Martin Henry Neumeyer was born in Jackson, Missouri on October 8, 1892. He attended De Pauw University where he obtained his B.A. in 1919, and was married the same year to Esther Sternberg. He had planned to join the ministry, and obtained his Bachelor of Divinity degree from Garrett Theological Seminary in 1921, he decided to pursue a career in sociology instead and obtained an M.A. from Northwestern University in 1922 and a Ph.D. from the University of Chicago in 1929.

He joined the Department of Sociology at the University of Southern California in 1927 as assistant professor, was promoted to associate professor in 1931, and to professor in 1938. He served as managing editor of *Sociology and Social Research* from 1954–1958, and as editor of SSR from 1961–1973. He became professor emeritus in 1961. He was elected President of the Pacific Sociological Society in 1941.

Esther Neumeyer was born in White Cloud, Kansas, August 30, 1893. She attended State Normal School (now State College), Cape Girardeau, Missouri, where she received a certificate in 1916; later she received an A.B. degree in 1930 and an A.M. degree in 1932 with a major in sociology from the University of Southern California. Her teaching experience included rural schools in S.E. Missouri, (1912–1915); junior high school in Decatur, Illinois (1916–1919); and public schools in Winnebago, Illinois (1919–1920). In Chicago she served as a social worker in the Chicago Women's (Protestant) Protective Association. In Los Angeles, California she taught in various schools, and in the continuation education program until 1950.

Her organizational membership included various Methodist churches, where her father and husband were ministers, and the Wilshire United Methodist Church; the Cleonion Literacy Society; Alpha Kappa Delta, Sociology Honor Society; Euterpe Opera (L.A. Chapter); Faculty Wives Club and Town and Gown, University of Southern California; and the Ebell Club of Los Angeles. Her name appeared in *Who's Who Among Women*. (Fourth Edition, 1966–67:850)

Martin Neumeyer was one of the very first sociologists to give attention to the play, recreation, and leisure phenomena. He published a 119-page mimeographed work entitled *Sociology of Play* in 1930 which he used in teaching Sociology 110, by the same title, at U.S.C. during the first semester in 1930. Immediately following the title page he placed a poem by Dennis A. McCarthey which read:

Give Them A Place to Play

Plenty of room for dives and dens,
(Glitter and glare and sin!)
Plenty of room for prison pens,
(Gather the criminals in!)

Plenty of room for jails and courts,
(Willing enough to pay;)
But never a place for the lads to race,
No, never a place to play!

Plenty of room for shops and stores,
(Mammon must have the best!)
Plenty of room for running sores
That rot in the city's breast!
Plenty of room for the lure that lead
The hearts of youth astray,
But never a cent on a playground spent
No, never a place to play!

Plenty of room for schools and halls,
Plenty of room for art;
Plenty of room for teas and balls,
Playform, stage and mart.
Proud is the city—she finds a place
For many a fad today,
But she's more than blind if she fails to find
A place for the boys to play.

Give them a chance for innocent sport,
Give them a chance for fun—
Better a playground plot than a court
And a jail when the harm is done!
Give them a chance—if you stint them now,
Tomorrow you'll have to pay
A larger bill for a greater ill,
So give them a place to play!

The purpose of *Sociology of Play* was to serve as a manual and source book for the study of play life in its sociological aspects. Both the book and the course Sociology 110: Sociology of Play, were designed around the following:

I. Introductory Note
The nature and requirements of the course, investigation, and research; sources of information

II. Play as a Factor in Modern Life
    A. The extent of play and leisure time activities
    B. The need and function of play

III. Theories of Play

    A. The early views of play
    B. The biological theories of play
    C. The psychological theories of play
    D. The sociological theories of play

IV. Play and the Group

    A. The play group as composed of interacting personalities
    B. Play as a cultural pattern, with special reference to the game and the dance
    C. Play and the gang
    D. Play and the crowd

V. The Development of the Play Movement

    A. The meaning of a social movement
    B. The play movement abroad
    C. The play movement in the United States
    D. Recent trends of the play movement

VI. Play Activities and Interests:

    A. General classification of play activities
    B. Play objectives
    C. Provision of play space and facilities
    D. The organization and administration of community recreation
    E. The program of activities

VII. The Community Play Program

    A. The problem of community recreation
    B. Play objectives
    C. Provision of play space and facilities
    D. The organization and administration of community recreation
    E. The program of activities

VIII. Commercial Amusements

    A. The nature and extent of commercial amusements
    B. The motion picture
    C. The modern dance

IX. Play Leadership

    A. The significance and types of play leaders
    B. The qualifications and training of play leaders.

He believed that while there was enough literature published on play, there was enough material dealing with it from a sociological point of view. Following is the list of readings suggested for the course, including the work of the man who initiated the course, Dr. Clarence E. Rainwater:

Bowen, W. P. and Mitchell, E. D. (1923). *The Theory of Organized Play Its Nature and Significance,* Barnes.
Curtis, Henry S. (1915). *Education Through Play.* Macmillan.
Curtis, Henry S. (1915). *Play Movement and Its Significance.* The Macmillan Co.
Cutten, F. B. (1926). *The Threats of Leisure.* Yale University Press.
Gulick, Luther H. (1920). *A Philosophy of Play.* Association Press.
Lee, Joseph (1915). *Play in Education.* Macmillan.
Lehman, H. C. and Witty, P. A. (1927). *The Psychology of Play Activities.* Barnes.
May, Herbert L. and Petgen, Dorothy (1928). *Leisure and Its Use: Some International Observations.* Barnes.
Nash, Jay B. (1927). *The Organization and Administration of Playgrounds and Recreation.* Barnes.
Rainwater, Clarence, (1922). *The Play Movement in the United States: A Study in Community Recreation.* University of Chicago Press.
Steiner, Hesse F. (1925). *Community Organization—A Study of Its Theory and Current Practice.* Century Co.
Thrasher, F. M. (1927). *The Gang.* University of Chicago Press.
Wood, Arthur (1928). *Community Problems.* The Century Co.

In 1935, H.S. Barnes of New York published the Neumeyers, *Leisure And Recreation: A Study of Leisure and Recreation in Their Sociological Aspects.* In the Introduction (Chapter I), the authors stated that society may find its greatest asset in the constructively-used leisure of its citizens, but leisure may become also the greatest menace to our civilization. (p. 1) The purpose of the volume was to point out the needs and problems and to describe the conditions of leisure and recreation in this society.

In Chapter II, entitled The New Leisure, the Neumeyers reviewed leisure among "primitive," intermediate, and modern societies and its recent extension. They attributed the growth of leisure in the 20th century to the machine. The machine had, directly or indirectly contributed to reduction of the working period, unemployment, modern convenience, transportation and communication, vacations and holidays, and early retirement. (pp. 19–25)

The conditioning factors of leisure, asserted the Neumeyers in Chapters III and IV (pp. 25–52), were geographical and ecological (natural resources, climate, topography, and geography); population (size, density, composition and distribution) . . . inventions and discoveries; economic conditions; political organization; education; and community life.

Chapter IV dealt with the changing uses of leisure. According to the authors, "when the work period was reduced the workers did not dash wildly to schools, libraries, museums, operas, and concerts to improve themselves," but commercial amusement centers became crowded (p. 53). Yet home activities increased more rapidly than outside activities. People became engaged in "such things as cultivating hobbies, caring for home grounds, reading magazines and newspapers, reading books, conversation, listening to radio, caring for flowers, carpentry and caring for vegetable gardens and pets. (p. 54) But the desires of people were more important to the authors than what people actually did. A study of the National Recreation Association was quoted showing that of the 34,683 wishes expressed by 5,000 people, 22,731 were for outside activity. These were not available because of the Depression. The Neumeyers concluded that special problems would arise in idleness and spectatoritis.

In Leisure and Personality (Chapter VI), the authors suggested that civilization cannot be measured in terms of mere material success but also in the progressive development in ourselves and others, of rational and rich personality, and in the establishment of a social order conducive to this end (p. 73). Although the term personality is baffling, nonetheless it encompasses certain traits which have an affect-effect relationship to leisure. Traits such as physical features, intelligence, temperament, character, concept of self, and social expression are very much affected by the social environment, including leisure. Personality grows through leisure and recreation. Character which is part of personality, is built through controlled recreation. Uncontrolled recreation and misuse of leisure lead to undesirable habits and attitudes such as drugs, "drinking, vice, gambling, dishonesty, disobedience, disloyalty" and others. (p. 82)

"It is important for social as well as personal welfare that the extra hours of leisure be used for personal cultivation and the improvement of the social order," (p. 85) so stated the Neumeyers in Chapter VII, Preparing for Leisure. But how?. Education for Leisure is the answer. Formal education alone will not achieve the desired end, although it may furnish a background. Public school curriculum should give consideration to the following (pp. 91–97):

- Wholesome reading and literary appreciation
- Creative literary expression
- Music and art
- Dancing and rhythmics
- Dramatics and pageantry
- Creative arts and crafts
- Scientific experimentation
- Games and sports

- Nature studies and activities
- Social recreation and sociability

There is also education through leisure. New interests are developed and new skills are acquired through leisure.

Although recreation activities are universal phenomena, they have witnessed an unprecedented increase in modern life (Chapter VIII). This is evidenced by the growth of public recreation and rise of commercial recreation. In the past it was thought that "play" was mainly a childhood activity; now the concept of recreation has grown in preference, being more conclusive and descriptive of the phenomenon at hand. The early theories of play and recreation were biological and physiological in character, followed by psychological interpretations, with more sociological contributions by the turn of the century (Chapters IX and X).

In addition to the elemental biological wishes, such as appetites, and thirst, human wishes may be grouped into:

1. desire for new experience,
2. desire for security,
3. desire for response,
4. desire for recognition, and
5. desire for aid.

Interests overlap with wishes and both "represent psychological inclinations and tendencies which predispose or impel a person towards or against certain types of activity." (p. 154) Whether an activity is recreation "depends on the attitude toward it, the primary motive behind it, and the conditions under which it is undertaken." (p. 160)

The Neumeyers believed that most writers have overlooked the importance of the group aspects of recreation (Chapter XI). They advocated that it is possible to discern major social processes in the recreation group, even in commercial recreation. Interaction, competition, accommodation, assimilation and imitation are but some of the social processes that take place in recreation groups. "Sports and games, shows and commercial attractions, dances, mass parades, and recreation fads partake of the nature of crowd behavior. (p. 172) On the other hand, recreation represents the culture from which it arose.

Influences of age, sex, and race were discussed by the authors in Chapter XII. They stated that each age period had its special interests, and cited studies that showed boys preferring active games and girls sedentary ones. (p. 190) Their desire to play school is a sort of compensation for their "inferior status." (p. 192)

The American society had gone through unequal social or cultural change which explained, to a considerable extent, the prevalence of social maladjustment as "spontaneous play groups so prevalent in crowded areas of the city are gangs in embryo form." (p. 200) The quest for new experiences seemed to be the most fundamental drive. In Chapter XIII, the authors advocated that leisure may be the root of many evils, such as delinquency and gangs, citing seven studies conducted in Los Angeles, Omaha, and New York to support their view. (pp. 201–206) Another outcome of the cultural lag was hoboism and wandering youth. And although shelters and camps were provided for them, recreational facilities or activities were not included, a must if there were to be any rehabilitation. (p. 211)

Commercial amusements such as motion pictures, radio, dance halls, amusement parks, and theatre exert tremendous influence (Chapter XIV), yet they "render a worthwhile service. Their value depends largely upon the quality of entertainment which they provide." (p. 244)

In Chapter XV, the authors reviewed the recreation movement in the United States as "a positive movement rather than a negative one because it seeks to bring about adjustments to situations through the organization of activities." (p. 249) The most phenomenal growth in recreation in the United States was promoted by two types of communal organizations: the public and semipublic. But in other lands (Chapter XVI), in Europe Asia, Latin America, and even Africa, the recreation movement has touched every country, manifesting itself differently "due to the divergencies in the social, political, economic and cultural heritage and geographic conditions." (p. 205)

In Chapter XVII, the author showed that public control and provisions of recreation in the United States is a "growing tendency as it should be, for the problem is so great and the opportunities so vast that private agencies are inadequate to meet the situation." (p. 322) But the activities provided by semipublic, private, and commercial agencies usually preceded the introduction of public provisions for recreation (Chapter XVII). Among these are some voluntary organizations whose activities are ends in themselves and are enjoyed for their own sake. (p. 360)

Recreation leadership means instruction and guidance (Chapter XIX), and the need is growing. "Few fields of service offer greater opportunities for intimate and direct influence depending upon the personality and character of the leader." (p. 368) Although there were few openings in the nascent recreation field, the author suggested that a college student interested in pursuing a career in recreation should combine courses in physical education, psychology, speech, music, and social science.

The study of recreation (Chapter XX) is difficult because of its complexity and its many variables. Yet it can be done through three techniques: the recreation survey, including observations; the questionnaire; and the recreation interview/case method. The authors warned that "the recency of interest in the problems of leisure and recreation account largely for the lack of scientific procedure in this field." (p. 387)

Leisure and Recreation was well received. A Scientific Book Club reviewer wrote:

> The authors evidently are well versed in their subject and their methods are in accordance with the standards of sound scholarship. Moreover, they clothe the results of their work in very readable style. While the book is intended especially for the use of students and the guidance of educators and recreation leaders, the ordinary layman who wants to inform himself on its theme will find it interesting reading.

And the *Journal of Home Economics* wrote:

> Dr. and Mrs. Neumeyer have made a fine contribution in this volume to our knowledge of the social aspects of human behavior in this particular field. Dr. Neumeyer is associate professor of sociology in the University of Southern California. . . . The book is apparently designed primarily as a textbook for students in normal schools and colleges, but it will be read with profit by educators, recreation leaders and social workers, and it is sufficiently interesting to appeal to the 'general reader' who is concerned with any of the problems of modern society. It is abundantly documented and its treatment is comprehensive.

PUBLICATIONS OF THE NEUMEYERS:

Sociology of Play. (1930). Mimeographed.

with Esther Neumeyer. (1936). *Leisure and Recreation*. New York: A. S. Barnes.

International Trends in Juvenile Delinquency. (1956). *Sociology and Social Research, 41* pp. 94–99.

Areas for Research in Leisure and Recreation. (1958). *Sociology and Social Research, 43* pp. 90–96.

Juvenile Delinquency in Modern Society. (1961). Princeton, N.J.: Van Nostrand.
Community Coordinating Councils As a Social Movement. (1961). *Sociology and Social Research, 45* pp. 265–273.

THOMAS E. RIVERS

1892-1977

By Charles Hartsoe
Virginia Commonwealth University

Courtesy Dr. Charles Hartsoe, Virginia Commonwealth University

"Building a Better World Through Recreation."

Thomas E. Rivers' career in recreation spanned a period of approximately 60 years. While recognized as a national leader during the formative years of the recreational movement, Rivers' principal influence was in developing recreation and leisure services on an international level. He was one of the leading forces in the creation of the World Leisure and Recreation Association (WLRA), and served as director general of WLRA from its inception in 1956 until his retirement in 1974.

Thomas Rivers was born on October 6, 1892, in Meridan, Mississippi. Upon graduation from Mount Hermon Preparatory School in Northfield, Massachusetts, he enrolled in the University of Wisconsin where he pursued an undergraduate program in social sciences. Late in his career, he was awarded an honorary Doctor of Humanities degree from Springfield College.

At the time of his graduation from college, World War I was still in progress. Shortly after receiving his degree, Thomas Rivers was inducted into the Army and assigned to a newly created civilian agency whose mission was to help local communities provide off-base leisure time activities for military personnel. War Camp Community Services (WCCS) was an organization created by the Playground and Recreation Association (now NRPA) to deal with the unprecedented leisure needs of a newly mobilized national military force. It was this early experience in dealing with the leisure needs of military personnel that helped shape Rivers' life long career.

Following World War I, Rivers continued on the staff of an expanded National Recreation Association, parent of the War Camp Community Service. Over the succeeding years, he held a number of prominent national staff positions, including that of a southern field representative, manager of personnel and placement services, secretary of the National Recreation School, and secretary of the National Recreation Congress, a position which he held for over 30 years. While on the staff of the National Recreation Association, Tom Rivers developed a reputation as one of the most effective fund raisers for recreation in the nation.

Rivers' interest in international recreation was undoubtedly stimulated by his responsibility for planning the first International Recreation Congress, held in Los Angeles, preceding the 1932 Olympic Games. This Congress, hosted by the National Recreation Association, attracted more than 100 delegates from 40 foreign countries. The success of this meeting prompted plans for a second international meeting to coincide with the 1936 Berlin Olympics. However, the potential for Adolph Hitler to expand Nazi propaganda caused the NRA to boycott the second international meeting and it was not until 1956 that another major international meeting on recreation and leisure was held. Rivers' global interest in recreation had continued in the intervening war years, and following World War II, he was instrumental in establishing a new International Recreation Service within the structure of the National Recreation Association.

The development of this new service was stimulated by an extensive worldwide trip made by Tom Rivers and his wife, Ruth, in 1952. During this trip, Rivers made contact with recreation leaders and public officials in several countries, including Italy, Spain, Portugal, Greece, Egypt, Jordan, Lebanon, Pakistan, India, Thailand, Philippines, Hong Kong, and Japan. While in Japan, he presented medals and citations from the National Recreation Association of the U.S.A. to several Japanese recreation leaders and represented the NRA at the Sixth Japanese Recreation Congress. This exploratory trip by Rivers made clear the exceptional opportunity for further development of recreation and leisure on an international scale. In September 1953, the National Recreation Association established an office in the Carnegie Endowment International Center to house the International Recreation Services headed by Tom Rivers. This new location was across from the United Nations in New York City.

The early efforts of this international initiative were focused upon responding to increasing requests from individuals and organizations in other nations seeking information, advice, and literature on America's experiences in establishing community recreation programs. In addition, formal relationships were established with other U.S. and United Nations organizations active in the international welfare scene. With help from the U.S. Department of State, Thomas Rivers was instrumental in organizing a Cooperative Community Recreation Project in which 19 foreign authorities responsible for recreation and youth services in 13 countries were brought to the United States for 4 months to study the recreation movement in America.

Rivers was soon to develop a reputation as the "global ambassador of recreation." In 1955, he undertook another major international journey which took him to 22 countries where he met with both professional and citizen leaders interested in recreation. This visit along with his 1952 trip helped lay the groundwork for organizing the 1956 International Recreation Congress held in Philadelphia, Pennsylvania. This Congress, planned by Tom Rivers, commemorated the golden anniversary of the National Recreation Association, and also served to launch the creation of the International Recreation Association. With the active leadership and support of the National Recreation Association, the International Recreation Association was established in Philadelphia on October 3, 1956. Thomas E. Rivers was appointed director general of the new organization, a position he held for 18 years. The initial objectives of the International Recreation Association were to:

1. Serve as a central clearinghouse for the exchange of information and experiences among recreation agencies of the world.

2. Aid countries to establish central recreation service agencies.

3. Forward the development of a world recreation movement designed to enrich the human spirit through wholesome use of leisure.

4. Encourage the provision of land and facilities, training of leaders, development of varied programs, and public interpretation of the values of play for children, recreation for youth, and creative use of leisure for all ages.

5. Provide a medium through which the recreation authorities of the world may work in unity on one of the common problems of man.

Under Rivers' leadership, the International Recreation Association quickly established worldwide identity. Within three years, the IRA had become financially independent and no longer required budgetary support from the National Recreation Association.

Many accomplishments stand out during Tom Rivers' 18 years as director general. Among his most significant accomplishments were helping to organize national recreation associations in Brazil, Pakistan, India, Korea, Columbia, and Israel; providing leadership for the 1964 World Congress which took place in Japan; assisting in the formation of the European Recreation and Leisure Association and providing an expanded international philosophy. This broadened philosophy was evidenced by an organizational name change in 1973 from International Recreation Association to World Leisure and Recreation Association.

A testimonial to Tom Rivers' philosophy and leadership was the creation of a worldwide Charter of Leisure. This document, developed over a 2½ year period by an IRA committee chaired by Norman P. Miller, then vice chancellor of the University of California, Los Angeles, became an important tool for furthering recreation and leisure on a worldwide basis. It is reproduced at the conclusion of the chapter to reinforce the vision of Tom Rivers for "Building a Better World Through Recreation."

CHARTER FOR LEISURE

Leisure time is that period of time at the complete disposal of an individual, after he has completed his work and fulfilled his other obligations. The uses of this time are of vital importance. Leisure and recreation create a basis for compensating for many of the demands placed upon man by today's way of life. More important, they present a possibility of enriching life through participation in physical relaxation and sports, through an enjoyment of art, science, and nature. Leisure is important in all spheres of life, both urban and rural. Leisure pursuits offer man the chance of activating his essential gifts (a free development of the will, intelligence, sense of responsibility, and creative faculty). Leisure hours are a period of freedom, when man is able to enhance his value as a human being and as a productive member of society.

Recreation and leisure activities play an important part in establishing good relations between peoples and nations of the world.

Article 1

Every man has a right to leisure time. This right compromises reasonable working hours, regular paid holidays, favorable travelling conditions and suitable social planning, including reasonable access to leisure facilities, areas, and equipment in order to enhance the advantages of leisure time.

Article 2

The right to enjoy leisure time with complete freedom is absolute. The prerequisites for undertaking individual leisure pursuits should be safeguarded to the same extent as those for collective enjoyment of leisure time.

Article 3

Every man has a right to easy access to recreational facilities open to the public, and to nature reserves by lakes, seas, wooded areas, in the mountains and open spaces in general. These areas, their fauna and flora, must be protected and conserved.

Article 4

Every man has a right to participate in and be introduced to all types of recreation during leisure time, such as sports and games, open-air living, travel, theatre, dancing, pictorial art, music, science, and handicrafts, irrespective of age, sex, or level of education.

Article 5

Leisure time should be unorganized in the sense that official authorities, urban planners, architects, and private groups of individuals do not decide how others are to use their leisure time. The above-mentioned should create or assist in the planning of the leisure opportunities, aesthetic environments and recreation facilities required to enable man to exercise individual choice in the use of his leisure, according to personal tastes and under his own responsibility.

Article 6

Every man has a right to the opportunity for learning how to enjoy his leisure time. Family, school, and community should instruct him in the art of exploiting his leisure time in the most sensible fashion. In schools, classes, and courses of instruction, children, adolescents, and adults must be given the opportunity to develop the skills, attitudes, and understandings essential for leisure literacy.

Article 7

The responsibility for education for leisure is still divided among a large number of disciplines and institutions. In the interest of everyone and in order to utilize purposefully all the funds and assistance available in the various administrative levels, this responsibility should be fully coordinated among all public and private bodies concerned with leisure. In countries, where feasible, special schools for recreational studies should be established. These schools would train leaders to help promote recreational programs and assist individuals and groups during their leisure hours, in so far as they can without restricting freedom of choice. Such service is worthy of the finest creative efforts of man.

ORIGIN OF THE CHARTER

In 1967, at the Geneva Symposium of some 16 agencies operating internationally in the field of play, recreation, and leisure, the International Recreation Association was requested to develop a Charter For Leisure. A committee consisting of the following was appointed:

Norman P. Miller, International Recreation Association(IRA)
Drummond W. Abernethy, International Playground Association(IPA)
Julien Falize, International Council for Health, Physical Education & Recreation(ICHPER)
Eugene-Marcel Guitin, International Center for the Study of Leisure(CIEL)
Fredrich Roskam, International Working Group on Sports Facilities(IAKS)

After 2½ years of work, it was completed at a final meeting in Geneva on June 1, 1970 and its announcement was made. It is now available in four languages: English, French, German, and Spanish. IRA believes this Charter for Leisure can be an important tool for use by authorities responsible for planning for leadership and facilities for play, recreation, and leisure-time services for all age groups.

We hope the Charter will soon be translated into many other languages, so that authorities may have it as an aid to extending recreation services throughout the world.

PARTIAL LIST OF RIVER'S PUBLICATIONS

My Sixty Years in Recreation Working for Life Enrichment. (1983). Alexandria, Virginia: National Recreation and Park Association.
Recreation Around the World. (1953). New York: National Recreation Association.
Thomas E. Rivers. *Recreation Magazine, XLVII,* p. 37.
Rivers, Thomas E.: World Service Through Recreation. *Recreation Magazine, XLVIII,* pp. 320–321.
Cooperative Community Exchange Project. (1956, September). *Recreation Magazine, XLIX,* p. 326.
The Launching of the International Recreation Association. *Recreation Magazine, L,* p. 12.

REFERENCES

Butler, George D. (1965). *Pioneers in Public Recreation.* Minneapolis: Burgess Publishing Company.

Knapp, Richard E. and Charles E. Hartsoe. (1979). *Play for America.* Alexandria, Virginia: National Recreation and Park Association.

In Memorium—Dr. Thomas E. Rivers—Founder and Builder of WRLA. (1977, September/October). *WRLA Bulletin, XX,* pp. 1, 2.

Prendergast, Joseph. (1952, October). An International Recreation Service. *Recreation Magazine, XLVI,* pp. 254–255.

Westland, Cor. (1987). IRA WRLA 1956–1986. Thirty Years of Service. An Historical Perspective. *World Leisure and Recreation, XXIX* (Special Anniversary Issue).

24

GEORGE HJELTE

1893–1979

By Gus Gerson
California Polytechnic University, Pomona

Courtesy Dorothy Meyer

"Full coordination was desirable
between municipal endeavor in public
recreation and the expansion of school
services in the same field.**"**

1973:18

George Hjelte was born in 1893 to immigrant parents of Swedish descent. His parents came to America in the 1880s, finally settling in the San Francisco Bay area. He was educated at the University of California, Berkeley, and majored in economics and physical education. He was an outstanding athlete in college. His sport was the evolving game of basketball, where he was selected as All Pacific Coast Conference, and All American in 1917.

Upon graduation, Mr. Hjelte was involved in the First World War. He entered officer training at the Presidio in San Francisco, and later was commissioned a Second Lieutenant. He served with the allied forces in Europe and earned the Belgium War Cross for bravery. He was discharged in England with the rank of Major. He stayed abroad for a short period and took graduate study at Cambridge University.

He returned to California in 1919 and continued graduate work at Berkeley. During these graduate years, he served as a graduate teaching assistant in physical education. Mr. Hjelte married twice. The union with his first wife produced two children, a son and a daughter, George DS. and Dorothy. His first wife died after a long illness. Mr. Hjelte died January 9, 1979 at the age of 85.

The city of Los Angeles in 1904 was the first to form a separate municipal recreation department with a commission to advise its operation. This department, called the Department of Playgrounds, was headed by a Stanford University graduate and athlete named Charles B. Raitt. The playgrounds of Los Angeles were fenced level lots, not turfed. Generally, there was a small shed on the grounds to house lime and athletic equipment. Indoor recreation centers were located in nine locations throughout the city. These buildings were composed of a multipurpose room (not a gymnasium), a kitchen, and several smaller rooms. The early centers contained small (less than official) bowling alleys.

The centers were not as comprehensive as some of the South Chicago Park District examples of Jane Addams and Mary E. McDowell, but were as multiuse as any found in the west. Only Oakland and Berkeley were as complete. Even though some midwestern and eastern examples were more advanced from a facility standpoint, recreation programs in these areas were "poor cousins" of the landscape architects and park authorities. Recreation programs were tolerated as a means of keeping "juvenile delinquents" (the poor and minorities) "off the streets" (actually, out of the parks).

The Raitt administration initiated two historically significant professional recreation concepts. The first was the requirement of a college degree for recreation directors; thus, putting these people on a par with teachers in California. Secondly, the first city-owned camping facilities were developed in the nearby San Bernardino Mountains as well as in the eastern slopes of the High Sierra Nevada Mountains.

In 1924, C. B. Raitt made a grave political error. He became an out-spoken supporter of what he perceived as a well-entrenched current city administration. But, a political coalition headed by George Cryder and George Dunlap, representing a group called the "Los Angeles Municipal League," favored a decentralized municipal form of government consist-ing of various city departments, each governed by separate commissions with considerable autonomy. It was an improvement on the commission-form of city government so popular at the turn of the century. Thus, in 1924, George Cryder was elected mayor with a substantial majority. Just prior to this, in 1923, the voters approved a $1.5 million (considerable in those days) bond issue for development of recreation and park facilities.

Mayor Cryder formed a Board of Freeholders to draft a new city charter. The charter created several new departments: a parks department, a library department, and a department of playgrounds and recreation. Each department was to be granted a fixed budgetary allocation and a fixed property tax allocation. Each was to be governed by a commission of citizens who had the power to designate the fixed funds virtually as they pleased. R. Van Griffith, a political reporter, supporter of the freeholders, and son of the donor of Griffith Park, was appointed chair of the com-mission.

At its first meeting, in 1925, C. B. Raitt was asked to resign. A nationwide search was instituted to replace him. A 32-year-old man applied for the position. His credentials were impressive. He had been an All American basketball player from the University of California, Berkeley, who com-piled an envious academic record with a dual major of economics and physical education while working part-time on the playgrounds of Oak-land. For two years following graduation, he served as assistant supervisor of physical education for the state of California. His next professional position was Superintendent of Recreation for the Berkeley Unified School District. The young man continued to move up in the world. George Hjelte became the superintendent (general manager) of the newly formed Playgrounds and Recreation Department for the City of Los Angeles.

The period of time between 1926 and 1930 was characterized by growth and expansion. There was ample money from the recreation budget allocations. A passed bond issue brought good property tax reve-nues into the municipal coffers.

Hjelte reorganized the department and brought to it a core of new employees, expanded its programs, and developed other facilities. Some of the innovations of this reorganization plan included public relations, industrial recreation, cultural arts, and four other program divisions.

Unbelievably, Los Angeles, prior to 1925, had no municipal swimming facilities. A part of Hjelte's reorganization was the implementation of an aquatics division. By 1930, several outdoor municipal pools were in operation, including the Olympic Swim Stadium adjoining the War Memorial Coliseum at Exposition Park.

A major innovation of the Hjelte era centered on the creation of comprehensive community centers located in neighborhoods of all socioeconomic statuses. Throughout the country at this time, the overwhelming number of municipally-operated recreation centers were located in low socioeconomic neighborhoods. Hjelte believed recreation was for everyone. He expanded the camps of the Raitt era and added children's day and overnight camps. The boys and girls camps in Griffith Park began at that time. Public beaches at Venice Pier and in San Pedro were adopted and developed by the department and became a prototype for the nation.

Because of Hjelte's experience in Berkeley as supervisor of Physical Education for the school district, he recognized the need for cooperation and coordination with the Los Angeles Unified School District. "Full coordination was desirable between municipal endeavor in public recreation and the expansion of school services in the same field. The situation calls for a conscious effort on the part of the two mutually independent public agencies to avoid working at cross purposes . . . ." (Hjelte, 1978:18) His belief in leisure services within the schools was to take a bizarre twist later.

The period between 1926 and 1929 were creative, expansion years. But there was trouble on the horizon. Several conditions brought about this change:

1. Mayor Cryder chose not to run for reelection and a new administration ensued under Mayor John C. Porter.
2. The city had contracted for the Olympic Games of 1932.
3. The stock market crash of 1929 (although L. A. did not feel the effects until late 1930) reared its ugly head.

The change of administration from Cryder to Porter brought the automatic resignations of the five recreation commissioners. Only one was retained. One of the new appointees included a politically ambitious lawyer named J. Paul Elliott. Elliott, later to be elected to the Board of Education and then to its presidency, agreed with Hjelte on the school's role in leisure but was not as sold on municipal recreation, and opposed many funding proposals.

Since the completion of the construction on the War Memorial Coliseum in 1921, it had been operated by the Community Development Assocation. The expectation was that it would be turned over to the Playground and Recreation Department within three years as required by the city charter. But the expansion of the Coliseum necessitated by the impending Olympics, needed an additional $500,000 to bring the facilities to Olympic standards. The Community Development Association not only refused to relinquish its administrative role, but also borrowed a large portion of additional funds from the city as well as the Playground and Recreation Department. (Only about $2,700.00 was repaid.)

Although the Depression had not yet greatly affected Los Angeles, it was obvious that financial support would not come from traditional property tax sources. City employees were asked to take a 10 percent reduction in pay. Despite the spector of the Depression, which was a time for employment conservation, Mr. Hjelte exhibited the strong professional ethics whch characterized his career. He resigned his position in March of 1930, and assumed the position as superintendent of Recreation of Westchester County, New York. He remained in New York for three and a half years.

In October of 1933, after the Olympics and after Elliott was elected to the Board of Education, and only after federal aid was promised, did Hjelte return to Los Angeles.

The Depression was an interesting time for recreation professionals. Despite the hardships, economic chaos, massive unemployment, and professional expansion, facilities and many programs continued to grow. Several factors contributed to this expansion. The first was the city charter which allowed for the employment of part-time recreation leaders with only the approval of the general manager and Commission. This charter inclusion was instrumental in bypassing the red tape of civil service rules and the payment of expensive full time employee's fringe benefits. Second was the availability of highly trained and skilled personnel for part-time work. This availability occurred because of the massive unemployment of artists and sportsmen. The third factor was the "Alphabet Soup" social programs of the Roosevelt Administration. This author, as a young recreation director in Los Angeles, remembers the stories of veteran directors who worked during the Depression years. One such director, Y. F. Hammatt, recalled having a large part-time staff of W.P.A. (Works Project Administration) and municipal art department employees, many of whom were highly skilled and well known ex-athletes.

By 1935, J. Paul Elliott, the former commissioner, had been elected president of the L.A. Board of Education. Also, the California State Legislature had passed a bill authorizing a permissive tax called the "Community Services Tax" which allowed school districts to levy up to ten cents per $100 (equivalency of a one mill levy in other states) of assessed valuation to fund the use of public schools for community services. California had had a "Civic Center Act" since 1917, but this act enabling the private and recreational use of schools in California did not authorize funding for that purpose. Now, 18 years later, the funding was possible. However, this funding was at the pervue of the local board of education.

Armed with this funding source, Elliott visited Flint, Michigan to observe the Flint Community School concept which was funded through the Charles Stuart Mott Foundation. Upon his return, he negotiated and the board approved the formation of the unified school districts Youth Services Division. Now Los Angeles had two multi-million dollar recreation departments.

The Youth Services Division was under the direction of Larry Houston and John (Jack) Merkley. The school program consisted of school playground activities at most elementary schools, and youth centers at most secondary schools. This division also had portable roller skating rinks, swimming pools, and performance trailers which traveled, according to a schedule, throughout the district. Coordination between the executives of these programs became more acute than ever. The Recreation and Youth Services Planning Council was formed for this purpose.

In 1937, an event occurred which may have prevented the political dismissal of George Hjelte. City department heads were successful in their bid to come under the protection of Civil Service Commission rules. The emergence of California as a true two-party state, (previously dominated by the Republican Party) caused concern that a political spoils system might occur at city management levels. In other words, city department heads could well be at the mercy of new mayors (as had been the case of C. B. Raitt) who would appoint political supporters to these positions.

In fact, this concern became a reality with the recall of Mayor Frank Shaw by Fletcher Bowron, a reform-minded candidate. Bowron suspected the city executives were tied to Shaw and would have fired all of them if they had not been protected by the new Civil Service provision.

In 1938 a tragic event became engraved in Hjelte's memories and his administration. During the Shaw-Bowron transition, the city had an opportunity to purchase 240 acres adjacent to Griffith Park. This land would provide recreation opportunities to the growing San Fernando Valley. Mr. Hjelte directed Bert R. Petticord to make a master plan of the two proposed areas. He developed a plan for a golf course, camp, and athletic facilities.

A cemetery concern also was interested in the property. Under California law at that time, any grounds with burial remains were protected perpetually as cemeteries. Using this legal loophole, the company, in the dead of the night, buried several bodies on the land. The tragedy was not only a professional loss of a badly needed recreation property, but a personal tragedy as well. "Bert R. Petticord, who was dedicated to the project, suffered a stroke and was hospitalized for 13 years in a nearby sanitarium. Ironically, upon his demise he was buried in Forest Lawn cemetery where the other bodies had frustrated his plan." (Hjelte, 1976:24)

The years of the Second World War were best described as a dichotomy. Despite the inevitable death and destruction of war, the demand for recreation increased on several fronts. First, the population was rising because of the war industries centered around Los Angeles. Secondly, troops stationed in the Los Angeles area crowded into the urban area, especially Hollywood. The United Services Organization, (USO) was created to aid efforts of private agencies and the recreation department. Thirdly, the National Community Service Agency (NCSA) was formed not only to augment the USO but to provide community recreation for the "Rosies the Riveters" working in the industrial complexes. Many Los Angeles recreational personnel not called into the service were granted leaves of absence to serve this organization. George Hjelte spent three months on leave serving this organization as an advisor to the entire Pacific Coast-North American area.

After his stint with NCSA, Hjelte served as a Naval Lieutenant Commander in Washington before being requested back to Los Angeles by Mayor Bowron. He was then asked by the Mayor to serve in the dual capacity of general manager of the playground and recreation department and director/executive officer of the Civil Defense Corps (the organization that provided the famous Air Raid Wardens of World War II).

The post-war period was characterized by change and population growth. The first main change was the consolidation of the playgrounds and recreation department with the parks department in 1947, into what is now the Department of Recreation and Parks. The industrialization of Los Angeles continued, bringing an influx of minority and blue collar workers. The department's previously middle class-based program was forced to adjust. One adjustment was the assumption of the management of some recreation programs within Federal Housing Projects. Eventually, there was even a housing district formed and managed by specialists for this socioeconomic group.

In 1945 the largest bond issue for recreation passed in Los Angeles. This, coupled with a previous issue in 1937, caused facilities including parks, playgrounds, recreation centers, swimming pools, golf courses, and camps to more than double. In addition, this money enabled the development of two regional parks, museums, and the Greater Los Angeles Zoo.

In 1961, the incumbent mayor, Norris Poulson, was defeated for election by the maverick mayor Sam Yorty. As is the custom, all members of the recreation commission resigned. Only one commissioner was retained by Yorty. Hjelte was to retire in 1962 at the age of 70 years. Although 70 is the mandatory age of retirement under the Civil Service system, the new commissioner appointed by Yorty certainly made Hjelte's retirement more attractive. Two of the Yorty appointments to the commission were later arrested for malfeasance of office (criminal use of public office for personal gain). One of the commissioners, Mel Pierson, was convicted and sent to prison. George Hjelte continued to serve as a consultant to the department for four additional years.

An interview with Maxine McSweeney Hjelte, George's widow, revealed that Hjelte was most proud of three professional accomplishments:

1. His initiation of cooperation between federal and state agencies, especially the Naval Department and the State Department of Physical Education;

2. His recreation philosophy which emphasized the learning of activity skills for all ages and socioeconomic groups;

3. His model for program planning which included three aspects: unstructured activities which he called "drop-in," scheduled skill development classes and activities referred to as "recurrent," and highly structured, larger in scope activities, usually culminating in an activity or celebrating a holiday or event, titled "special event."

He was the author and/or coauthor of four books (two of them revised into 2nd editions) and literally hundreds of journal articles. An accomplished and sought after public speaker, he was the keynote speaker at several professional conferences. Some other professional accomplishments not listed in the chronological order were:

1. One of the founders of the California Professional Recreational Organization (CPRS) and the recreation fraternity, Pi Sigma Epsilon.

2. Formulation of recreation master plan for several cities, including New York, Columbus, Tulsa, Kansas City, Pasadena, Long Beach, and Torrance. Through these studies, he developed his published standards for recreation facilities vis a vis population.

3. Past president of the American Recreation Society, and a fellow and board member of the American Academy of Physical Education.

William Escherich, (Hjelte, 1971: forward) said this of George Hjelte ". . . aspects of this man, which can be observed both personally and through his writings, are his outstanding character, modesty, total integrity, and resourcefulness." The history of the development of recreation from 1925 until 1962 in the City of Los Angeles indicates that Mr. Escherich was correct in his assessment.

PARTIAL LIST OF HJELTE'S PUBLICATIONS

Administration of Public Recreation. (1941, 1971). Westport, Conn: Greenwood Press. Reprinted.

with Jay S. Shivers. (1972, 1978). *Public Administration of Recreational Services.* Philadelphia: Lea and Febiger. Second edition.

The Development of a City's Public Recreation Service 1904–1962. (1978). Los Angeles: Public Service Publications.

Footprints in the Parks. (1977). Los Angeles: Public Service Publications.

Hudson, Susan Diane. (1974, August). George Hjelte, Recreation Administrator. Doctoral Dissertation. Utah: University of Utah.

INTERVIEWS

Ms. Dorothy Meyer (Mr. Hjelte's daughter).

Mrs. Maxine McSweeny Hjelte (Mr. Hjelte's widow).

Mr. Al Goldfarb—Public relations L.A. City Department of Recreation.

Mr. Sydney Kronenthal—Department of Human Services of Culver City, California.

25

FOSTER RHEA DULLES

1900–1970

By Hilmi Ibrahim
Whittier College

"**R**ecreation in America may be compared to a river—its course adapting itself to the nature of the country through which it flows, the main stream continually augmented by tributaries, and the river bed itself ever growing both broader and deeper."

A History of Recreation
1965: vii

Foster Rhea Dulles was born in Englewood, New Jersey to a business-man father. He attended Princeton University obtaining his B.A. in 1921. He served as a foreign correspondent for many newspapers: the *Christian Science Monitor,* Bejing, 1922; the *New York Herald Tribune,* Paris, 1923–1925; and the *New York Evening Post,* 1927–1933. He joined academe, teaching in a number of Eastern colleges, and obtained his Ph.D. from Columbia in 1940.

Foster Rhea Dulles wrote 20 books (See Pioneer's Publications), among which is *America Learns to Play: A History of Recreation.* The first edition appeared under this title in 1940. In 1965 the second edition appeared as *A History of Recreation: America Learns to Play.* It is the first, and still the only book that is devoted to the history of recreation in America.

While having published the only volume devoted to the rise of recreation in America, Foster Rhea Dulles, although not in any way closely related to the recreation profession or leisure studies, has added signifi-cantly to our understanding of the rise of all forms of play in America. He believed that in the early settlement days play and recreation were no more than thin trickles, forcing their way into a forbidden terrain which by the 18th century gathered volume and flowed quietly and steadily into the 19th century. They were transformed in the 20th century into riotous torrents, breaking all barriers, to be the full flood that covers the total terrain of today's America.

Initially, there was a detestation of idleness in that the common welfare could not permit a "mispense of time." The Virginia Assembly in 1619 decreed that "any person found idle should be bound over to compulsory work." It prohibited gaming at dice or cards, strictly regulated drinking, provided penalties for excess in apparel, and rigidly enforced the sabbath observance. (Dulles, 1965:5) Massachusetts and Connecticut followed suit. The Puritanical influence was at its peak.

As the economic security of the communities that stretched along the eastern section of the country from Maine to South Carolina increased, life began to change in the opening years of the 18th century. Farm festivals and husking bees became popular. Hunting, fishing, shooting matches, and horse races became common. While the simple country folk of New England were asserting their rights to play, "the more wealthy and leisured class was even less restrained by earlier prejudice. Prosperity induced a more liberal attitude and the barriers which once had blocked all worldly pleasures were being let down." (Dulles, 1965:45)

During these years, the frontier was being pushed farther west. There, a new nation was being born. Its settlers were no longer displaced Eng-lishmen, but people born on American soil filled with new American ideals. They were tougher and more adaptable to their environment. They had less opportunity for social gatherings as the frontier offered them a hard and lonely lifestyle. The wealth of game along the frontier was greater and shooting matches became more popular than in the colonies. Horse racing became a universal recreation, as well. The importance of physical strength in pioneer life gave impetus to jumping contests, wrestling matches, throwing the long bullet, hurling the tomahawk, and flinging the rail. But bees were still popular and neighbors came from miles away to aid and participate in the contests. Dinners became gargantuan feasts, after which dancing would commence. The Virginia Reel, country jigs, and shake-downs were danced on the forest floors as the fiddler played. (Dulles, 1965:77)

In the meantime, the Eastern seaboard was changing. The simple agri-cultural communities were becoming complex urban centers in the open-ing decades of the 19th century. A gradual growth of commercial recre-ation was the beginning of what has now become a vast entertainment industry. Dulles points to the fact that while European pleasures were essentially exclusive and aristocratic like Europe itself at that time, the rise of a working class imbued with the ideals of Jacksonian democracy created the demand for popular entertainment. (1965:84–85) He lamented the shift from active to passive recreation which did not make for a healthy adjustment, and which was not redressed until after the Civil War with the rise of organized sport.

A cultural awakening was taking place at mid-century, as was self-education in the Lyceum movement along with public lectures. Also, theatre was coming of age and found a great challenge from the American circus, a native product with its combination of little menageries, bands of acrobats and equestrian performers. The theatre found it necessary to give up the classics to meet the demand for undiluted entertainment, burlesque, and melodrama. (Dulles, 1965:100–135)

Dulles suggested that urbanization broke the traditional patterns of recreational activities in America towards the middle of the 19th century. Restrictions on time and space deprived the people of their familiar games and contests of village life. "If they could not play or compete, they could at least get the thrill of vicarious participation by cheering on their favorites from a grandstand," (1965:137) thus the beginning of spectator sport. Sport became a professional affair. Horse racing, foot racing, and prize fighting headed the list. Fascination with parades began then, as well.

A basic need for outdoor exercise, combined with a call to improve national health, served to break down the barriers that stood in the way of the development of organized participatory sports. The first among them was baseball. Croquet got men and women outdoors for an activity that they could enjoy together. So did archery and lawn tennis. Roller skating was introduced in 1863. But it was bicycling that became the craze. A few years later, football was to be the first intercollegiate sport, and basketball and volleyball were played by the YMCA members. (1965:182–203)

Dulles described the lack of public recreational facilities and programs at that time and wrote:

> Imperial Rome had sought to appease the restlessness of its labouring masses by providing the free spectacles of the circus and gladiatorial combat. Imperial America had its amusement palaces, its prize fights, its concert-saloons, for which the modern working man had to pay." (1965:211)

Towards the close of the 19th century, the electric trolley began to provide holiday substitutes for the theatre, the circus, the dance hall, bowling lanes, billiard parlors, and sports arenas. Amusement parks were in full swing and became the holiday Mecca of millions of workers. In the meantime, the social world was represented by the few wealthy who gave elaborate fancy dress balls, went to the opera, and played polo at their country clubs. (Dulles, 1965:211–247)

The church and fraternal orders found it necessary to enter the arena of leisure. To make up the restraints it placed on worldly pleasures, the church provided its own forms of entertainment. The church supper included innocuous entertainment. At the fairs, bazaars, and festivals which were intended for fund raising, fishing ponds, guessing games, and relays took place. Elaborate ceremonies and rituals began to take shape in fraternal lodges providing a relief from the dull routine of the now industrial America. Women were no longer left out. They formed the auxiliaries which provided them with social recreation. (Dulles, 1965:248–270)

While the city dweller was enjoying the new recreational diversions brought about by urbanization, mechanization, and commercialization, the life of the rural resident suffered from inertia. It took a philosopher like Emerson to find joy in solitude, reading, and physical labor that country life required. "But not all the world was a philosopher," wrote Dulles. (1965:272) Special events began to form. The Grange meeting, a social gathering, a country dance, the Fourth of July picnic, the annual country fair and the coming of the circus were remembered for months afterwards with continuing pleasure.

In 1895, three events took place that would alter, not only how and with what Americans played, but their very lifestyle. Closely following Thomas Edison's invention, two young men created the kinetoscope, which produced a jerky flickering moving picture on a screen in Atlanta, Georgia. A pioneer race for the new horseless carriages took place in Chicago on Thanksgiving Day of that year. Guglielmo Marconi succeeded in working the wireless telegraph, the forerunner of radio and television.

In the early years of the 20th century, an electric theatre was established in Los Angeles solely for the exhibition of moving pictures. In 1905, the first nickelodeon was opened in McKeesport, Pennsylvania, signalling the real boom. Popular amusements had generally evolved from diversions of the wealthy and took a long time to become popular. The nickelodeon was the common man's amusement from the beginning in America, while in Europe, particularly in France, cinema took on a sophisticated role. (Dulles, 1965:292)

Great improvements took place in movie production and business before World War I, such as clear cut, distinct pictures, multi-reel films, movie stardom, and comfortable theatre. While the talkies came about in 1928, the Depression led to a drastic decline in attendance. To combat the decline, the double feature was inaugurated, also bank nights, lucky numbers, and bingo. By the end of the 1930s, the movies were taking their place as the first source of amusement in America. After World War II, musical extravaganzas, science fiction, war stories, horror films, and westerns attracted record numbers. (Dulles, 1965:287–311)

While the movies were for the masses, the automobile was for the upper classes in that the motorist was a picture of arrogance of wealth with all its independence and carelessness, asserted Dulles. (1965:314) The automobile was the plaything for the rich. It was not until the 1930s that the automobile opened up broader horizons in the field of recreation, to the sport arena, amusement park, and the open country. About that time the automobile trailer made its appearance to add to the migratory impulses of vacationing Americans who were responding to the popular slogan "See America First!" New England became a summer vacation land, Florida a popular winter resort, and the National Parks and Forests of the West were favored destinations.

By the end of 1922, a new entertainment industry was born: radio. It was the most novel amusement America had ever known and it made spectacular advances. Improvements in technique and organization took place in 1924 when nationwide hookups were installed for a national political convention. It was no longer the minstrel show, the vaudeville team, or the circus that spread the new songs; it was the radio. Classical music, piano recitals, concerts, and opera appealed to a few. Along with the radio came the phonograph and the record which Americans spent more on, at that time, than on musical instruments, books and periodicals, and sporting goods combined. Every study on how people spent their free time, in these years, showed that listening to music was the most popular recreation, to the decline of reading, card playing, and conversing. (Dulles, 1965:335—336)

With the coming of the Depression, federal programs were introduced, such as the Works Progress Administration which, in 1937, allocated 10 percent of its expenditure for new parks and recreational facilities. Dulles advocated that this added to the already enthusiastic feelings for sport and physical activities. (1965:346)

"Sport For All" is the title of the chapter in which Dulles showed the expansion of sport into schools, colleges, and clubs, including women and minorities. Sociologists have tried to analyze the role of sport in American life using every possible angle, yet the fact remains that Americans were sold on spectator, as well as participatory sport.

In the 20th century, the American people continued to enjoy diversions other than commercial entertainments and sport. Crazes and fads swept people off their feet now and then. Table games also played an important role in American life. Dancing remained a popular pastime over the years. Gambling, which was limited to a few, became an acceptable form of recreation for many and by many. Hobbies of all sorts became an important part of Americana. (Dulles, 1965:366–385)

In the closing chapter, which Dulles entitled "The New Leisure," he wrote:

The people of no other country and no other age had ever had anything like the leisure, the discretionary income, or the recreational choices of the American people in the mid-twentieth century. It was overwhelming—the democracy had come into its recreational heritage. It has achieved both leisure and the means to enjoy it. Even though they might not always have used leisure to the best advantage, the American people had to learn to play. (1965:397)

PARTIAL LIST OF DULLES' PUBLICATIONS

The Old China Trade. (1930). New York: Houghton. Reprinted, AMS Press, 1970.

Eastwood Ho: The First English Adventurers to the Orient: Richard Chancellor, Anthony Jenkinson, James Lancaster, William Adams, Sir Thomas Roe. (1931). New York: Houghton. Reprinted, Books for Libraries, 1969.

America in the Pacific: A Century of Expansion. (1932). New York: Houghton. 2nd edition, 1938; reprinted De Capo Press, 1969.

Lowered Boats: A Chronicle of American Whaling. (1933). New York: Harcourt.

Harpoon: The Story of a Whaling Voyage. (1935). New York: Houghton.

Forty Years of Japanese-American Relations. (1937). New York: Appleton.

America Learns To Play: A History of Popular Recreation 1607–1940. (1940). New York: Appleton. 2nd edition published as A History of Recreation, 1965.

The Road to Teheran. (1944). Princeton, N.J.: Princeton University Press.

Twentieth Century America. (1945). New York: Houghton. Reprinted, Books for Libraries, 1972.

China and America: The Story of their Relations Since 1784. (1946). Princeton, N.J.: Princeton University Press. Reprinted, Kennikat Press, 1967.

Labor in America. (1949). New York: Crowell. 3rd edition, 1966.

The American Red Cross. (1950). New York: Harper. Reprinted, Greenwood Press, 1971.

America's Rise to World Power. (1955). New York: Harper.

The Imperial Years. (1956). New York: Crowell.

The United States Since 1865. (1959). Ann Arbor, MI: University of Michigan Press. 2nd edition, revised and enlarged, 1969.

Americans Abroad. (1964). Ann Arbor, MI: University of Michigan Press.

Prelude To World Power: American Diplomatic History. 1860–1900. (1965). New York: Macmillan.

Yankees and Samurai: America's Role in the Emergence of Modern Japan. 1791–1900. (1965). New York: Harper.

The Civil Rights Commission, 1957–1965. (1968). East Lansing, MI.: Michigan State University Press.

American Policy Toward Communist China, 1949–1969. (1972). New York: Crowell.

REFERENCES

Bowker, Benjamin. *Books.* April 7, 1940, p. 7.

Condit, Abbie. *Springfield Replican.* April 28, 1940, p. 7.

Duffus, R.L. *New Republic.* June 10, 1940 (102), p. 801.

Hollybrook, S.H. *Booklist.* May 1, 1940 (36) p. 340.

Handlin, Oscar. *Journal of Home Economics.* April 26, 1940:(33) p. 45.

Meyer, D.H. Pratt. *Autumn,* 1940, p. 20.

Sylvester, Harry. *Boston Transcripts.* April 13, 1940, p. 2.

Wecter, Dixon. *Wisconsin Library Bulletin.* May, 1940 (36), p. 97.

26

CHARLES K. BRIGHTBILL
1910–1966

By Charles Hartsoe
Virginia Commonwealth University

Courtesy Dr. Charles Hartso, Virginia Commonwealth University

"If *He asks what I did for immortality, I sired a girl and a boy, wrote a book, and planted a tree.***"**

Charles K. Brightbill's influence was at the core of major developments taking place within the field of recreation from the end of World War II up until his death in 1966. Few, if any, recreators had as diversified a career as did Brightbill. His professional experiences included work at the municipal and federal levels of government, as an assistant with a national non-profit voluntary agency, and culminated with his position as head of the recreation department at the University of Illinois. His service spanned an era in which recreation was markedly influenced by the Depression of the '30s, World War II, and the technological and economic boom that followed.

Charles Kestner Brightbill was born on February 15, 1910, in Reading, Pennsylvania. Upon graduation from high school, he enrolled as a commerce and finance major at Pennsylvania State University. One of his more notable achievements as an undergraduate student was being selected as drum major of Pennsylvania State's Marching Blue Band. While in college, Brightbill spent his summers working as a picnic specialist for the Reading Department of Playgrounds and Recreation. In this position, he planned and conducted picnics and special events for community groups in the Reading area. His summer work experiences in recreation played a major role in helping to shape his future career which was to begin following the completion of a Master's degree in Business Administration at the University of Pennsylvania in 1933.

It was at the age of 23 that Charles Brightbill accepted his first full-time job as supervisor of Special Activities for the Reading, Pennsylvania Department of Recreation. It was at a time when one-third of the nation's workforce was unemployed. The Depression of the 1930s introduced the country to the problems of forced free time brought on by unemployment, which prompted the federal government to assume a pioneering role in human welfare. Brightbill's first position involved the supervision of 25 federally-funded W.P.A. workers assigned to develop a cultural recreation-education program for the city of Reading.

Following his experience in Reading, Brightbill accepted the position of superintendent of Recreation for Decatur, Illinois. There he developed the system into one of the best in the nation for a city of its size. Decatur became the model for the film, "Playtown, U.S.A.," produced by the Athletic Institute.

In 1937, as a result of his work in Decatur, Brightbill was invited to join the staff of the National Recreation Association where he served as New England District Representative. In this capacity, he traveled extensively throughout the six New England states, rendering consulting services to communities.

Just prior to the outbreak of World War II, Charles Brightbill accepted a promotion with the Office of Community War Services, Federal Security

Agency. In this assignment, he was responsible for the federal government's work in coordinating recreation activities in war-impacted communities in the New England region. He subsequently became Associate Director of this federal agency where he shared responsibility for overseeing the operations of more than 3,000 USO programs and numerous other war recreation services for civilians.

Following World War II, Brightbill was recruited to head the Recreation Service of the Special Services Division of the Veterans Administration where he served from February 1947 to February 1949. During this period, he was responsible for the planning, development, and supervision of the VA's pioneering recreation program in veterans hospitals.

Upon completing his service with the Veterans Administration, Brightbill served for a period of two years as the first and only executive secretary of the President's Committee on Religion and Welfare in the Armed Forces. This committee was created by President Harry S. Truman in October 1948 to advise and recommend action on matters pertaining to the religious and welfare needs of men and women in the armed forces. Among the studies he directed were Free Time in the Armed Forces, The Military Chaplaincy, and Community Planning for the Peacetime Serviceman.

While serving with the President's committee, Charles Brightbill was approached by the University of Illinois regarding his possible interest in a newly authorized faculty position at the University. Brightbill initially declined the offer; however, the University persisted and ultimately prevailed. In 1951, he accepted the position and remained there until his death in 1966.

One of Charles Brightbill's major convictions was his belief in government as the social service of man. In this context, he viewed recreation as a legitimate and essential function of government. To him, the community was the focal point of organized recreation. He felt that the task of providing community recreation was not spontaneous, but rather required planning, organization, development, and intelligent evaluation. Through his experiences, he encountered a variety of situations and problems that served to stimulate his interest in defining fundamental principles related to organizing and administering a community recreation program. Brightbill, along with Harold D. Meyer, noted educator from the University of North Carolina and long time advocate of public recreation, published a book in 1948 entitled Community Recreation: A Guide to its Organization and Administration. This book, along with its subsequent revisions, became a standard text for students and teachers, as well as a general reference for recreation and park administrators. It also marked the beginning of a continuing literary partnership between Charles Brightbill and Harold Meyer.

In addition to his strong commitment to community recreation, Brightbill was also a proponent of the importance of state and federal government leadership in the area of recreation. Following World War II, he became one of the principle advocates for the creation of a federal recreation service.

Brightbill was a well-respected leader within the profession. He served as president of the American Recreation Society and held leadership positions in other organizations. He saw much to be gained from all segments of the profession working closely together and he contributed significantly to this end. Brightbill was a strong advocate of the concept of citizen and professional cooperation in the field of recreation and parks. He contributed greatly to developing the principles that helped bring about the merger of professional and citizen groups to form the National Recreation and Park Association.

One of the most personally rewarding and productive phases of Brightbill's career was his work at the University of Illinois. Under his leadership, professional preparation in recreation at the University grew from a small undergraduate program to a nationally-recognized program involving undergraduate and graduate education, research, and public service. His personal concern for students won Brightbill their respect and affection. He always took time to listen and to give personal attention to the problems of his students, somehow sensing the capacity of each one.

Perhaps Brightbill's greatest influence upon the recreation movement was through his philosophical writings. He was recognized as one of the leading philosophers within his field at the time of his death.

His three major books on philosophy were *Man and Leisure: A Philosophy of Recreation*, published in 1961; *The Challenge of Leisure*, a revised and condensed version of *Man and Leisure*, written primarily for the layman and published in 1963; and *Educating for Leisure Centered Living*, a searching examination of how Americans must prepare for a leisure-centered society, published in 1966. The most popular and widely circulated of these was *The Challenge of Leisure* which was selected as one of ten books for the recommended freshmen reading list at the University of Illinois in 1965 and 1966.

In July of 1963, Brightbill was asked by an associate for a statement of his personal philosophy. The thoughts he selected to express his philosophy were summarized from his work, *The Challenge of Leisure*. He entitled his summary, "A Point of View," which follows:

Leisure should be thought of more as an opportunity than a problem . . . it can no more be divorced from the element of time than it can be completely separated from work . . . it is the endless ways it can be used which make it significant . . . leisure is time beyond that required for existence and substance, it is discretionary time . . . to look upon leisure as a respite from work is never to discover its full potential . . . leisure is man's eternal opportunity to overcome his inner improvements, although it is no guarantee he will do so . . .

. . . Because the recreative use of leisure deals almost exclusively with the enthusiasm of mankind, it is impossible to set limitations upon it . . . the recreative pursuit is best identified by the words attitude, freedom, and self-fulfillment . . . recreation may well be the only known way of running away from and toward life at the same time. It can shore up our self-respect and dignity by animating and generating an appreciation of our own abilities to accomplish. It can help us recognize that inward satisfactions precede outward delights. While it may help us through the years, it does not neglect the past; it recaptures life as a child knows it. Its focus is more upon living now than hoping to exist tomorrow. The proper use of leisure can help tighten spiritual bonds, encourage higher codes of ethics and morals, help heal and rehabilitate the ill and handicapped, and even add to our material wealth. But those are intentions it sets and victories it claims not primarily for itself. The only threshold upon which the recreative use of leisure has ever soundly stood is the chance for everyone to live a decent, satisfying, and creative kind of existence . . .

. . . In the end, only the individual man can make his life zestful, exciting and satisfying. Only he can put his life together in the new patterns and images. The aspirations and the intensities of purpose come at high tide when they come from within us. Somebody can teach us how to address a golf ball, but we have to hit it.

. . . In a world which places a high premium on science, too often as a means of keeping one nation more powerful than another, it is easy to forget that the most important concern of the human race should be man. Not powerful, affluent and possessive man, but resourceful, selfless, creative man—and with leisure, recreative man.

. . . Leisure ought to be the time for achieving human balance, the elusive but desirable state between underdevelopment and overdevelopment; and above all, it should be the time for cultivating ourselves in the whole creation . . .

Charles Brightbill had much to say about life and leisure. His strength of character was ever apparent in his struggle with ill health. In January 1963, after his usual noontime swim, Brightbill fell and it was discovered that his spinal column was fractured. Later in that year, it was determined that he had multiple myeloma, an incurable malignancy of the bone marrow. He suffered three additional lumbar fractures prior to his death on August 23, 1966. The period of his terminal illness proved to be one of the most productive of his career. During that time, he continued to teach, write, and participate in professional affairs. He retained his keen sense of humor and refused to permit any discussion of his illness. Charles K. Brightbill was a crusader within the recreation movement. His beliefs in recreation, his vision of its importance in our society, his empathy and understanding of people and situations made him an effective leader, spokesman, and arbitrator for the profession. Through his writings, Brightbill placed his profession within the context of the society in which he lived. He projected with wisdom and vision the increasing importance of recreation in our lives.

PARTIAL LIST OF BRIGHTBILL'S PUBLICATIONS

Federal Security Agency. Office of Community War Services. (1944). *Community Recreation Comes of Age.* Washington, D.C.: Government Printing Office.

Teamwork in Community Services, 1941-1946—A Demonstration in Federal, State, and Local Cooperations (1950). Washington, D.C.: Government Printing Office.

The President's Committee on Religion and Welfare in the Armed Forces (1949). *Community Planning for the Peacetime Serviceman.* Washington, D.C.: Government Printing Office.

Free Time in the Armed Forces (1951). Washington, D.C.: Government Printing Office.

Report on the National Conference on Community Responsibility to Our Peacetime Servicemen and Women (1949). Washington, D.C.: Government Printing Office.

The Military Chaplaincy (1950). Washington, D.C.: Government Printing Office.

Educating for Leisure-Centered Living (1966). Harrisburg, PA: The Stackpole Company.

How To Make Recreation A Family Affair (1958). Booklet No. 30. Chicago, IL: F.E. Compton Company.

Man and Leisure: A Philosophy of Recreation (1961). Englewood Cliffs, NJ: Prentice-Hall, Inc.

What Comes Naturally (1965). *Background Readings for Physical Education.* Edited by Ann Paterson and Edmond C. Hallberg. New York: Holt, Rhinehart, and Winston.

Parks and Recreation in Minneapolis. Vol. I: Policies, Procedures and Practices of the Minneapolis Board of Park Commissioners (1965). Urbana, IL: Field Service, Department of Recreation and Park Administration, University of Illinois.

and Langston Clair; Duncan, Ray (1948). *Community Recreation: A Guide To Its Organization and Administration.* Boston: D.C. Heath and Company.

and Meyer, Harold D. (1953). *Recreation: Text and Readings.* Englewood Cliffs, NJ: Prentice-Hall, Inc.

and Meyer, Harold D. (1956). *Community Recreation: A Guide To Its Organization* (1956). 3rd Edition. Englewood Cliffs. NJ: Prentice-Hall, Inc.

and Meyer, Harold D. (1956). *Recreation Administration: A Guide To Its Practices* (1956). Englewood Cliffs, NJ: Prentice-Hall, Inc.

and Meyer, Harold D. (1950). *State Recreation—Organization and Administration* (1950). New York: A. S. Barnes and Company.